Response to

Response to Student Writing

Sarah Warshauer Freedman
University of California, Berkeley

With
Cynthia Greenleaf
University of California, Berkeley

Melanie Sperling
University of California, Berkeley

National Council of Teachers of English
1111 Kenyon Road, Urbana, Illinois 61801

For Bob and Rachel

Book Design: Tom Kovacs for TGK Design

NCTE Stock Number 40823

This project was funded by the National Institute of Education (NIE-G-083-0065) and the Office of Educational Research and Improvement Center for the Study of Writing (OERI-G008690004), with supplementary funding provided by the Spencer Foundation. However, the opinions expressed herein do not necessarily reflect the position or policy of the funding agencies, and no official endorsement should be inferred.

Library of Congress Cataloging in Publication Data

Freedman, Sarah Warshauer.
   Response to student writing.

   (NCTE research report; no. 23)
   Bibliography: p.
   1. English language—Composition and exercises—
Study and teaching (Secondary) 2. English language—
Composition and exercises—Evaluation. I. Greenleaf,
Cynthia. II. Sperling, Melanie. III. Title. IV. Series.
PE1011.N295 no. 23 [LB1631] 808'.042'071273 87-24894
ISBN 0-8141-4082-3

Contents

Acknowledgments   vii

1. Introduction   1

2. Design   11

3. Response Practices: Range and Helpfulness   49

4. Values about Writing: Underpinnings and
   Structuring of Response   110

5. Summary of the Research   155

6. What Have We Learned and Where Do We Go
   from Here?   160

References   165

Appendix A: The National Writing Project Surveys   173

Appendix B: Assignment Sequences   200

*Appendix C: Note-Taking Conventions and
Procedures for In-Class Data Collection*   204

*Appendix D: Criteria for Determining What Was
to Be Recorded on Camera*   205

Appendix E: Supplementary Tables   206

*Appendix F: Would You Buy a Used Car from
This Man? Questions for Character Analysis*   217

Appendix G: Student Writing Samples   219

Acknowledgments

This project belongs to the teachers and students from the National Writing Project sites who participated in the surveys and to Art Peterson and Mary Lee Glass and their students who opened the doors of their classrooms during the spring of 1984. The contributions come from those who live the results; I am the record keeper for the actions and thoughts of these fine teachers and their students. I only hope to have communicated here the essence of what my research team and I learned from them, so that our readers can experience some of what we encountered in our months reviewing returned questionnaires and sitting daily in the ninth grade.

Special thanks go to James Gray, who gave one hundred percent of his support — both intellectual and practical — and to Miles Myers, who helped me conceive the initial idea for this project during a five-hour discussion on a return trip from an NCTE convention. Selma Monsky of Berkeley's Survey Research Center offered sage advice on the design of the survey as did Arthur Applebee and Robert Calfee. Calfee also helped conceptualize the analysis of the surveys. Janet Kodish typeset the survey forms on the computer, a process that involved many hours and demanded constant care. Mayland Cann-Ortiz ably provided advice on the statistics and executed the computer runs. Melissa and Charles Fox helped set up the audio recording plan for the classrooms. John Gumperz and Jenny Cook-Gumperz served as ongoing advisors to us as we collected and analyzed the mounds of data from the two local classrooms.

Both Larry Lynch, principal at Gunn High School, and Arthur Fibush, principal at Lowell High School, facilitated our work in every way possible, arranging for equipment storage, assisting with the installation of microphones, and writing special letters to the students' parents to explain the research and gain their support.

Both the research and my ideas have been enhanced by the collaborative relationship that I have enjoyed with several Berkeley graduate students who served as coresearchers with me: Melanie Sperling and Cynthia Greenleaf, who aided me during data collection and the first phases of analysis, and more recently, Jane Bennett, who has worked on the ninth-grade peer-group data. Leann Parker's intellectual and practical contributions encompassed many areas, from developing systems for cataloging data to assisting with the videotaping. Many of the ideas presented here belong to these students. Ernest Grafe provided much support in producing the final manuscript.

A number of my colleagues read and responded to versions of this manuscript. As a learning writer, I depend on such response. Special thanks for comments on the entire manuscript go to Lillian Bridwell-Bowles, Robert Calfee, Colette Daiute, Marcia Farr, Linda Flower, Jim Gray, Art Peterson, Melanie Sperling, and Tom Hilgers.

Finally, I want to thank my family. My husband, Bob, encouraged me and provided support throughout a long and arduous process. My daughter, Rachel, was in seventh grade when the project began; as I watched her pass through ninth grade, she allowed me clearer insights into the minds of the ninth-graders I observed.

1 Introduction

For many years, writing teachers have acknowledged that responding to their students' writing is central to their teaching. As early as 1903, in their classic book on the teaching of English, Carpenter, Baker, and Scott express sentiments that many would agree with today (although we might prefer the more neutral term "response" to their "criticism"):

> The . . . question, How shall written work be criticized? is one of the most important in the whole problem of teaching English. Upon the value of the criticism success in teaching composition finally depends. (142)

Simultaneously acknowledging the importance of response, teachers throughout the years have voiced frustration about how to make their response effective. In fact, there is even evidence that response can confuse writers and promote negative attitudes toward writing (e.g., Brannon and Knoblauch 1982; Sommers 1982). Most teachers have at least overheard the following typical student complaint: "But I used lots of details in this paper because Mrs. North told me that was a good thing, and now Mr. South tells me I have too many details." In the bleakest scenario, students develop a folk theory about response in which they believe that the nature of the response is dictated solely by the responder's taste. They become frustrated when they perceive inconsistency in "tastes" and receive mixed messages about their writing. They give up trying to learn to write, and often, in frustration, adopt a strategy of learning to please a particular teacher at a given time and then consciously, upon encountering the next teacher, try to forget everything they "learned" so that they can start anew to satisfy the next teacher's taste. Teachers express similar complaints: a feeling of having to "start over" with each new class, a feeling of discontinuity in writing instruction.

The following quotation from Jody, a college freshman, dramatizes these points and emphasizes just how difficult the task of responding to student writing is as she chronicles the development of her attitudes about her teachers' advice. On a questionnaire returned to her college writing teacher during the first class of her freshman year, Jody writes:

1

> I like English, but I've had so many different English teachers, all saying different things about my writing, that I really can't know what to believe. All teachers want different things, and it's hard to please all of them without changing my way of writing. Hopefully you won't try and change the way I write, but just try and help me on the things I do badly.

In a conference the next week with her teacher, Jody elaborates further:

> English is really easy, 'cause it's easy to get a good grade, if you know what the teacher wants. So that's what I've been doing, you know, all through grammar school and high school. You just like, you know, in your first paper or something you write, and they'll say, "Oh you should do this, or you should do this," and you go, "Uh ha, I know what they want," and then you just write the way they want and they go, "Great! Excellent writing." You know. Houh! Okay, that's this semester taken care of. You have a new teacher, and they like this. So you say, "Okay, I'll put that in my writing." And they just love you for it. But then you end up in college, and you don't know how to write, for yourself. You just write for other people.

Other students, like Jody, understand the importance of having a personal investment in their writing but are less successful at playing the school game. These students often do not interpret negative response to their writing so matter-of-factly; instead, they react personally: "Criticize my writing and you criticize me as a person." To protect themselves, if the response environment feels unsafe, these students, like Jody, pull back and do not invest themselves in their writing. Or they may shield themselves in another way by not "attending" to the response, by shutting it out.

A major difficulty with response in schools is that it is often coupled with grades and functions to justify the grade rather than to teach the student (Sommers 1982). As Purves (1984) emphasizes, teacher-responders must take multiple roles; however, the institutional role of the evaluator frequently makes it difficult for the teacher to assume other reader roles successfully (Applebee et al. 1984; Britton et al. 1975).

These difficulties with response lead to one central question: How can response support the teaching and learning of writing? Given the importance of response to learning to write, we need to understand what teachers can do to begin to overcome some of the difficulties that have traditionally been associated with it. The research reported in this monograph will address this key question.

The Study

To begin to learn about how to overcome the traditional barriers to effective response, I designed a study that would uncover how the most successful teachers of writing in the nation, as a group, respond to their students. The study has two parts: (1) a national survey of the response practices of 560 successful (K–12) writing teachers from diverse communities, and a survey of 715 of their secondary students (grades 7–12); and (2) an ethnographic study of how response is accomplished in the classrooms of two successful ninth-grade teachers in the San Francisco Bay Area. The surveys are designed to provide information from a large number of teachers and students and to help focus the ethnographic observations, whereas the ethnography is designed to provide details about the workings of response that could not be obtained in the surveys' self-report form.

Ninth grade was selected as the focus for the ethnography because it is a transitional year, when teachers commonly raise their expectations of their student writers. Ninth grade marks the start of the final phase of secondary education. At a transition point, response can be especially important in helping students meet new demands.

So that the response practices of the two teachers could be compared most easily, the observations focused on the teaching of a single type of writing: academic argumentation.[1] The academic argument was selected because it is commonly assigned in ninth grade and is associated with rising expectations and the transition to high school. Academic argumentation was also selected because teachers often report that it is difficult to teach.

The decision to focus on the teaching of academic arguments should not be taken as an endorsement of the position that this kind of writing is inherently more demanding cognitively or more difficult to learn than any other type of writing. Points of view on the issue of genre and cognitive complexity vary (compare Olson [1977] and Scribner and Cole [1981] for a survey of the different positions, and Street [1984] for a critical discussion of the issues). The most compelling arguments are against any direct association of genre and cognitive complexity (Scribner and Cole 1981; Street 1984); as Traugott (1985) points out, complexity relates more to how communication functions, than to genre per se.

A further decision was made to select ninth-grade teachers who differed from each other in approach. Since the experience of the National Writing Project suggests that there are different models of success in the teaching of writing, the goal was to find two teachers who offered important contrasts and to observe differences in successful practice; to obtain, then, a tightly focused but diverse picture of response as it functions during teaching and learning.

The research approach for both the survey and the ethnography — a focus on learning from successful practice — is somewhat novel in research on writing. In recent years, research on written language has moved from an emphasis on experiments with different classroom techniques (e.g., Braddock, Lloyd-Jones, and Schoer 1963), to case studies of individual students during the writing process (e.g., Emig 1971), to a reconceptualized reemphasis on teaching and learning in school settings (e.g., Applebee 1981 and 1984; Heath 1983; Heath and Branscombe 1985). Throughout, the aim has been for the researcher to inform the teacher of these new trends through research studies or through teacher-researcher collaboration, as in Heath (1983) and Heath and Branscombe (1985).

This study of response takes a different perspective. Although the hope is to provide teachers with information through research, the research focuses on what successful teachers know and do and how their actions affect their students. Successful teachers and their students, then, become the sources of information about response. This approach leads the researcher to join with teachers and students in order to study teacher knowledge and the effects of teaching, and then to synthesize the teacher's and the researcher's observations about student learning. The approach should lead to enriched theories of the teaching and learning of written language in general and of the response process in particular. It should also uncover difficulties in the classroom that may well be out of the hands of the classroom teacher and that cannot be understood through studies such as this one at the classroom level, but rather require studies of the organizational structure of the schools.

What Counts as Response?

Just by reading the current literature on response, we know that today's enlightened teachers and researchers agree that response includes more than the written comments teachers make in the margins of their students' finished pieces of writing. Indeed, the professional literature focuses much of its attention on the peer response group (e.g., Elbow 1973; Gere and Stevens 1985; Healy 1980; Moffett and Wagner 1976; Mohr 1984; Murray 1984; Nystrand 1986) and the individual conference (e.g., Calkins 1983; Freedman 1981; Freedman and Katz 1987;

Freedman and Sperling 1985; Graves 1983; Kamler 1980). However, few discussions of response go beyond descriptions of formally structured peer groups, conferences, and written comments.

Response, as defined in this study, includes other activities as well and may not differ much from what we include as the teaching of writing. Response includes all reaction to writing, formal or informal, written or oral, from teacher or peer, to a draft or final version. Response may occur as a formal part of a classroom lesson or informally as teachers and peers have brief and seemingly casual conversations. Although response is a reaction — that is, it is evoked by a previous "writing" action — the act of writing could include anything from a tentative list of ideas to a polished piece. Response can also occur in reaction to talk about an intended piece of writing, the talk being considered a "writing" act. Response may be explicit, such as: "I like that idea" or "You need a comma before the 'and' " or "Can you explain more precisely what Mary looks like; you say, 'Mary is pretty' but as your reader, I want to know what makes her pretty" or "Reread your essay to see if you can find sentence fragments." Or response can be less explicit. For example, a student could tell a teacher she planned to write, "The children asks the mother" and the teacher could respond, "Yes, the children ask the mother." In such a case, the writer would be expected to follow the teacher's model for subject-verb agreement. Or the teacher might also respond, "Who else might the children ask?" The writer would then be expected to infer from the teacher's curiosity that it might be desirable, from the teacher's point of view, to include more information.

Theories about the Role of Response in Learning to Write

Theories relevant to learning to write suggest that for learning to take place, all types of response must play a central and positive role in teaching and learning. Although there is no widely accepted theory of writing acquisition per se, at least two powerful theoretical traditions seem key: theories of how intellectual skills, such as mathematical problem solving and writing, are learned in school (e.g., Anderson 1982; Gagne 1974) and theories of how oral language is acquired (e.g., Cazden 1979; Clark and Clark 1977; Ochs 1979; Snow and Ferguson 1977). Learning to write involves both intellectual accomplishments gained primarily in school and linguistic accomplishments that are part of the more general acquisition of language. Response is central to both.

Those who study the intellectual skills learned in school focus on response or feedback that occurs mainly when the "teacher" gives explicit and often value-laden comments to the "learner" about his or her learning process or product. General theories about how intellectual skills are learned in school explain why this type of feedback is necessary for learning. Through feedback, learners come to distinguish for themselves when they are performing well from when they are not. Further, feedback helps them figure out how to take corrective action when they are not performing well. Theoretically, feedback operates this way across intellectual domains, from the learning of mathematical problem solving to the learning of writing. In a related vein, many who study reading (e.g., Brown 1982; Flavell 1981; Langer 1986) and writing (e.g., Bereiter and Scardamalia 1982, in press; Flower 1980; Langer 1986) advocate teaching learners of written language to become aware of their cognitive processes by self-consciously monitoring those processes.

However, theories that are concerned with feedback in oral language learning stress social processes. Response is part of a teaching-learning interaction; both teacher and student or speaker and hearer play a role in its accomplishment. When children learn to talk, the parent or other responder gives feedback, which is often indirect and usually occurs in a natural and highly supportive social setting. The nature of the feedback varies according to cultural norms, but regardless of the feedback patterns, children learn to talk (Heath 1983).

Theories of the acquisition of intellectual skills and of natural language learning suggest a model of response to student writing that considers response as both a social and a cognitive process — a point of view perhaps best articulated by Vygotsky (1978) and his interpreters and followers (Wertsch et al. 1984; Leontiev 1981).[2] Vygotsky (1978) argues that *collaboration* underlies the teaching-learning process: "Learning awakens a variety of internal developmental processes that are able to operate only when the child is interacting with people in his environment" (90). Vygotsky emphasizes the importance of the *social* nature of *cognition* or individual learning.

While Vygotsky argues that collaboration is crucial to the learning process, he argues at the same time that collaboration must lead the learner, at some future time, to *independence* in performance. Vygotsky continues, "Once these processes [the ones being learned] are internalized, they become part of the child's independent developmental achievement" (90). Bruner (1983), in a discussion of how children acquire oral language, also stresses the importance of the eventual independence of the learner from the teachers. Bruner proposes a "handover principle" in caretaker-child interactions in which the caretaker "would introduce a new procedure and gradually 'hand it over' to the child as his skills for executing it developed" (60). From a Vygotskian point of view, it is through such a process of collaboration that writers receive response, but it is crucial to remember that the goal of collaboration and response is to help the learner become independent of the collaborator. These ideas are reminiscent of those emphasized in 1903 by Carpenter, Baker, and Scott, who note that through response, they expect that the teacher will aim

> to increase the pupil's knowledge of the subject, and to raise his standard of judgment; in brief, to make him self critical. The less necessary to him the teacher becomes, the better is the teaching. (142)

Vygotsky's theory also provides insights into how successful collaboration and response must be arranged to lead to independent production. According to Vygotsky, it is critical that collaboration be in tune with the child's level of development. When Vygotsky considers development, he thinks of not one but two levels, the actual or completed level and the potential level toward which the child can reach. He calls the space between these levels the "zone of proximal development" and defines it as follows:

> It is the distance between the actual developmental level as determined by independent problem solving and the level of potential development as determined through problem solving under adult guidance or in collaboration with more capable peers. (85)

It follows that the most useful response takes place within the zone — above the actual developmental level but not beyond the potential level.

Response, then, ideally is a process of what I call *collaborative problem solving*. The problems must be within the writer's developmental grasp, and the writer must gradually become more competent, that is, more independent of the responder. For example, when a child tells or writes a story and the listener or reader asks questions that get the child to fill in gaps in meaning or that stimulate the child to consider what the reader might not understand, the listener or reader provides support. Assuming that the child is developmentally ready to learn to consider these reader needs without the support, the child, in time, will internalize the kind of information listeners need for understanding stories. The responder helps the child solve the problem of anticipating the reader's needs by providing the child with examples of the kinds of questions real readers ask about stories. This theory does not argue that any writer ever becomes completely independent from responders; it is just that as writers grow, the kind of response they need changes. Professional writers need response, but they tackle more difficult tasks than they did as schoolchildren and the kind of response they need changes with time. In other words, learning, and therefore the writer's need for response, never ends.

The concept of collaborative problem solving is similar to other teaching techniques that have gone by a number of names, each with related but slightly different meanings: scaffolding, reciprocal teaching, and procedural facilitation. *Scaffolding* is a term usually applied to caretaker-child interactions during the early stages of oral language acquisition (e.g., Bruner 1983; Cazden 1979; Greenfield 1984; McNamee 1980; Ninio and Bruner 1978; Ochs 1979; Rogoff and Gardner 1984; Snow and Ferguson 1977; Wertsch 1979; Wood, Bruner, and Ross 1976; see also Applebee 1981; Applebee and Langer 1983; and Applebee 1984 for discussions of scaffolding in classroom teaching-learning situations). The expert intervenes with a supportive tool for the learner as the learner needs the help; the focus is on what the expert provides for the novice. *Reciprocal teaching* involves tutors working with students to provide support during reading instruction (Brown, Palinscar, and Purcell, in press; Palinscar and Brown 1984); the tutors gradually release control to the learner. The focus is on teaching the learner to take on the role of the teacher; the learner is taught to ask the kinds of questions the teacher would ask about a reading passage and then to answer those self-generated questions. *Procedural facilitation* involves a system of support during the writing process in which students are made aware of their cognitive processes and are helped to engage in productive procedures (Bereiter and Scardamalia 1982). The focus is solely on support for cognitive activities. Reciprocal teaching and procedural facilitation both focus on a particular type of collaborative problem solving or scaffolding — that which concentrates explicitly on cognitive and metacognitive processes. Scaffolding, although not limited to metacognitive processes, focuses mainly on the process of providing the support. The difference between collaborative problem solving and scaffolding is that collaborative problem solving focuses on the interaction and the social-cognitive activity rather than mainly on the support side of the activity.

This monograph is based on the theory that the achievement of cognitive gain depends on the substance of social interactions. Mehan (1976) provides an interesting example of the interplay between the social and the cognitive. He points out how children seek hints when taking individually administered standardized intelligence tests; that is, they play a central role in seeking the assistance they need. It is important, then, to think of the concept of collaborative problem solving not just as a way of teaching but as jointly accomplished teaching and learning. Both the teacher and learner negotiate the parts they play.

To conclude, when Vygotsky's theoretical insights are applied to response to student writing, it becomes clear that response (1) should be collaborative between a writer and someone more expert on the issue being discussed, (2) should try to help developing writers solve writing problems or write in ways that they could not alone, and (3) should lead to independent problem solving.

Given this theoretical background, it seems clear that for response to be effective, teacher experts must collaborate with learning writers with the aim of helping the writers become independent. This collaboration must result in a process the writer could not have engaged in without expert guidance and should result in a product the writer could not have produced without such guidance; in such cases, the collaboration takes place within Vygotsky's "zone of proximal development."

The response of successful teachers will be viewed through this theoretical lens. The research will explore the social and cognitive nature of collaborative problem solving in the classrooms of successful teachers of writing. Further, the research will take a broad view of response, and with a national survey, will look to the teachers and their students to illustrate the possibilities for response.

Research Questions

The project has three aims: (1) to understand better how response can function in helping students improve their writing, (2) to define more precisely the concept of response, in the hopes of enriching the traditional views and definitions, and (3) to understand how successful teachers accomplish response, and to learn what they do and do not know about response to student writing. Thus, the research focuses on the following specific questions:

1. Under positive instructional conditions, what is the range of response students receive in school? What characterizes response that students and teachers feel is most helpful? Least helpful?

2. In successful classrooms, what values about writing are being transmitted during response (what is the basis of the substance of the response)?

3. In these classrooms, how are different types of response related to one another during the teaching-learning process?

Overview of the Monograph

This introductory first chapter is followed by Chapter 2, which focuses on the design and procedures for conducting the survey and the ethnography and provides a description of the samples for both parts of the study. Chapter 3 offers a discussion of the range of response practices, their distribution in both the survey and ethnography, and their perceived helpfulness. Chapter 4 turns to the values underlying response for the teachers in the survey and the ethnography. It includes illustrations from the ethnography to show how two teachers with different teaching styles integrate whole-class discussion, peer groups, individual conferences, and written comments on their students' writing. Chapter 5 summarizes the study and the findings. Chapter 6 offers a candid assessment of the remaining difficulties in response to student writing and ends with suggestions for teaching and research.

Notes

1. I use the term "academic argument" to avoid traditional labels for "modes of discourse" since there is so much debate about the meanings of the category systems in current use. I include under the label "academic argument" pieces of nonfiction in which students are asked to take a point of view and argue for that point of view. Britton et al. (1975) describe the pieces as "transactional." In Kinneavy's (1971) terms, they are "persuasive." In the classrooms studied here, topics ranged from opinion pieces on controversial issues to analyses of characters in literary works.

2. Some of the ideas for looking at the teaching and learning of writing as social and cognitive processes grew out of conversations with Arthur Applebee, Wallace Chafe, Anne Haas Dyson, Shirley Brice Heath, and Judith Langer.

2 Design

National Surveys: Procedures for Selecting Teachers and Students

A sample of successful teachers for the survey was gathered through the National Writing Project (NWP) network. At the time of the survey, the NWP consisted of 116 affiliated sites, located in forty-three states and the District of Columbia, three foreign countries (England, Canada, and Australia), and segments of the Department of Defense school system and the private American schools in the Far East. Each site is located at a university and is organized by a site director who is a member of the university faculty.

As the first step in gathering the sample, each of the 116 directors was sent a letter asking for the names of six of the most outstanding teachers of writing in his or her region, two at the elementary level (grades K–6), two at the junior high level (grades 7–9), and two at the senior high level (grades 9–12). Ninth grade overlaps in the junior high and senior high sample because of the variable organization of American schools, with ninth grade frequently part of either junior high/middle school or senior high school.

The NWP site directors were uniquely positioned to select a sample of successful teachers for the survey, as can be seen in the description provided by James Gray, director and founder of the NWP, of how each site functions:

> The site directors identify successful teachers of writing in their geographical areas from all levels of instruction. They invite these master teachers to come together on university campuses for intensive five-week-long Summer Institutes focusing on three closely interrelated activities: demonstration by teachers of their most successful classroom practices, study of current theory and research in the teaching of composition, and practice in writing in a variety of forms — personal, literary, persuasive, and expository. The aims of the institute are simple: to provide teachers a setting in which they can share classroom successes, to help them broaden and make more conscious the grounds of their teaching, to give teachers of writing an opportunity to commit themselves intensely and reflectively to the process of writing, and finally to identify and train a corps of writing teachers who can effectively

teach the techniques and processes of teaching writing to other teachers.

The success of any Writing Project site depends on the director's ability to identify and work with successful local teachers.

Each nominated teacher was sent a survey and a personal letter explaining the purpose of the research and how he or she was chosen. Two of the six teachers from each site were selected randomly to help gather the student sample; one taught at the junior high level and one at the senior high level. These teachers were asked to select four students enrolled in a class in which they taught writing, two high-achieving and two low-achieving students, with each pair including one male and one female. Each teacher in this subset of the nominated teachers, then, also received four surveys for students.

Development of the Survey Forms

Survey development took approximately six months. It involved (1) deciding on the information about response practices that could be gathered from a survey, (2) formulating questions to get that information and putting those questions in a professional yet friendly tone and format, and (3) pilot testing and then revising drafts of the surveys. Different but parallel survey forms were developed for elementary and secondary teachers, who are in different teaching situations, and students, who talk about the educational process in less technical language than their teachers. All surveys focused on the role of response in the teaching and learning of writing.

A number of experts in writing research and survey design offered suggestions on various early versions of the surveys.[1] As the forms were reviewed by the experts and discussed by the project staff, they were tested informally with local teachers and students who not only completed the surveys but also gave information about items that were difficult to interpret or answer. Such items were revised and then tested on more teachers and students.

The forms were formally piloted by seventeen teachers from kindergarten through twelfth grade and fifty-four secondary students. Responses from the larger group of teachers and students led the research team to eliminate items that provided too small a spread of response or that remained ambiguous.

Elementary and Secondary Teachers

Both teacher forms contained questions on the following seven topics:

1. teachers' perceptions of the effectiveness of different practices in the teaching of writing, with a focus on response;

2. teaching strategies emphasized, with a focus on response;
3. teachers' reasons for teaching writing;[2]
4. kinds and amounts of writing emphasized in the curriculum;
5. characteristics of the teaching situation, such as the number of classes taught by the teacher, the number of students taught, the ability level of the students;
6. demographic information about the school; and
7. personal information about the teacher.

Secondary Students

The questionnaires for secondary students focused on four of the seven topics covered in the teachers' surveys:

1. students' perceptions of the effectiveness of different practices in the teaching of writing, with a focus on response;
2. teaching strategies emphasized by the teacher in the survey, with a focus on response;
3. kinds and amounts of writing emphasized by the teacher in the survey; and
4. personal information about the student.

Students were not asked about their teachers' reasons for teaching writing, or for information about the teaching situation or school. The teacher and student questionnaires can be found in Appendix A.

Procedures for Conducting Surveys

Questionnaires were mailed to the nominated teachers in early April, 1984. Usual procedures were followed for getting returns on mail surveys[3] and for ensuring the anonymity of the participants.[4] By the end of June, about two and one-half months from the time of the original mailing, survey collection ended.

Response Rates

The NWP site directors proved extraordinarily helpful in nominating teacher-participants, with 90.5 percent giving names (only 10 of the 116 site directors did not respond (Table 2.1). Of those responding, all but a few provided six names in the specified categories.

Of the directors who did not nominate teachers, several were from relatively inactive sites, several could not be reached, and two chose not to participate. The directors' response rates were fairly consistent

Table 2.1

Response Rate from Site Directors within Geographic Regions

Geographic Region	Number Contacted	Number Responding	Percentage Responding
Northeast	12	12	100
North Central	25	23	92
South	37	31	84
West	33	33	100
Foreign American	5	3	60
Foreign non-American	4	4	100
Totals	116	106	90.5

across the geographic regions in the U.S. (divided according to U.S. Census categories [Bureau of the Census, 1980]) and across foreign sites divided to separate foreign American schools and local foreign schools. Response was slightly lower from the southern region (84 percent) and still lower from the foreign American schools, although the small number of foreign American schools makes that figure unreliable.

The return rate for teachers and students, by geographic regions, appears in Table 2.2. The overall 87 percent teacher and 87.2 percent student response was significantly higher than expected. In general, 50 percent is considered an adequate return for mail surveys, 60 percent is considered good, and 70 percent or over is considered very good (Babbie 1973, 165). In his survey of secondary teachers, Applebee (1981) reports an overall return of 68 percent, with a higher rate of 75 percent from English teachers (20).

In this study, as expected, the response for elementary teachers, none of whom received student surveys, was slightly higher than for the secondary teachers, many of whom had the more complicated task. Like the site directors', the teachers' returns were fairly evenly distributed geographically.

Many of the teachers who did not participate sent letters or telephoned to explain why. One felt that she was not an excellent teacher; another said that she had nothing to say other than that she encouraged her students to write. Others missed the deadline for various personal reasons. A number of the teachers who did participate sent letters and lengthy explanations about answers to questions. One teacher noted that she framed the letter asking for her participation, it being the only official word of encouragement she had received in years.

Table 2.2

Response Rate from Teachers and Students within Geographic Regions

Geographic Region	Elementary Teachers			Secondary Teachers			All Teachers	Secondary Students		
	Number Contacted	Number Responding	Percentage Responding	Number Contacted	Number Responding	Percentage Responding	Percentage Responding	Number Contacted	Number Responding	Percentage Responding
Northeast	24	22	91.7	49	39	79.6	83.6	88	61	69.3
North Central	44	37	84.1	91	76	83.5	83.7	176	157	89.2
South	60	55	91.7	125	107	85.6	87.6	232	194	83.6
West	66	62	93.9	141	119	84.4	87.4	268	234	87.3
Foreign American	6	5	83.3	12	9	75.0	77.8	32	16	50.0
Foreign non-American	7	6	85.7	19	11	57.9	57.7	24	24	100.0
Missing Region	—	4	—	—	8	—	—	—	29	—
Totals	207	191	92.3	437	369	84.4	87.0	820	715	87.2

Characteristics of Teachers, Schools, and Students

The personal characteristics of the teachers who participated in the survey are presented in Table 2.3.[5] Most of the elementary teachers held bachelor's degrees in education while their secondary counterparts' degrees were in English. The subject area trends for the master's degrees were the same. Significantly more of the secondary than elementary teachers held master's degrees. In both groups, only a small number of teachers had received or were working on doctorates.

The teachers were mostly female: 86.9 percent at the elementary level and 77.2 percent at the secondary level, which is a significant difference. The average number of years teaching experience was fourteen. These teachers were slightly more experienced than the English teachers in Applebee's (1981) survey who averaged 12.8 years in the classroom (23). Some difference could be expected given the later date of this survey and the rise in the average age of the teaching force.

The average age of the teachers in the sample was forty-one. A comparison of the age distribution of these teachers with Applebee's shows that this group contained fewer teachers under thirty years of age — 6.1 percent as opposed to Applebee's 24.1 percent — and more in the forty to forty-nine age bracket — 39.5 percent as opposed to Applebee's 14.2 percent (Applebee 1981, 22).

The schools in which the teachers taught (Table 2.4) were fairly evenly spread across the United States with a somewhat higher percentage in the West and a somewhat lower percentage in the Northeast. Because the Writing Project began and remains headquartered on the West Coast, this distribution may be an artifact of the larger number of active sites in the western states and the more frequent contact between the western site directors and teachers with the research staff. Only a small percentage of the sample taught in foreign countries.

Most of the teachers taught in small towns or in suburbs of large metropolitan areas, although a substantial number taught in urban areas. U.S. Census statistics (1983) show that 74.8 percent of the U.S. population can be found in metropolitan areas (over 50,000 population) and 25.2 percent in nonmetropolitan areas (19). The surveyed population is fairly typical, with 39.4 percent coming from nonmetropolitan areas (rural and small town).[6]

The schools in which the teachers worked were predominantly public. The elementary schools were significantly smaller than the secondary schools. U.S. Bureau of the Census statistics (1983) show the same pattern; an average-sized elementary school has 391 students, and an average-sized secondary school has 730 students (64).

Table 2.3

Characteristics of Sampled Teachers

Characteristics	Percent of Teachers Reporting			Chi-square Tests Elem. vs. Sec.
	Elementary ($n = 191$)	Secondary ($n = 369$)	All ($n = 560$)	
Education[a]				
Undergrad. major				
English	12.6	61.2	44.7	212.95***
Education	61.6	10.6	27.9	($df = 7$)
Other	25.8	28.2	27.4	
	($n = 190$)	($n = 369$)	($n = 559$)	
M.A.				
Yes	52.1	67.5	62.5	12.62***
	($n = 190$)	($n = 369$)	($n = 559$)	($df = 1$)
Working on	55.6	59.5	57.8	.320
	($n = 90$)	($n = 116$)	($n = 206$)	($df = 1$)
Major area				
English	10.6	52.9	39.7	81.58***
Education	76.8	35.4	48.2	($df = 7$)
Other	12.6	11.7	12.1	
	($n = 142$)	($n = 314$)	($n = 456$)	
Ph.D.				
Yes	3.3	2.8	3.0	.08
	($n = 182$)	($n = 351$)	($n = 534$)	($df = 1$)
Working on	11.4	13.1	12.5	.26
	($n = 149$)	($n = 282$)	($n = 431$)	($df = 1$)
Major area				
English	4.3	47.8	33.3	16.43*
Education	82.6	45.7	58.0	($df = 7$)
Other	2.1	6.5	8.7	
	($n = 23$)	($n = 46$)	($n = 69$)	
Gender				
Female	86.9	77.2	80.5	7.52**
	($n = 191$)	($n = 369$)	($n = 560$)	($df = 1$)
Age				
Below 30	7.4	5.4	6.1	1.73
30–39	40.0	40.4	40.2	($df = 4$)
40–49	38.4	40.1	39.5	
50–59	12.6	11.4	11.8	
60+	1.6	2.7	2.3	
	($n = 190$)	($n = 369$)	($n = 559$)	

Characteristics	Averages			t Tests
	Elementary	Secondary	All	
Years of teaching experience	13.33 ($sd = 6.31$) ($n = 191$)	14.35 ($sd = 6.69$) ($n = 369$)	14 ($sd = 6.57$) ($n = 560$)	−1.77 ($df = 404$)
Age	40.79 ($sd = 8.04$) ($n = 190$)	41.26 ($sd = 7.94$) ($n = 369$)	41.10 ($sd = 7.97$) ($n = 559$)	.66 ($df = 377$)

[a] For the three questions asking teachers about their majors, there were originally eight categories. Since relatively few teachers majored in any discipline other than English or education, the remaining six categories were collapsed into the category "Other" for purposes of reporting percentages. For the chi-square tests, all categories were used, and so there are 7 degrees of freedom.

*$p < .05$.   **$p < .01$.   ***$p < .001$.

Table 2.4

Characteristics of Sample Schools and Classes

Characteristics	Percent of Teachers Reporting			Chi-square Tests
	Elementary $(n = 191)$	Secondary $(n = 369)$	All $(n = 560)$	
Region				.23
Northeast	11.8	10.8	11.1	$(df = 5)$
North Central	19.8	21.1	20.6	
South	29.4	29.6	29.6	
West	33.2	33.0	33.0	
Foreign American	2.7	2.5	2.1	
Foreign non-American	3.2	3.0	3.1	
	$(n = 187)$	$(n = 361)$	$(n = 548)$	
Metropolitan status				1.00
Rural	9.6	7.6	8.3	$(df = 5)$
Small town	31.4	31.0	31.1	
Suburban	28.7	30.7	30.0	
Urban—large	10.6	12.0	11.5	
Urban—not large	15.4	14.7	14.9	
Other	4.3	4.1	4.1	
	$(n = 188)$	$(n = 368)$	$(n = 556)$	
School type				.41
Public	93.7	92.6	93.0	$(df = 2)$
Private, nonparochial	4.2	4.4	4.3	
Parochial	2.1	3.0	2.7	
	$(n = 191)$	$(n = 367)$	$(n = 558)$	
Enrollment				117.46**
Under 500	60.1	19.2	33.4	$(df = 3)$
500–999	33.0	36.2	35.1	
1000–2499	6.9	42.1	29.9	
2500+	0	2.5	1.7	
	$(n = 188)$	$(n = 354)$	$(n = 542)$	

Student Socioeconomic Status[a] in Selected Class	Percent of Teachers Reporting Student Income at Each Level			t Tests
	Elementary $(n = 191)$	Secondary $(n = 369)$	All $(n = 560)$	
Well-to-do	30.0	35.8	33.8	-1.88 $(df = 376)$
Basic necessities	57.2	56.1	56.5	.38 $(df = 379)$
Less than basics	12.8	8.0	9.7	3.07* $(df = 283)$
	$(n = 186)$	$(n = 365)$	$(n = 551)$	

[a] Since the answers for socioeconomic status were originally reported in percentages, t tests were computed for each level of the variable.

* $p < .01$. ** $p < .001$.

Continued on next page

Table 2.4 — *Continued*

Normal Class Load	Percent of Teachers Reporting	
	Usual Secondary Teacher	This Teacher
4 classes or below	5.4	34.1
5 classes	66.7	47.7
6 classes	26.9	16.3
7 classes or above	1.1	1.9
	(*n* = 279)	(*n* = 369)

Teachers were asked to estimate the percentage of students in their class who fell into each of three general socioeconomic categories: those whose families could not afford basic necessities, those whose families could afford only the necessities, and those whose families could afford luxuries. The teachers said that their students came mostly from families that could afford the basic necessities, with the elementary schools having a significantly greater number of poverty-level students.[7]

The secondary teachers reported that the usual teaching load in their schools was between five and six classes, a load significantly above the four classes recommended for English teachers by the National Council of Teachers of English. However, 52.8 percent of the teachers in the sample taught fewer classes than was normal at their school while 44.7 percent taught a normal load. Only 2.4 percent of the teachers exceeded the normal teaching load for their school. Undoubtedly some of the teachers were part-time and others had administrative responsibilities — factors that would skew the numbers of classes taught but information that was not gathered in the survey. Still, the fact remains that, on the whole, these teachers kept their teaching load relatively low.

The elementary teachers taught grades one through six, with a few teaching a grade above the sixth-grade level (Table 2.5). The central tendency was skewed toward grades four through six, perhaps because some Writing Project site directors, when asked to nominate teachers, understood that they were only to nominate from the upper-elementary grades. Most of these elementary teachers taught a single grade; however, 19 percent taught combination classes, with most of those teaching upper-grade combinations.

The teaching situation of the secondary teachers is reported both for the class selected as focal for the questionnaire and for all their classes considered together (Table 2.6). The teaching situation across

Table 2.5

Characteristics of Elementary Classes: Grade Levels

Grade Levels	Percent of Teachers Reporting
Grade taught	
1	12.6
2	14.2
3	20.5
4	30.0
5	36.3
6	35.3
above 6	6.8
	($n = 190$)
Combined classes	
One grade only	66.3
1 only	6.8
2 only	5.8
3 only	8.4
4 only	13.7
5 only	14.2
6 only	17.4
Two adjacent	
grades combined	19.0
1–2	1.1
2–3	1.6
3–4	4.2
4–5	3.7
5–6	8.4
More than two grades	
or two nonadjacent	
grades combined	14.7

all of a teacher's classes cannot be compared statistically with the teaching situation in the selected class because the selected class was one in the total number of classes and therefore was part of the figure for all classes. However, the survey results do not indicate any apparently unusual trends for the selected class.

For the most part, the secondary teachers taught grades seven through twelve. The grade levels were relatively evenly distributed with a few more teaching eleventh and twelfth grade than ninth or tenth and with fewer teaching seventh than eighth. Ninth grade, sometimes part of junior high and sometimes part of senior high, could have been included by the site directors as part of the junior or senior high group and so had the strongest chance of being sampled as either the highest grade in a junior high or middle school or the lowest grade in a high school.

Table 2.6

Characteristics of Secondary Classes

Current Teaching Situation	Percent of Teachers Reporting	
	All Classes	Selected Class
Subject area		
English	90.4	95.6
Social studies	4.4	2.6
Other	5.2	1.8
	(n = 365)	(n = 341)
Grade levels		
pre-7	2.4	1.9
7	19.9	17.7
8	25.0	25.1
9	18.0	16.1
10	15.6	13.6
11	25.8	24.8
12	27.6	28.6
	(n = 367)	(n = 367)
Combined classes		
One grade only	77.9	80.4
pre-7 only	1.4	0
7 only	15.6	13.9
8 only	19.7	20.7
9 only	12.4	12.5
10 only	6.6	7.4
11 only	9.7	10.6
12 only	12.5	15.3
Two adjacent grades combined	13.0	11.2
pre-7–7	0.05	0
7–8	2.6	2.2
8–9	0.09	0.3
9–10	0.08	0
10–11	0.08	0.5
11–12	7.9	8.2
More than two grades or two nonadjacent grades combined	9.0	8.4
Class status		
Required	68.0	69.5
Option in required area	18.0	17.9
Elective	14.0	12.6
	(n = 369)	(n = 364)
Class length		
Year long	75.6	75.5
Semester	20.3	21.5
Other	4.1	3.0
	(n = 369)	(n = 367)

Therefore, it is surprising that ninth grade was not better represented. These successful secondary teachers tend to gravitate toward the upper grades in their schools.

Like the elementary teachers, most of the secondary teachers taught one grade level in a class. Combinations, which occurred less frequently for the secondary teachers than for the elementary teachers, were found mostly for eleventh and twelfth grade.

Like the classes taught by the teachers in the Applebee sample (1981, 22), the classes these secondary teachers taught were usually required of students and ran for the entire school year.

A comparison of the secondary and elementary teachers gives additional information (Table 2.7). First, both the elementary and secondary teachers perceived their students as able; both groups reported a larger percentage of their students above average than below average.[8] Elementary teachers had larger classes than the secondary norm but not larger than the secondary teachers in this study; class size was lower than what is often reported. The elementary class size has a median of 26.41, not significantly different from the median for the focal class for the secondary teachers but significantly larger than the median of 24.98 reported by secondary teachers for the usual class at their schools.[9] Only about 5 percent of the elementary and secondary students were labeled nonnative speakers of English. The elementary teachers reported using computers in their classes significantly more than the secondary teachers did.

On their questionnaires, the secondary students gave information about themselves (Table 2.8). Roughly half of the students were males and half were females. They were fairly evenly distributed across grade levels, and, not surprisingly, showed the same imbalances in grade-level distribution that the teachers did. Most reported making A's and B's in the writing class taught by the teacher in the survey. After graduation, the higher-achieving students were more inclined than their lower-achieving peers to expect to go to a four-year college and were less inclined to expect to enter a two-year college or to have no plans for education beyond high school. Most of the students in both groups expected to complete four years of college.

Establishing the Teachers' Success: How These Teachers Differ from Usual Writing Teachers

The teachers in this survey were identified by Writing Project site directors as among the most outstanding teachers of writing in their

Table 2.7

Comparisons between Elementary and Secondary Classes

	Percent of Teachers Reporting			
		Secondary (n = 369)		
	Elementary (n = 191)	All Classes	Selected Class	Tests of Significance
Ability level of students				
Above average	33.2	32.5	35.2	
Average	45.7	24.8	25.5	
Below average	21.2	14.4	13.5	—
Mixed	n/a	28.3	25.8	
	(n = 187)	(n = 369)	(n = 364)	
Teach writing	—	95.1	100.0	—
		(n = 369)	(n = 365)	
Use computer	44.3	19.5	21.1	chi-square = 32.16*
	(n = 185)	(n = 369)	(n = 365)	(df = 1)
Percent nonnative speakers of English taught	5.1 (n = 186)	5.4 (n = 366)	—	t test = −.20 (df = 334)

	Medians				
		Secondary Teachers			
	Elementary Teachers	Usual Class	Focal Class	All Teachers	Chi-square Tests[a]
Class size	26.41 (n = 182)	24.98 (n = 367)	26.46 (n = 361)	25.44 (n = 549)	(a) 3.51 (df = 1) (b) 18.83* (df = 1)

[a] The first chi-square (a) compares the elementary classes with the secondary focal classes. The second chi-square (b) compares the elementary classes with the teachers' reports of the usual enrollment in a secondary class at the teacher's school.

* $p < .001$.

Table 2.8

Characteristics of Sampled Students

Characteristics	Percent of Students Reporting
Gender	
Female	50.6
Male	49.4
	(n = 706)
Grade level	
below 7	2.3
7	12.7
8	21.5
9	14.9
10	8.8
11	19.4
12	20.5
	(n = 707)
Grades in sampled class	
A	40.1
B	35.2
C	19.6
Below C or other	5.1
	(n = 710)

	Percent Reporting			
Expectations[a]	High-Achieving Students	Low-Achieving Students	All Students	Secondary Teachers
Plans after graduation				
None past high school	10.9	25.9	18.3	22.8
Vocational school	5.4	3.4	4.4	14.3
1 or 2 years of college	6.9	15.0	11.0	18.5
At least 4 years of college	78.8	53.8	66.3	44.3
	(n = 349)	(n = 353)	(n = 702)	(n = 364)
Chi-square test	49.47*			
	(df = 3)			

[a] Differences between the students' and their teachers' responses cannot be determined because the number of categories for this variable differed across the questionnaires. On the student questionnaire there were six categories, the additional categories being specifications of the category "none past high school," which included work full-time, work and then go to college, and military service. Percentage comparisons were made across the categories by combining these three student categories and including them in the category "none past high school."

* $p < .001$.

regions. Seeking independent confirmation of site directors' judgments, the research team hypothesized that if these teachers were especially successful, they would answer certain questions differently than participants in Applebee's (1981) survey, who were selected to be above average but not necessarily especially successful.[10]

Two sets of items were paralleled with sets used in Applebee's survey. The first concerned the amount of writing students are asked to do and the second concerned the reasons teachers give for teaching writing. Applebee found that the teachers he surveyed had students write infrequently, required only brief pieces, and that the teachers had restricted reasons for teaching writing. They did not combine the teaching of writing as a craft with the teaching of writing as an instrument of thought, nor did they combine the teaching of writing to transmit information with the teaching of writing to connect students' school and personal experiences.

We hypothesized that both our secondary and elementary teachers would have students do more writing than the teachers in the Applebee survey and that these groups would teach writing for multiple reasons. The two hypotheses were confirmed: both sets of paralleled items showed significant differences in the expected directions between these teachers and Applebee's. The survey results concerning the amount of writing required follow, and the data on the teachers' reasons for teaching writing form the foundation for Chapter 4.

The Writing Their Students Do

The teachers in this sample reported that their students were doing a significant amount of writing (Table 2.9). First, the teachers claimed to teach writing in 95 percent of their classes.

Much of the writing was being done during class time, with in-class pieces averaging about a page in length. At the time of the survey, 96.9 percent of the elementary teachers and 87 percent of the secondary teachers had their students writing in class, and 59.8 percent of the elementary and 68.7 percent of the secondary teachers had their students doing out-of-class writing. Both groups of teachers were significantly more likely to assign in-class writing than out-of-class writing. The elementary teachers leaned more strongly in the direction of in-class writing than the secondary teachers did, and the secondary teachers had their students doing significantly more at-home writing than did the elementary teachers.

In regard to in-class writing, most of the teachers (both elementary and secondary) had their students producing one-page pieces, followed by a substantial number of teachers who also used writing for copying

Table 2.9

Amount and Length of Writing: In-Class and Out-of-Class

	In-Class		Out-of-Class		
	Elementary (n = 191)	Secondary (n = 368)	Elementary (n = 189)	Secondary (n = 367)	t Tests[a]
Percent answering that writing is occurring	96.9	87.0	59.8	68.7	(a) −9.87*** (df = 188) (b) −6.19*** (df = 366)
Chi-square tests (df = 1)		13.02***		3.97*	

	Percent of Teachers Reporting "Yes"				
	In-Class		Out-of-Class		Chi-square Tests[b] (df = 1)
Writing Behavior	Elementary (n = 185)	Secondary (n = 320)	Elementary (n = 113)	Secondary (n = 252)	
Copying, note-taking or sentences	45.4	42.2	23.0	11.5	(a) .37 (b) 7.19**
Up to 250 words (1 page)	69.7	58.8	49.6	25.4	(a) 5.59* (b) 19.56***
251–500 words (1–2 pages)	28.6	26.3	37.3	33.7	(a) .23 (b) .13
501–1000 words (2–4 pages)	6.5	3.8	18.6	38.5	(a) 1.38 (b) 13.24***
Over 1000 words (more than 4 pages)	2.2	.6	5.3	13.1	(a) 1.23 (b) 4.17*

[a] The first test (a) measures the difference in the means of the elementary students doing in-class writing versus those doing out-of-class writing. The next t test (b) compares the mean of the secondary students doing in-class writing with those doing out-of-class writing.

[b] The first chi-square test (a) measures the difference in elementary and secondary in-class writing; the second (b) measures the difference between elementary and secondary out-of-class writing.

* p < .05.   ** p < .01.   *** p < .001.

and note taking, and next a significant number who had students write one- to two-page pieces. There was only one significant difference between secondary and elementary teachers: more elementary than secondary teachers had their students writing in-class pieces of one page or less.

For writing done at home, the pattern shifted dramatically toward longer works, especially for the secondary sample. The elementary teachers had students doing significantly more copying and note taking and more pieces of less than one page. The secondary teachers had students writing significantly more pieces of two to four pages. Although at-home writing of more than four pages was occurring for relatively few students, it was occurring significantly more for secondary students than for elementary students.

Table 2.10 contains the comparison with Applebee's sample.[11] Applebee found that teachers in his sample required little extended writing, usually less than a page. Across the board, teachers in this survey assigned more writing than Applebee's English teachers. Teachers in the Applebee survey required significantly more writing of one page or less and of one to two pages; in contrast, the teachers in this sample required significantly more pieces of two to four pages and of over four pages.

The teachers in this sample also gave students a longer time to complete their writing, on the average 5.03 days for elementary students, and 5.21 days for secondary students, an insignificant difference across the two groups ($t = .46$ with 1 degree of freedom). Applebee reported that teachers in his sample expected written work to be completed in less than a week and often in less than two days (55).

Table 2.10

Length of Out-of-Class Writing: Secondary Sample and
Applebee's Secondary English Sample

	Percent of Teachers Reporting "Yes"		
Length of Writing	Secondary ($n = 252$)	Applebee's Secondary English ($n = 139$)	Chi-square Test ($df = 1$)
Up to 250 words (1 page)	25.4	59.7	45.29**
251–500 words (1–2 pages)	33.7	46.8	6.50*
501–1000 words (2–4 pages)	38.5	10.08	35.59**
Over 1000 words (more than 4 pages)	13.1	3.6	9.21**

* $p < .05$.   ** $p < .001$.

Comments from the Students

In their questionnaires, students provided additional evidence that their teachers were extraordinary. The students were asked one open-ended question, "When you are trying to write better, what helps you most and why?" They were also given space to add comments. Student comments were analyzed on a subset of 100 randomly selected surveys. The comments were placed in four categories indicating the sources of help as they learned to write: (1) help from their current teacher, (2) help from the act of writing, (3) help from other readers (parents, siblings, friends, other teachers), and (4) help from the act of reading (from reading books to reading the writing of peers). Of the 100 students, only 8 chose not to respond to the question. Of the 92 who responded, 62 percent mentioned the role of their current teacher, 40 percent the role of writing itself, 28 percent the role of other readers, and 17 percent the role of reading. The importance of the teacher, then, was mentioned by the most students.

Since it is likely that the teachers would select students who liked them to complete the questionnaires, we would have to compare the comments of these students with comments from students similarly selected from classrooms of "usual" teachers. However, such data are not available. Still the content of the students' comments points to these teachers as special. When writing about their teachers, the students stressed particular qualities and techniques that set these teachers apart. The teachers were described as patient, hardworking, and understanding about the difficulty of writing. Their directions were clear. They were constructive critics who made their students think for themselves rather than telling students what to do. Typically, they helped students throughout the writing process, giving them valued guidance, especially when students were in the process of generating ideas and then revising.

Several student comments provide a sense of the students' feelings. A ninth-grade girl writes about her teacher's important personal qualities:

> My Intro. to Lit. and Comp. teacher is a very patient teacher. I like her because she takes pride in all the student's work and helping them when they have a problem in their assignment.

An eleventh grader quips, "Mrs. M. is a very helpful and good teacher. She gets involved and doesn't sit on her tush all day."

A twelfth-grade boy praises his teacher's approach to response:

> My present English teacher is the best one that I have encountered in high school. She gives constructive criticism without *attacking* me. I can talk to her and most students do talk to her.

About her teacher's curriculum, a seventh-grade girl comments:

> I really like this class because we arent being given a book and being said to "copy" this and "copy" that. I like the idea of having my own due dates and doing my own work at my own pace. I know I am learning alot more about myself and English than I have in any other of my classess.
>
> P.S. Mrs. M. is also verry understanding and helpful.

Many of these comments say as much about the negative past experiences these students have encountered in school writing as they do about their current, more positive experience.

Summary and Discussion

The teachers participating in this survey were selected as the most outstanding in their region by the 116 site directors of the National Writing Project. In all, 560 teachers participated. They represented every geographic region in the country and every grade level from kindergarten through grade twelve. The secondary teachers selected 715 student participants in a way that yielded almost equal numbers of males and females and higher- and lower-achieving students. These teachers were selected for their special expertise in teaching writing and for being highly experienced; other than that, they seem representative of the general population of teachers.

However, they were atypical in a number of significant ways. First, these teachers had their students do more than the usual amount of writing. Overall, they assigned relatively long pieces (an average of one page for in-class pieces and two to four pages for out-of-class pieces at the secondary level), assigned them often (most students were writing at the time of the survey), and gave their students more time than usual (over a week) to complete their written work. Both secondary and elementary teachers assigned an especially large amount of in-class writing.

Although one could argue that the amount and extent of the writing reported here is still not great, it is at least significantly greater than has been reported previously and can provide a realistic goal toward which other teachers could aspire.

The secondary teachers were also atypical in that almost all were English teachers with college degrees in English. In spite of the recent emphasis on "writing across the curriculum," with the National Writing Project taking a leading role in that movement in this country, few of these secondary teachers taught in disciplines other than English. It still seems to be true that when we look for specialists in teaching writing, we turn to the English department. A great deal remains to be done to help teachers outside English departments become expert in using writing within their subject-matter classes. In addition, it seems necessary to encourage English teachers such as these to play a major role in the cross-curricular movement.

These teachers seize control over their environment and make it support them. They are not victims. A high percentage of the teachers report teaching fewer classes than the usual teacher at his or her school. And as a group, they only have about twenty-five students in their classes, a figure lower than the one they report for other classes at their schools and certainly lower than the number usually reported in the press. Nevertheless, they still find the teaching load difficult to manage and see it as a barrier to what they could do given more ideal conditions.

A final, outstanding mark of this sample of teachers is that they have positive perceptions of their students' abilities and high expectations for them. Corresponding to their teachers' faith in their abilities, the students perform well and have high expectations for themselves. The teachers perceive more of their students as above-average achievers than below average. Most of the students report making A's and B's and say that they plan to complete four years of college. Even though the students clearly form the higher- and lower-achieving groups that we asked the teachers to select (the groups receive significantly different grades), all exhibit relatively positive self-concepts of themselves as writers. The teachers' perceptions and the high student goals may be partly an artifact of the teaching situations of the teachers. Although they teach in varied types of schools and communities, for the most part they teach in relatively affluent public schools. Their students, on the whole, are not faced with the problems of poverty. The teachers teach relatively few nonnative English speakers. Even though a few teach students who traditionally are considered difficult, the number is small.

As a society, we need to understand more about why such teachers, as a group, do not tend to tackle our most challenging educational problems. Ironically, these are the very teachers who are most needed to contribute to an understanding of how to help students who traditionally fail to succeed. Clearly, there are many excellent teachers of such students; it is just that this sample did not yield high numbers of them. Ideally, the Writing Project site directors would have recommended more of such teachers than they did. Even from the site directors in the major metropolitan areas in the U.S., more teachers were recommended from the suburbs of these areas than from the inner cities.

**Ethnography in Two Ninth-Grade Classrooms: Procedures for
Selecting Teachers and Classrooms**

Two teachers in the San Francisco Bay Area were to be selected to
participate in the ethnography. The teachers had to meet initial selection
requirements of being (1) known successful teachers of writing, (2)
ninth-grade teachers during the spring of 1984, (3) teachers of academic
writing to ninth graders, (4) willing to participate in the study (which
would include allowing intensive observations and audio- and videotaping of their teaching and their students' learning over a period of
several months and also assisting with the analysis of the data), and
(5) different from one another.

A preliminary list of candidates thought to meet these requirements
was generated by James Gray and Mary K. Healy, who were in charge
of the in-service teacher training programs of the Bay Area Writing
Project and who work closely with hundreds of local teachers each
year. Their list was supplemented by lists from local school personnel
and teacher-leaders in the community who know the reputations of
local teachers of writing. Through this process, thirty-five highly recommended teachers emerged.

The research team[12] conducted preliminary screening interviews with
each of the thirty-five. These first telephone interviews determined
whether the teachers were scheduled to teach or could be scheduled to
teach ninth grade during the spring term when we would be observing,
whether they would be teaching academic writing to ninth graders as
a normal part of their curriculum, and whether they were willing to
consider participating in this project. No one whom we contacted was
unwilling to participate, but only seventeen of the thirty-five teachers
planned to teach ninth graders and academic writing during the spring.

One member of the research team, either one of the two ethnographers or I, observed each of the seventeen teachers teaching at least
one class (if possible, ninth grade) during the fall of 1983. The
observation was followed by an extensive interview with the teacher
about his or her teaching philosophy, curriculum, response practices,
and plans for the spring class that we might observe. At this point,
some teachers were eliminated for logistical reasons: the classroom was
not large enough to accommodate a team of researchers with video
equipment or was located in an environment where ambient noise was
too great to gather usable audio recordings. For example, one teacher's
school was located at the intersection of three major freeways in San
Francisco; it would have been impossible to collect audible audiotapes
in any classroom in the school.

Several teachers were eliminated because school philosophies forced them to engage in teaching practices that ran counter to their philosophies. For example, one teacher's local proficiency test measured students' knowledge of formal grammatical terms; the teacher had to spend a significant portion of his class time on the teaching of these terms even though that was not, in his judgment, what his students most needed to learn.

In making the final choices, characteristics of the teachers and the school site became a consideration. Although a number of the remaining teachers would have been excellent candidates for the project, the research team agreed that the two teachers we selected: (1) had an understandable sense of purpose — a clear rationale for what was being taught and why, (2) had students who seemed to be engaged in the class and learning what the teachers were intending to teach, (3) had exceptionally high expectations for their students that their students seemed to be meeting, and (4) offered a contrast with one another along the lines of their gender, their teaching style, and the communities in which the schools were located.

Descriptions of the Selected Teachers

The selected teachers, Mary Lee Glass of Gunn High School in Palo Alto and Art Peterson of Lowell High School in San Francisco, are leaders among writing teachers, have participated in the invitational summer programs of the Bay Area Writing Project, have received special recognition in their school districts for their abilities as writing teachers, and are considered by their principals and by the professional community to be model teachers. Both publish their own writing in journals and books.

Glass is chair of her English department and holds major offices in state and national professional organizations. During the time we observed her class, she was the program chair for the National Council of Teachers of English Secondary Section meeting, made a trip to Council headquarters for business, and was elected president of the California Association of Teachers of English. She also starred in the Gunn High School community musical, *Kiss Me Kate,* which ran to sell-out crowds for a two-week period. With twenty-four years of teaching experience — twenty of those years at Gunn — she has taught substantially longer than the fourteen years of the average survey participant. Like many of the secondary teachers participating in the survey, she holds an M.A. in English.

Peterson has taught in the San Francisco Unified School District for twenty-three years (again substantially longer than most teachers in the survey). During the time we observed his class, he had just completed a revision of the writing curriculum at his school, was selected to become a mentor teacher in the first year of the state of California's mentor teacher program, and had signed a contract with a publisher to write the teacher's companion to *The Preppie Handbook.*[13] He also was serving on the advisory board for teacher-training programs at a nearby university. Before joining Lowell's English department six years before, he taught social studies and English in a San Francisco junior high school. His academic background is in social studies, making him different from most of the survey participants; he has an M.A. in American history.

Both Glass and Peterson expressed their teaching philosophies in writing. Selections from their statements give a flavor of their views about the teaching of writing (see Freedman [1985] for complete copies of their statements).

Glass writes the following about her teaching:

> How can we expect children to learn their way into thinking coherently, expressing themselves effectively, speaking with authority and voice and transitions, polishing with grace and art, if all we have done is talk about writing, about topic sentences, about paragraph structure, but we have not practiced? Practiced what? All of it — saying it, seeing it, saying it better, trying it out on others, becoming aware that we hear when one phrase says it better, learning that making mistakes is not only not fatal but necessary to becoming better.
>
> Simultaneously with practice, the student of writing must learn to evaluate — his own, her peers', the masters' writing. And in that fact lies yet another dimension of practice and dilemma for the teacher of writing, for he must, like coaches and drill sergeants and counselors, be all things at the right time to all students. . . . Clearly, evaluation must become an automatic part of the practice, an informal exercise in expression and revision as well as the formal statement translated into a grade at the end of the quarter, an easy and comfortable nonthreatening part of the process of growth and thinking, an acknowledgment that we can all see and hear and judge what is 'better' rather than depend entirely upon the teacher who grades the paper to tell us how good it is.

Peterson discusses his techniques for responding to student writing and makes a point similar to Glass's about the importance of nonthreatening practice: "Learning to write is not like learning to hang glide. The hang glider needs to learn all of the 'dos' and 'don'ts' before he puts on wings and tries to fly. But a writer can only learn to write by practicing, and he needs to understand that, in writing, no crash is fatal." Also about practice he says,

Some truths about teaching and learning writing seem so simple-minded they are embarrassing to recite. For instance: Students learn to write by writing. What could be more obvious? Yet for years I ignored this truism. I filled class periods with lots of talk about writing but very little writing. We would begin to write, (I seemed to be saying) when we learned to write better. This idea only sounds like it comes from Joseph Heller. . . . There may be no way to relieve the agony that comes with sorting out jumbled ideas. However, with practice this process comes to be understood as a prelude to the emotional rush that accompanies an idea clearly expressed.

Peterson, too, wants students to learn to evaluate, but he sees students working in groups to "share" rather than to "evaluate." He continues by making a further distinction: "I came to recognize that sharing and evaluating need to be separated. . . . I saw [as] my job to respond so as to help students develop a common criterion for judgment." He also asserts, "I've found the traditional method of response — meticulous correction of errors and an evaluative grade — seldom works." Just as he separates "sharing" and "evaluation," he separates "response" and "grades." Peterson says, "When the revisions stop, my comments stop. I do not comment on the paper I grade. . . . My students need to understand that they can learn to write competently if they will learn to understand that writing is a process, not a slapdash task, and that good grades on written work are quite often a by-product of the care and attention this process demands."

The Setting for the Observations

Both teachers taught college preparatory classes at high schools in which most students are headed for college. Both schools have been designated as being one of the top high schools nationwide.[14] In spite of this similarity, the schools and student bodies are strikingly different in most other respects.

Gunn High School

Gunn High School, where Glass teaches, is located in Palo Alto, an intellectual, middle-class suburb of San Francisco whose character derives in large part from two sources: (1) nearby Stanford University, and (2) the high-tech industry that dots much of the surrounding area, known as Silicon Valley. Stanford imparts to the community an atmosphere typically associated with college towns, including book-stores, cafés, restaurants, shops that cater to "academic tastes," and a broad range of music, drama, film, and art. Silicon Valley communicates, if only indirectly, the value our society places on science, technology, and "growth industry." Gunn draws students who, in good measure, come from homes connected to one of these two cultural sources. Another, smaller group of Gunn students, giving the school a bit of cultural diversity, come from a segment of Palo Altans who could be characterized as an upwardly mobile blue-collar ethnic mix of Asians, Blacks, and Hispanics and other Caucasians.

Although one sees Asians, Hispanics, and Blacks at Gunn, one would not characterize the school as an ethnic or cultural melting pot. The students are mostly white, from middle-class and upper-middle-class families. Many of them enjoy the privileges associated with the type of suburb they live in, having read many books, experienced as observers or participants both sports and the arts, and traveled in this country and abroad. They come, for the most part, from homes that place great value on academic success. Students' scores on standardized tests tend to be well above the national average, and they come to Gunn with respectable grade point averages from feeder middle schools or junior high schools, as well as from private schools.

Gunn High School itself is a modern structure of wood, concrete, and glass. Architecturally striking, the school was built to allow students and teachers to be outdoors a great deal; the buildings are connected by covered outdoor walkways and are interspersed with stretches of well-groomed lawn. In order to get from class to class, one traverses these walkways, often crossing from one building to another. The school site resembles, therefore, a small college. In fact, the architecture might be thought to echo the view held by many Gunn parents, teachers, and students, that this high school is getting students ready to attend colleges or universities.

Lowell High School

Lowell High School in San Francisco, where Peterson teaches, is characterized as an "academic" school; that is, most courses there satisfy high school prerequisites for college entrance; "nonacademic" courses (for example, "shop" courses or home economics) are not offered. Located in a middle-class residential neighborhood that was built up mostly in the late forties and fifties, Lowell has for a neighbor a large suburban-type shopping center. Its location, then, although in the city, resembles in some ways a modest suburb: neat row houses with trees and small lawns, and a neighborhood shopping center. Yet Lowell draws students from all over the city, not just from the neighborhood in which it is located. For, unlike other San Francisco public high schools, it enrolls any student who meets its academic entrance requirements, currently a B+ grade average from junior high school and high scores on the Comprehensive Test of Basic Skills (CTBS).

Students at Lowell are, for the most part, academic achievers. While all ethnic groups are represented there, most students are Asian, followed by Caucasians. There are more females than males. Yet these students reflect diverse cultural backgrounds, coming from the wealthiest and the poorest of San Francisco neighborhoods and from working class as well as middle- and upper-middle-class homes. They have in common high grade point averages from feeder middle schools and junior high schools (some are private and parochial schools) and above-average scores on the CTBS. Lowell also has some students who have problems in English classes because English is their second language and others who have difficulty because they came from less than rigorous junior high and middle schools from which they got unrealistically good grades. In a sense, then, there are two Lowell populations: the struggling students and the real academic cream of the San Francisco public schools. Lowell's reputation is based on the second group, who are, for the most part, students who plan to go to a college or a university when they graduate. In fact, Lowell is considered "college prep."

The building in which Lowell is located was built in the early sixties, although the school itself dates back over 125 years, being San Francisco's oldest "living" high school. The current building is a two-story concrete structure, punctuated by many windows and surrounded by lawn. All classrooms and offices are located along indoor halls. While the school is built around a central courtyard, much social activity — including lunch and snack eating — occurs inside, in the hallways. Lining the hallway walls are bulletin boards and glass cases displaying, among other things, pictures of and articles about distinguished Lowell alumni. Lowell students are thus daily reminded that they walk in halls echoing with a spirited 125-year-old tradition of excellence that has yielded much academic and professional success.

A Comment on Choices of Teachers and Settings and an Aside on the Teaching of Academic Writing

Both Glass and Peterson, as well as most of the teachers we could locate who teach academic writing to ninth graders, teach in predominantly college preparatory high schools. Every private school teacher we talked to teaches academic writing to ninth graders, as do most teachers in wealthy suburban public schools with academic orientations. In addition, these teachers teach other forms of writing, including imaginative and personal experience writing, play writing and journalistic writing. The teachers we interviewed who were working with non-college-bound students, as well as most of those working with inner-city students, were not teaching academic forms of analysis or exposition at this grade level nor were they headed in that direction. Instead, they focused, for the most part, on the personal experience narrative.

The teachers seem to be following the dictates of the curriculum of their school, and many seem unaware of the differential nature of their curriculum. They personally do not seem to believe it is inappropriate to teach academic writing to non-college-bound students or to inner-city students; they just don't do it. Applebee et al. (1984) found that weaker students in the academically oriented schools he studied were exposed to a variety of forms of writing, unlike their more successful counterparts, who were restricted almost solely to academic or informational writing. From a wider but less formal look at Bay Area schools, I found that the non-college-bound students received little exposure to at least one type of writing — the type essential to success in the academic community and perhaps beyond.

Before beginning this research, I was unaware of the distribution of the teaching of academic writing in the local curriculum. Originally, I hoped to study at least one teacher in an urban public school that does not cater exclusively to the college-bound student as Lowell does. Unfortunately, it was not possible to locate a teacher in such a school who met the other criteria. I could have selected a teacher from an inner-city school and abandoned the criteria of limiting the study to teachers who were teaching academic writing; however, I maintained the criteria for two reasons. First, it was necessary to limit the focus and to establish points of similarity across the two settings. Thus, not only the grade level but also the type of writing being taught during the observations was controlled. Second, academic writing was selected because it is commonly *used* to support teaching students the patterns of abstract reasoning necessary to success in school (Goody and Watt 1963; Olson 1977), even though academic writing is not the only route to teaching abstract thinking and certainly does not guarantee that such thinking will be practiced (see Scribner and Cole 1981; Street 1984; Traugott 1985). On a strictly pragmatic level, since academic writing is part of academic success in many disciplines, lack of exposure to this type of writing may well lead to diminished academic opportunities. Thus, it seemed important to study how students are initiated into academic ways of writing, both for the benefit of those who routinely receive the initiation and for those who do not.

It is important finally to stress the belief that students are handicapped when they lack exposure to a wide variety of types of writing in school. This is true for all students, in all instructional contexts, and includes experience with all types of writing, from the personal experience narrative to the academic essay to the writing of stories and plays.

Procedures for Selecting Focal Students

The observations in each classroom focused on four students, the maximum number that could be followed effectively. The aim was to examine responses to their writing from their peers and their teachers and to study the oral responses as well as the written comments that they received. Neither the teacher nor the students knew that any students were receiving particular focus until after all classroom observations were completed.

Within each class, the focal students differed in their past academic achievement levels. They were selected on the basis of their scores in reading and vocabulary on the Comprehensive Test of Basic Skills (CTBS), which all California students take in eighth grade, as well as their grades in junior high and in the first semester of ninth grade. We chose two higher-achieving, and two lower-achieving students who also differed along gender and cultural lines because we wanted a sample that was representative of the classes we were observing.

Characteristics of Classes and Focal Students

Mary Lee Glass's Class

Glass's class was an "honors" section in communication with a curriculum covering both writing and speaking. Relatively speaking, the students were all high-achieving; however, there was still diversity in the group. Of the 33 students, 12 were boys and 21 girls. Of these students, 26 were Caucasian and 7 were Asian. All the Asians were of Chinese heritage except for one of Middle-Eastern descent; 4 were female and 3 were male.

For our focal students, we selected Julie, a highly motivated Asian girl; Jim, a quiet but high-achieving Caucasian boy; Allison, a very shy, lower-achieving Caucasian girl; and Derek, a gregarious, lower-achieving Caucasian boy.[15]

Julie had an impressive student file and looked to us to be a representative high achiever in language arts; she was among the top students in this class. In the first semester of ninth grade, Julie made all A's on her report card, a pattern consistent with that in her junior high years. Her percentile scores on the CTBS ranged from 90 to 98, with a 97 in vocabulary, purportedly the best single score for predicting achievement in language arts. (These CTBS national percentiles are higher than the district percentiles. Julie's 97, for example, translated to an 80 for the district.)

Another high achiever, Jim, differed primarily from Julie in being a Caucasian male, because his records were only a hairline below hers. On the CTBS, Jim's percentile scores ranged from 88 to 98, with a 98 in vocabulary, the district equivalent being 86. His first semester report card for ninth grade showed a B and two A−'s among the A's; however, in World Culture, the first semester English class, he received an A.

Just as Julie and Jim showed promise as high achievers, Allison seemed to promise difficulties. Interestingly, her CTBS percentile score hit a high of 95 in mechanics but her low score of 77 was in vocabulary, equivalent to a district percentile of 33. Also, in ninth grade, her first semester report card showed two C's, one of them being in the English course, World Culture. Considering the rest of the students in Glass's class, Allison's past record was among the poorest.

Again keeping in mind that low-achieving students in this honors course would not parallel the mainstream of low-achieving students, we chose our fourth focal student, Derek. Derek's CTBS percentile scores ranged from 52 to 92; his vocabulary score was 65, translating to a district percentile of 20. His first semester report card for ninth grade showed one C+ in Spanish, one A in physical education, a B+ in World Culture, B− in science, P (Pass) in photography, and B− in European History.

Art Peterson's Class

Peterson's class was a regular ninth-grade English class with a curriculum centered on literature and writing. Although Peterson's class was not designated as an honors group, he felt that they were similar to honors groups at Lowell. Further, unlike Gunn, Lowell is in fact an honors-only school, since academic criteria are used for admission.

The class contained 27 students, 14 of whom were Asian, 1 Black, 3 Hispanic, and 9 other Caucasians. Like the total school population at Lowell, the great majority — 21 — were female.

Thus, we selected focal students to represent this ethnic and sexual imbalance: three females and one male; two Asians, one Black, and one Caucasian. The sample included Lisa, a highly motivated, outgoing, Chinese-American girl; Donald, a quiet but high-achieving Chinese-American boy; Candace, a coquettish, lower-achieving Caucasian girl; and Rhonda, a sociable, lower-achieving Black girl.

Lisa had CTBS percentile scores in language arts that ranged from 81 to 96 percent, with a vocabulary percentile at 86. She made all A's in her first semester at Lowell. At Lowell a straight-A showing is not to be taken lightly; "grade inflation" does not seem to have afflicted this school. Lisa was thus a clear-cut choice for a high-achieving student and as an Asian female, she represented the majority at Lowell.

If past records are good predictors, Donald's promised us another high achiever. His CTBS percentile scores in language arts ranged from 96 to 99, and his grades from his first semester at Lowell included only one B among all A's. His first semester English grade was an A.

Candace's records marked her as a low achiever. The only Caucasian in our group, her CTBS percentile scores ranged from 59 to 81, with her vocabulary percentile score at 71. Her first semester report card for ninth grade showed a C in English, three other C's and two D's. She had the lowest grade record of any of our focal students, and we were interested in following Candace's progress in our study since she had made the necessary grades to be accepted into Lowell the year before. However, in the end we were unable to follow Candace. She attended class infrequently, rarely wrote anything, and appeared to have rather severe personal problems. She eventually had to leave Lowell.

We chose our last focal student, Rhonda, primarily for her having received a D in English in her first semester at Lowell. This low grade was unusual for the students in Peterson's class but went along with the other D and two C's she received her first semester, although she did also receive two B's (one in physical education). Rhonda's CTBS percentile scores in language arts ranged from 60 to 92, with an 81 in vocabulary. Like Candace, she appeared to represent an interesting combination of certain low achievements, but with the potential for a great deal of growth.

Collecting Ethnographic Data

Videotape and audiotape recordings were collected in Glass's classroom from January through mid-April, 1984, and in Peterson's from mid-April through mid-June of that year. Besides recordings of the main channels of teacher-student interactions, separate tape recordings were made of all peer group meetings. In addition, an ethnographer took field notes in each classroom every day. All materials prepared by the teacher were collected as were all student writing assignments, including drafts done out of class when feasible. These data form a comprehensive record of school-based response to the students' writing.

Curriculum Sequence

Both classes were a semester rather than a year in length and began in January; thus, students and teacher first met in January. The observation schedule that we chose allowed us to observe parallel segments of the curriculum in each classroom — times when academic writing was the focus. Fortunately, the teachers planned their curriculum so that we could complete observations in one class before moving on to the next. However, since both classes began in January, in order to see how both teachers got acquainted with their students and established the classroom rules, we observed both classes during their first week. Fortunately, since Glass's class met in the early morning and Peterson's in the late morning, it was possible to visit both classrooms on the same day.

An overview of the curriculum sequence that we observed in each class gives the general context for the activities that became the subject of the ethnography.[16]

Mary Lee Glass's Class

During the ten weeks that we observed Glass's classroom, the students wrote three major papers; gave oral presentations, some of which were based on the paper topics; and kept personal "process logs," or running accounts of how their writing was progressing as well as what they thought about it and about their assignments. The four oral/written assignments were (1) an oral and written account of an interview with a fellow student; (2) an oral group presentation of a commercial; (3) a written study of an interesting place (Glass calls these "saturation reports") and (4) a written "opinion" essay. Interspersed were additional assignments, which were often short "practice writings."

Throughout the ten weeks, what stood out was the class's work on generating and molding content for their essays. They moved from the concrete topic of the fellow-student interview to the more abstract topic of an issue about which they had opinions. They learned strategies for focusing their writing, developing their generalities, getting an audience interested, and organizing their ideas.

Glass emphasized, through the process of peer-, teacher-, and self-evaluation, the effect writing has on a reader, reminding the students implicitly and explicitly that their writing and speaking were meant to communicate something to someone. She helped her students make discoveries for themselves, frequently withholding her expertise. Her approach to *collaborative problem solving* involved her in using her expertise to structure a learning environment that aimed at guiding students through specific activities and introducing procedures that would teach them strategies for writing and self-evaluation.

Art Peterson's Class

During the seven weeks that we observed Peterson's classroom, the students wrote three major papers, all based on their observations, descriptions, and analyses of a person, either real or fictitious. The three major essay assignments included (1) a character study of a friend or acquaintance; (2) a character study of a well-known contemporary figure; and (3) a character study of one of the figures in Dickens's *Great Expectations*. The students did a small amount of research on their well-known contemporary figure as the basis for the second of these papers, and over the span of the seven weeks, they read *Great Expectations* as the basis for the third of these papers. Each of these written assignments included practice writings and other prewriting activities related to the topic, several rough drafts, and teacher-student conferences and peer response during the writing process. A major part of classroom activity was group work, especially that in which students worked with words, sentences, and paragraphs, with groups competing with one another to produce the best writing in these categories. Crafting a piece of writing involved an extended process, with some students progressing more quickly than others, but with all students being held to final, teacher-imposed deadlines for each major piece of work.

Peterson emphasized writing as a process of crafting and recrafting text, developing with his students a master-apprentice relationship in which he frequently conferred with individual students both in class and in his office, lending his expertise and shaping successful texts through suggestions or specific examples from other writers, student as well as nonstudent. His approach to *collaborative problem solving* involved him in using his expertise to structure a learning environment in which students practiced the craft as they wrote alone and in group collaboration, learning strategies by testing their products on each other and on the master teacher.

Procedures for Collecting Data

During every day of observation, one of the two ethnographers was in charge of videotaping (the Technician) and the other of compiling ethnographic field notes (the Scribe). When present, a third assisted with equipment and took supplementary field notes. In each classroom, the following primary data were collected:

1. detailed field notes of all classroom sessions during the five-month period, written by the Scribe;
2. videotaped recordings of all class sessions during the three-month period, collected by the Technician;
3. audiotaped recordings collected with (1) an overhead microphone for the class and a wireless microphone attached to the teacher,

(both of which fed into a stereo audio recorder that was simul-taneously fed into the audio portion of the videotape, so that an audiotape cassette duplicating the audio portion of the videotape was created), (2) a backup audiocassette recorder with a single microphone placed in a different part of the classroom, (3) a separate audio recording for each peer group during peer-group discussions, and (4) audio recordings by the teacher of all out-of-class conferences;

4. copies of all drafts of the focal students' writings; and

5. copies of all written teacher or student comments about the pieces of focal students' writing.

The following secondary data were collected:

1. notes on informal conversations with teachers, students, and other school personnel;

2. two audiotaped, day-long interviews of the teachers by the in-vestigators about the substance of the instruction and about the progress of each focal student (held after all classroom data were collected);

3. two two-hour, audiotaped interviews between the investigators and each focal student: one in which the focal students filled out the national survey while discussing each item, and a second in which focal students discussed the effects of different types of response on their production of a selected piece of writing and also discussed their understandings of the different responses (held after all classroom data were collected); and

4. written statements from each teacher about their goals for the assignment sequence we observed and about their teaching phi-losophy.

Scribe's Procedures and Conventions

At the staff meetings that took place before the observations began and during the first week of observations, the research team developed note-taking conventions and procedures for in-class data collection. These conventions and procedures were refined during the first few weeks of ethnographic observations and are described in Appendix C.

During class, the Scribe was situated away from the students' desks but provided with a clear view of the class as a whole and, particularly, of the four focal students (see the diagram of Glass's classroom in Figure 2.1 and Peterson's classroom in Figure 2.2).

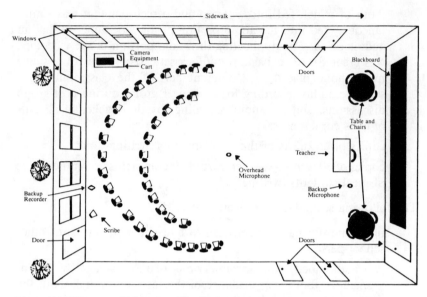

Figure 2.1. Diagram of Mary Lee Glass's classroom.

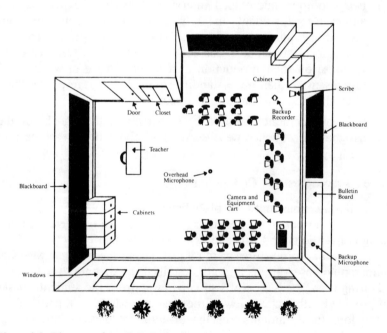

Figure 2.2. Diagram of Art Peterson's classroom

Technician's Procedures and Conventions

The classroom duties of the Technician included making decisions about camera shots (criteria for decisions are given in Appendix D), monitoring audio quality,[17] and taking supplementary notes about classroom events and keying those notes to the tape-recorded data.[18] Finally, the Technician functioned as a supplementary Scribe, describing events in the classroom and student behaviors that the official Scribe might miss from her angle of vision.

The video camera and recording equipment were placed in the left rear of each classroom, a spot that afforded a view of most of the classroom.[19] The camera was sometimes moved a few feet to enable a better view of focal students during class or group activities, but in general remained stationary in the far corner.

Summary

Two successful ninth-grade teachers from California were selected to participate in the ethnography: Mary Lee Glass of Gunn High School in Palo Alto, and Arthur Peterson of Lowell High School in San Francisco. Although both were teaching college preparatory classes, they offered a contrast of teaching styles, gender, and school location. To collect parallel data in the two classrooms, we arranged our observations at a time when both would be introducing their students to academic writing.

The observation period spanned ten weeks in Glass's classroom and seven weeks in Peterson's. Four students in one class and three in the other, selected to represent the range of students in their classes, were focal to the study. Each classroom was observed and activities were tape-recorded (audio and video) daily during the observation period.

In this way, we obtained a comprehensive record of response in two ninth-grade classrooms and could focus on the effects of response for a variety of types of students in each class.

Notes

1. The experts consulted were: Arthur Applebee and Robert Calfee from Stanford University's School of Education; James Gray, Mary K. Healy, Miles Myers, Leo Ruth, and Herbert Simons from the University of California at Berkeley's School of Education; and Selma Monsky from the University of California at Berkeley's Survey Research Center.

2. The set of questions on this topic is identical to a set of questions on Applebee's (1981) survey of secondary teachers.

3. The procedures were (1) giving no return deadline to the teachers but sending reminder postcards directly to those teachers who had not returned their materials within two weeks after the mailing; (2) telephoning site directors before a month had passed, and asking them to contact those teachers who still had not returned the forms, while simultaneously sending a second reminder postcard to teachers whose materials were still outstanding; and (3) placing follow-up telephone calls during the next month to those site directors with two or more teachers from their sites who still had not returned surveys. Note that no telephone calls were made to international sites or directly to teachers.

4. Participants' anonymity was ensured since all surveys were coded before they were mailed. All respondents were asked not to place their names on the surveys or the return envelopes. Each student received his or her survey in a separate manila envelope. Before returning the completed form to the teacher for mailing, the student was asked to replace the survey in the envelope and to seal it. The teacher then mailed the students' sealed envelopes, along with his or her own survey in the stamped, self-addressed return envelope that was enclosed. This procedure seemed to ensure the students' anonymity; at least, all student surveys were returned in their sealed envelopes. All forms were returned directly to the research staff.

5. To prepare the survey data for the first and subsequent analyses, members of the research team proofread each returned survey to clarify ambiguous responses and to note instances of missing data. Data were then entered into the computer at the Survey Research Center at the University of California at Berkeley with a specially developed data entry program. Every answer was entered twice, independently by different research assistants. Then the program detected discrepancies in the entries. When discrepancies were detected, the original items were checked and data entry errors corrected. This process yielded a clean data set. Once the data had been entered, they were transferred to the IBM/CMS system where SPSSX programs were used for statistical analyses.

Frequency statistics were run for individual items in all surveys. These data are used for describing the characteristics of the samples and for comparing the elementary and secondary teacher samples along demographic lines. Either a chi-square test, or a t test following the Welch (1947) and Aspen (1949) model was used to assess differences between individual variables across the elementary (K–6) and secondary (7–12) samples. The chi-square compares categorical variables across the samples. The Welch-Aspen t test compares noncategorical or continuous variables across the samples, when the two groups have separate variance. For this t test, the degrees of freedom are computed based on separate variance estimates. A matched-pairs t test was used to compare two variables within the same sample.

6. The 39.5 percent is probably even closer to the Census figure of 25.2 percent because some teachers who classified their area as small town in this survey might be classified as metropolitan by the Census.

7. This trend may be correlated to another trend reported by the Census (1983), showing that the percentage of ethnic minority students decreases in the higher grades (146).

8. The two samples cannot be compared statistically because there was an unequal number of categories for this question on the elementary and

secondary questionnaires and because of differences in the meanings of the categories. The elementary teachers were asked to report the percentage of their students who were above average, average, and below average; the secondary teachers were asked to assess the students from just one of their classes and were asked whether these students were predominantly above average, average, below average, or of mixed ability.

9. Because the range of reported class sizes was great on the elementary surveys (some of these teachers may have been resource teachers), the median rather than the average proved the truest measure of class size. So that the two samples could be compared, the median was used for secondary classes as well.

10. Although Applebee's sample only included secondary teachers, the comparisons were planned for both the secondary and elementary teachers in this study since there was no better comparison group for the elementary teachers. The only major nationwide study of writing in the elementary school (Graves 1978) did not include systematic teacher surveys.

11. To understand the comparison, one must know that Applebee asked his teachers whether they typically or occasionally assigned pieces of writing of the lengths we asked about (56). Although the teachers in our sample reported assigning a piece of a particular length at the time of the survey, this assignment may or may not represent their typical practice; nevertheless, it seems reasonable to conclude that across the sample the question elicited a sense of what was typical for the group. A comparison between these secondary teachers and Applebee's secondary English teachers was made since 95 percent of the secondary teachers in this survey taught English and since the English teachers in Applebee's survey proved to be the subset of his sample that taught the most writing.

12. The research team for the ethnography, at this point, consisted of Miles Myers and me, assisted by Cynthia Greenleaf, who became head technician, and Melanie Sperling, who became head scribe.

13. This book is now published: Peterson, Art. 1986. *Teachers: A Survival Guide for the Grown-Up in the Classroom,* New York: New American Library.

14. The ratings of the high schools were done for *Money Magazine* and appeared in their September, 1981, article, "The Twelve Top Public High Schools in the U.S."

15. Pseudonyms are used for the names of all students.

16. Appendix B gives further detail about the activities in each classroom.

17. To ensure clear, high-quality audio recordings, two microphones were used. One was an omni-directional microphone which was plugged into a permanent extension cable attached to the ceiling of the classroom. The other was a diversity wireless microphone worn by the teacher. Each microphone fed into a separate channel of a stereo audio recorder which was connected by cables to a stereo video recorder. A backup tape recorder was placed in a corner of the classroom opposite the master audiotape recorder, in case of master recorder failure.

18. The Technician noted video counter numbers that could then be correlated with the more elaborate notes taken by the Scribe. The Technician also noted video counter numbers when the camera was moved or the camera shot shifted.

19. To get the maximum amount of the classroom on videotape, the camera's zoom lens (focal length from 12.5 mm to 75 mm) was normally placed at the widest angle setting. This setting captured approximately one-third of the classroom on the frame at a time. Although we could have captured more students on camera with a wider angle lens, the loss of detail, particularly in facial expressions, was too great.

3 Response Practices: Range and Helpfulness

Introduction

Teachers have only so much time to respond to their students' writing, so the ways they use that time is crucial. This chapter explores how both the successful teachers who participated in the national surveys and those who participated in the ethnographies chose to use their instructional time and how the teachers in the surveys and their students evaluated their use of that time. The surveys provide a broad look at response patterns across 560 teachers (K–12) and 715 of their secondary students. The ethnographies both illuminate the broad patterns in the surveys and show how, within the broad patterns, there is room for variety and diversity of response activities across two ninth-grade classrooms.

Most studies of response to student writing have not considered questions about the distribution of response or about teachers' and students' attitudes toward its helpfulness. The one large-scale study of how teachers distribute response (Dillon and Searle 1983) found that Canadian teachers (K–12) respond almost solely with written comments to final versions of their students' writing.[1] I hypothesized that findings about the response practices of the successful teachers I studied would contrast with Dillon and Searle's findings and with other findings from large-scale studies of how writing is generally taught (e.g., Applebee 1981, 1984 and Graves 1978).

The following are examples of specific questions to be addressed in this chapter:

> How helpful do successful teachers of writing find different types of response for their students' writing?
>
> Do the teachers concentrate on one or two types of response, or do they use a number of types of response?
>
> Do they respond to their students' writing mostly by writing comments on completed pieces, or do they more often have their students meet in peer-response groups over early drafts?
>
> Do such teachers usually confer with their students individually?

Do their patterns of response shift from one grade level to the next? for different types of students?

What do their students think about the response they are receiving?

The first section of the chapter will focus on the survey questions that ask about different kinds of response to student writing — about response during the writing process, response to final versions of student writing, and response from different sources — from peers, from teachers, from the writer. The questions assess both the frequency and the helpfulness of the varied response practices, from the points of view of the teachers and their students. The survey questions cover standard types of response to writing commonly discussed in the literature.

The second section of the chapter moves to the ethnography with a focus on how Glass, Peterson, and their students spend their time when response to student writing occurs. The analysis measures the frequency of occurrence of different types of response in the two classrooms. These measures supplement the self-report measures of how response is distributed according to the teachers and students in the surveys (reported in the first part of the chapter) with observations of how these students and teachers actually spend their time. This quantitative analysis of how response is distributed in the two classrooms also provides direction for a more detailed qualitative analysis of classroom life in Chapter 4.

The Surveys

The 560 teachers of grades K–12 who completed the surveys were identified by site directors of the National Writing Project as among the most successful teachers of writing in their regions. The 715 students came from the classes of half of the secondary teachers who completed surveys. The teachers selected four students: two males and two females and within these groups one higher- and one lower-achieving student.

The first step in this analysis of the surveys involved grouping related questions into summary scales. When groups of individual questions are related conceptually, respondents oftentimes answer them in a consistently patterned way. When this happens, it is possible to treat the group of questions as a single question or a summary scale. Grouping related questions in this way makes it possible to look at fewer individual questions and therefore simplifies the data analysis task.

For the teacher surveys in this project, I identified eight sets of conceptually related questions that could potentially become eight summary scales:

1. questions having to do with the helpfulness of response during the writing process (Q1 to Q1E),[2]
2. questions having to do with the helpfulness of response after the writing is completed (Q2 to Q2E),
3. questions having to do with the helpfulness of different responders (the teacher, parents, peers, and the like) (Q3 to Q3E),[3]
4. questions having to do with the frequency of use of different teaching techniques (Q15 to Q27),
5. questions having to do with the helpfulness and frequency of teacher response (Q1C, Q1D, Q2C, Q2D, Q22, Q23),
6. questions having to do with the helpfulness and frequency of peer response (Q1B, Q2B, Q3A, Q20),
7. questions having to do with the helpfulness and frequency of self-response (Q1E, Q2E), and
8. questions having to do with the frequency of assigning different types of writing (Q11A to Q11G).

Some questions fall in more than one set because they are related to more than one concept. For example, a question about the helpfulness of peer response during the writing process is grouped with the set of questions about response during the writing process (1) and the set about peer response (6).

Insofar as the surveys were parallel, questions on the student survey were grouped according to the same conceptual sets as the teachers'. The sets of questions for the student surveys included:

1. questions having to do with amount of writing (Q1 to Q2),
2. questions having to do with the helpfulness of response during the writing process and after the writing is completed (Q28 to Q29E),
3. questions having to do with the helpfulness of different responders (Q30 to Q30F),[4]
4. questions having to do with the frequency of assigning different types of writing (Q9 to Q15),
5. questions having to do with the frequency of use of different teaching techniques (Q16 to Q27),
6. questions having to do with the helpfulness and frequency of teacher response (Q16 to Q19, Q27, Q28A, Q28C, Q28D, Q29A, Q29C, Q29D, Q30C),

7. questions having to do with the helpfulness and frequency of peer response (Q20, Q21, Q28B, Q29B, Q30A), and

8. questions having to do with the helpfulness and frequency of self-response (Q28E, Q29E).

The following example illustrates the scaling procedure. On the teacher surveys, the first set of conceptually related questions all ask how helpful the teachers find some aspect of response during the writing process. If each teacher gives similar answers to every question about response during the writing process (though the answers will differ for different teachers), then there will be perfect consistency. By contrast, if each teacher gives highly differentiated answers depending on the question, then there will be inconsistency, and it will not be possible to create a summary scale from this set of questions.

Perfect consistency is unlikely, and so whether or not a set of questions can be considered a summary scale depends on how far respondents lean in the direction of consistency. The level of consistency of the replies for the questions in the set can be determined by calculating an alpha coefficient. An alpha of .60 or above is generally taken as evidence that the respondents have relatively consistent opinions about the helpfulness or frequency of the questions in the set. Not all questions in a set may fit on a scale. The consistency of individual questions can be measured by the item-total correlation. An item-total correlation of .20 or higher is evidence that a question fits on the total scale. When a question does not fit on a scale, it is eliminated and the scale statistics are recomputed. Sometimes even when an item has a correlation above .20, dropping it creates a significant rise in the scale alpha; in such cases the item is dropped. The revised scale alpha and item-total correlations are then reevaluated to determine whether the remaining questions form a summary scale.

The process of forming the teacher scale for "the helpfulness of response during the writing process" segment turned out to be one of the more complex since most of the original six questions did not form a scale. The scale statistics for the six questions are presented on the first summary scale on Table 3.1.[5] The alpha coefficient for the scale containing all six questions is .45. This alpha indicates that the respondents were relatively inconsistent in answering different questions about the helpfulness of various kinds of response during the writing process. A look at the corrected item-total correlation for individual questions shows correlations below .20 for three of the six — peer response (.09), teacher grades (.13), and student self-assessments (.19). New scale statistics were calculated after dropping these three questions

Table 3.1

Teacher Summary Scales

	Means	Standard Deviation	Corrected Item-Total Correlation	Rescaled Corrected Item-Total Correlation
Helpfulness of response during the writing process				
Q1 Helpfulness response on early drafts	3.71	.53	.43	.45
Q1A Individual conference with teacher on early draft	3.71	.54	.31	.45
Q1B Peer group reaction to early draft	3.37	.70	.09	
Q1C Teacher comments on early draft	2.86	.89	.30	
Q1D Teacher grades on early draft	1.56	.77	.13	
Q1E Student self-assessment on early draft	3.16	.76	.19	
			Alpha .45	.62
Helpfulness of response after writing				
Q2 Helpfulness response on completed writing	3.27	.66	.57	
Q2A Individual conference with teacher on completed writing	3.42	.66	.43	
Q2B Peer group reaction to completed writing	3.36	.70	.33	
Q2C Teacher comments on completed writing	2.91	.86	.50	
Q2D Teacher grades on completed writing	2.56	.88	.31	
Q2E Student self-assessment on completed writing	3.33	.69	.31	
			Alpha .67	
Helpfulness of response from different responders				
Q3 Helpfulness response from different people	3.51	.56	.47	
Q3A Helpful response from classmates, friends	3.48	.62	.28	
Q3B Helpful response from parents	2.89	.68	.45	
Q3C Helpful response from teacher	3.61	.52	.27	
Q3D Helpful response from other teachers	3.12	.66	.49	
Q3E Helpful response from other adults	2.99	.66	.54	
			Alpha .69	
Frequency of response-related teaching techniques				
Q15 Topic introduced with in-class discussion	3.79	.50	.22	.25
Q16 Use examples of professional writing	2.60	.83	.25	.20

Continued on next page

Table 3.1 — *Continued*

	Means	Standard Deviation	Corrected Item-Total Correlation	Rescaled Corrected Item-Total Correlation
Frequency of response-related teaching techniques, *continued*				
Q17 Make aware of audience	3.38	.74	.39	.42
Q18 Focus on selected problems	3.39	.73	.29	.32
Q19 Use examples of student writing	3.18	.78	.38	.42
Q20 Students work in peer groups	2.98	.93	.36	.42
Q21 Comments on rough drafts	3.36	.78	.35	.43
Q22 Mark problems/errors on finished writing	1.69	.92	.13	
Q23 Assign grades to finished writing	2.83	1.12	.03	
Q24 Respond about strengths-weaknesses	3.66	.57	.32	.21
Q25 Assignments sequenced by design	3.05	.94	.29	
Q26 Publish student writing	2.75	.84	.22	.38
Q27 Individual student conferences	2.73	.82	.26	.38
			Alpha .61	.69
Written response from teachers				
Q1C Teacher comments on early draft—helpfulness	2.86	.89	.41	
Q1D Teacher grades on early draft—helpfulness	1.56	.77	.42	
Q2C Teacher comments on completed writing—helpfulness	2.91	.86	.47	
Q2D Teacher grades on completed writing—helpfulness	2.56	.88	.55	
Q22 Mark problems/errors on finished writing—frequency	1.69	.92	.35	
Q23 Assign grades to finished writing—frequency	2.83	1.12	.44	
			Alpha .70	
Response from peers				
Q1B Peer group reaction to early draft—helpfulness	3.37	.70	.54	
Q2B Peer group reaction to completed writing—helpfulness	3.36	.70	.35	
Q3A Helpful response from classmates, friends	3.48	.62	.54	
Q20 Students work in peer groups—frequency	2.98	.93	.39	
			Alpha .66	
Response from writer				
Q1E Student self-assessment on early draft	3.16	.76	.36	
Q2E Student self-assessment on completed writing	3.33	.69	.36	
			Alpha .53	

N = 560.

one at a time, but the alpha coefficient only rose to .52 and the correlation for one of the remaining questions, the teacher's written comments, dropped from .30 to .29. By deleting that question from the set, the alpha rose to .62. Thus, a two-question scale is formed. It turns out that the teachers do not hold consistent opinions about most types of response during the writing process. The teachers give consistent replies only about the helpfulness of general response during the process and about conferences. The mean for these questions (Table 3.1) shows that the teachers considered both of these types of response to be extremely helpful (3.71 on a 4-point scale, with 4 being the most helpful).

Once a scale is formed, it is possible that individual item means will vary significantly from one another. To determine how the group feels about the individual items on a scale, paired t tests compare differences in the means.

To conclude, if the teachers (or students) are consistent in their assessment of the relative helpfulness or frequency of any of the questions within a given set, then those questions about which they give consistent replies form a summary scale. Summary scales are useful in testing whether another variable, say teaching experience, affects response to student writing. The trend will be the same for all questions on the same scale.

When questions do not fit on a summary scale, there are two possible reasons: (1) vaguely or unclearly worded questions could lead different respondents to interpret the questions differently (these would be "bad" questions and would not fit on any scale), or (2) the set of questions cannot easily be summarized; respondents do not reply to the individual questions in a similar way.

Teachers' Opinions about Response

Helpfulness of Response during the Writing Process

Significant and important inconsistencies among the teachers are evident in the area of the helpfulness of varied kinds of response during the writing process (Table 3.1). The teachers gave somewhat inconsistent replies about the helpfulness of their written comments and very inconsistent replies about the helpfulness of peer-response groups, grades, and student self-assessments. They consistently valued response during the writing process in general and conferences, however. One teacher, in a comment written on her questionnaire, articulates her feelings about conferences: "To me the most helpful response to student

writing is immediate verbal help on the first drafts, actually sitting with
a student and helping him put the words on paper."

Other than conferences, the teachers do not show a consistent sense
of the most and least productive types of response during the writing
process. The teachers' comments written on their questionnaires indicate these inconsistencies. For example, some teachers who value
conferences highly also value peer response, but others do not. One
teacher who ranks peer groups almost as helpful as conferences writes
about groups:

> One of the best methods of response to initial writing is the read-
> around-group. I've experienced great success using that with my
> students early on as they write. I've also had great success using
> response groups early on, so that students work with their peers
> as they initially begin a project. That provides them with feedback
> needed to get underway. It also provides them with a greater
> degree of commitment to their writing.

The same teacher also discusses the importance of expanded audiences
beyond the teacher, and of the peer group as a way of providing that
expanded audience.

Another teacher who rates peer groups with a 4 (very helpful) and
conferences with a 2 (not too helpful), thinks groups can accomplish
a number of things: "Students work in small response groups which
comment constructively on ideas, questions for interviews, rough drafts
(along with editing of same)."

By contrast, an eighth-grade teacher ranks general response and
conferences as 3 (somewhat helpful), but peer groups as 2 (not too
helpful). She admits, "I only have to say that I have not had good
responses from using peer-group work in writing. This may be due to
the age group I work with."

Comments about written response during the process show a similar
pattern. A teacher who rates general response, conferences, and peer
groups with 4s (very helpful), drops to a 2, or not too helpful, for
written comments. This teacher remarks, "Too many marks too early
can be discouraging to students." However, another who gives 4 ratings
to general response, conferences, and peer groups, ranks written response
almost as high, with a 3. This teacher comments:

> My students have responded enthusiastically and with understand-
> ing when my comments were relevant to today's language that is
> sometimes used by teenagers. Example: Where's the beef? —
> meaning you need more content or ideas to express the topic or
> support the topic.

These teachers show marked contrasts in how helpful they feel peer groups and written comments are as compared to conferences and response during the process in general. Teachers with different senses of the success of some kinds of in-process response relative to others answer the questions about response during the process inconsistently.

One reason the teachers judge some kinds of in-process response differently from others may have to do with how the teachers define the activities. Certainly the two teachers' remarks about written comments show different senses of how comments could be used. The one who does not see them as successful sees them as "marks" or corrections; the other teacher's comments are thought-provoking questions posed in a language that she finds appeals to her students.

Similarly, the teachers have different senses of what peer response is for. They judge the success and relative helpfulness of groups according to their own notion of what the groups are supposed to accomplish, and therefore relate groups to other types of in-process response differently. When evaluating in-process response, such as peer groups or written comments, we would understand the practices better if we had clearer definitions of the activities and the functions we intend certain response activities to serve.

Underlying these unstable definitions of terms referring to the teaching of writing is a lack of clarity about what it means to teach the writing process. In his study of writing in secondary schools, Applebee (1984) concludes that the process approach has failed. He argues that "process-oriented activities are not appropriate to the typical uses of writing in the high school classroom" (187). He claims that the schools mainly teach writing for the purpose of examining the writer, and that process instruction will not work while students write for this purpose. Process instruction would more likely work if the schools used writing to aid students during their learning process. Applebee's solution seems oversimplified since written products do count in our society and since writing serves multiple functions, some of them evaluative. Furthermore, it is unclear how a process approach and writing to be examined are mutually exclusive.

However, Applebee is certainly right that the schools overemphasize the evaluative function of writing and underemphasize its functions in learning. Even more to the point is his claim that "the process approach to writing instruction has been inadequately and improperly conceptualized" (188). Applebee formulates the problem as follows: "Instructional applications have lacked a framework for integrating process-oriented activities with an analysis of the demands that particular contexts for writing pose for particular students" (188). Too little is known about how to integrate the findings from research on the writing process into actual classrooms.

The results of this questionnaire seem to point to a related problem. In group instruction (whole class or small group), many teachers seem to conceptualize teaching the writing process as teaching a rather formulaic set of procedures — prewriting, writing, revising. With such a conceptualization it is possible to ignore the problem-solving processes of individual students. And it is the problem-solving processes, not the procedures in and of themselves, that are central to the teaching of writing. Thus, teachers are likely to be consistent in their judgments of the success of the individual conference because they can attend to the individual's process, but it is possible that the teachers feel varying degrees of satisfaction about other kinds of instruction because it is so easy for the real goal to get lost in the procedures teachers must develop to manage the group.

Helpfulness of Response after Writing

In contrast to the inconsistency of the teacher replies to questions about the helpfulness of different types of response during the process, the teachers give consistent replies about the relative helpfulness of different types of response once a piece of writing is complete (second summary scale, Table 3.1). All the questions concerning response to completed writing fit well on the scale; that is, none show a corrected item-total correlation lower than .20, and the scale alpha is .67. Individual teachers make few distinctions among the relative helpfulness of different types of response to final versions of student writing. The average from all the items provides a trustworthy summary.

Given the large number of items on this summary scale, I used paired t tests to compare mean values the group of teachers assigned to different types of response to final versions (Figure 3.1). As a group, the teachers believe that the most effective response to final versions comes in individual, teacher-led conferences and peer groups, followed by student self-assessments (which the teachers consider significantly less helpful than conferences but not significantly less helpful than peer groups). Self-assessments are followed at a significant distance by teachers' written comments, with grades coming last. Interestingly, the more conventional kinds of response to final versions — grades and written comments — are seen by teachers as the least valuable.

Helpfulness of Response from Different Responders

The teachers are also consistent in their ratings of the helpfulness of response from different responders (third summary scale on Table 3.1), with a scale alpha of .69 for all questions.

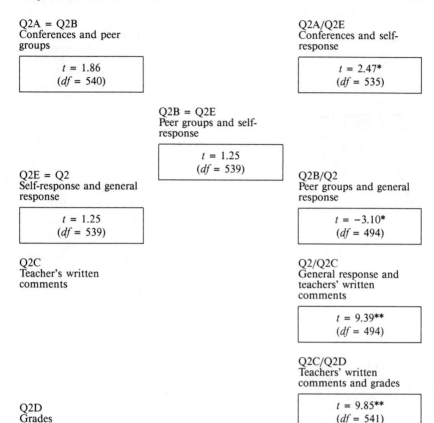

Q2A = Q2B
Conferences and peer
groups

| $t = 1.86$ |
| $(df = 540)$ |

Q2A/Q2E
Conferences and self-
response

| $t = 2.47^*$ |
| $(df = 535)$ |

Q2B = Q2E
Peer groups and self-
response

| $t = 1.25$ |
| $(df = 539)$ |

Q2E = Q2
Self-response and general
response

| $t = 1.25$ |
| $(df = 539)$ |

Q2B/Q2
Peer groups and general
response

| $t = -3.10^*$ |
| $(df = 494)$ |

Q2C
Teacher's written
comments

Q2/Q2C
General response and
teachers' written
comments

| $t = 9.39^{**}$ |
| $(df = 494)$ |

Q2C/Q2D
Teachers' written
comments and grades

Q2D
Grades

| $t = 9.85^{**}$ |
| $(df = 541)$ |

$^* p < .01.$ $^{**} p < .001.$

Figure 3.1. Teachers' assessments of the relative helpfulness of different types of response after writing: matched pair *t* tests.

Paired *t* tests on the differences in the means for questions on the scale (Figure 3.2) show that the group of teachers felt they were the most helpful responders to their students' writing, with classmates, other teachers, and parents and other adults following in that order.

In-Process Response versus Final Version Response

Although the teachers hold inconsistent opinions about the helpfulness of different types of response during the writing process and hold consistent opinions about the relative helpfulness of different types of response after a piece of writing is finished, they report that response during the writing process is significantly more helpful to students than response after a piece of writing is finished. The helpfulness of response

Q3C
Teacher

Q3 = Q3A
General response and
response from classmates

$t = .16$
$(df = 480)$

Q3D
Other teachers

Q3E = Q3B
Other adults and parents

$t = 1.90$
$(df = 466)$

Q3C/Q3
Teacher and general
response from others

$t = -3.66*$
$(df = 474)$

Q3A/Q3D
Classmates and other
teachers

$t = 9.51*$
$(df = 503)$

Q3D/Q3E
Other teachers and other
adults

$t = 5.06*$
$(df = 474)$

* $p < .001$.

Figure 3.2. Teachers' assessments of the relative helpfulness of different responders: matched pair t tests.

during the writing process and the helpfulness of response to final versions are compared in Table 3.2. Interestingly, the most important kind of response, response during the writing process, is the kind about which the teachers show the most inconsistencies.

Frequency of Response-Related Teaching Techniques

The next summary scale on Table 3.1 indicates how often these teachers use different types of response-related teaching techniques (questions 15 to 27 on the elementary questionnaire used on the table are equivalent to 16 to 28 on the secondary questionnaire in Appendix A).[6] The inconsistencies are particularly interesting here. Independent of the teacher's other practices is the frequency of assigning grades, of marking every problem or error on student writing, and sequencing

Table 3.2

Comparison of Teachers' Judgments about the Helpfulness of
Response during the Process versus Response to Final Versions

	Mean Helpfulness (4 = most helpful; 1 = least helpful)	*t* Test
Response during the process	3.71 *(sd* = .53)	1.89* *(df* = 498)
Response to final versions	3.27 *(sd* = .66)	

* p < .001.

assignments. The teachers employ these practices without any pattern in reference to their other practices.

I next compared the means for those practices that the teachers used consistently. Figure 3.3 shows that the group of teachers reports discussing topics with their students significantly more than any other practice. Next most often, they comment on strengths as well as weaknesses in their students' writing. Then they respond to selected problems, make their students aware of an audience, and comment either orally or in writing on drafts. Significantly less often, they use examples of student writing. Even less often, they use peer groups and have their students publish their writing. Still less frequently, they hold individual conferences. Least frequently of all, they use models of professional writing.

Although the teachers value conferences more than peer groups, they use them less. As one teacher writes on her questionnaire, "I wish there was more time for individual writing conferences. Since there is not, I find training students to respond to each other vital!" Another asserts, "I definitely feel that I could teach writing more effectively with a decreased student/teacher ratio. I find it quite difficult to assign the number of writings or schedule individual conferences with the frequency I would like when I have thirty-one students." In the margin beside the question about the helpfulness of conferences, another writes, "limited time and the large number of students prevent these from being as effective as they could be." This teacher's eighth-grade class contained twenty-seven students, a class size many public school English teachers would regard as relatively small.

The most frequent practice, discussions about topics, lends itself well to whole-class interactions, the most traditional form of classroom organization and one suitable to large groups of students. Although

Q15
Topic with discussion

Q15/Q24
Topic with discussion and
response to strengths and
weaknesses

$t = 4.20**$
$(df = 556)$

Q24
Response to strengths and
weaknesses

Q24/Q18
Respond to strengths and
weaknesses and selected
problems

$t = -7.87**$
$(df = 554)$

Q18 = Q17
Selected problems and
awareness of audience

$t = -.32$
$(df = 555)$

Q17 = Q21
Awareness of audience
and comments on drafts

$t = .36$
$(df = 556)$

Q18 = Q21
Selected problems and
comments on drafts

$t = .54$
$(df = 554)$

Q19
Examples of student
writing

Q19/Q21
Examples of student
writing and comments on
drafts

$t = -4.72**$
$(df = 556)$

Q20
Work in peer groups

Q20/Q19
Work in peer groups and
examples of student
writing

$t = 4.35**$
$(df = 556)$

$* p < .01.$ $** p < .001.$

Figure 3.3. Teachers' assessments of the relative helpfulness of different teaching techniques: matched pair t tests.

Q26
Publish student writing

Q20/Q26
Publish student writing
and work in peer groups

$t = 4.88**$
($df = 554$)

Q27 = Q26
Individual conferences
and publish student
writing

$t = .48$
($df = 555$)

Q16
Use professional models

Q16/Q27
Use professional models
and individual
conferences

$t = -2.79*$
($df = 557$)

$* p < .01.$ $** p < .001.$

Figure 3.3, continued.

these teachers found ways to cope within the institutions in which they worked, they make frequent pleas for the necessity of improved teaching conditions. In response to an open-ended question, "Is there anything else you would like to tell us about how you teach writing or how you think it should be taught?", the following comments about institutional difficulties are typical:

> Limitation of class size or an extra planning period for teachers of composition is the key. Most of us know what we're doing, but we don't have the time to do it properly.

> I strongly recommend smaller class size for writing courses.

Also revealing is how these teachers coped. One reports "spending thirty hours or more at home/week"; another characterized herself as "masochistic." Another "wish[es] for twelve more hours in a day!"

Written Response from Teachers

The next scale on Table 3.1 marks the first of three regroupings of items from the other summary scales. These new scales combine teachers' assessments of helpfulness and their reports about the frequency of different practices. This scale about teacher response includes only teachers' written responses, since the items having to do with teachers' oral responses did not fit on the scale.

Figure 3.4 shows that the means for the group indicate that the teachers find the most helpful kind of written response to be written comments on completed writing and on early drafts. They consider grades less helpful than they are frequent. The teachers mark all problems on completed writing less often than they give grades. Rated least helpful of all are grades on early drafts.

Response from Peers

The summary scale for peer groups follows the scales on written response (Table 3.1). The teachers have a consistent sense of the helpfulness and the frequency of use of peer groups both during the writing process and at the point of the final version.

The teachers as a group find peer response helpful, but judge its specific uses less helpful (that is, peer response during the process and to final versions). Although peer groups are considered helpful, they are not used often in relation to how helpful they are judged (Figure 3.5).

Response from Writer

The last scale on Table 3.1 groups the only two questions that ask about having students respond to their own work. The alpha is relatively weak at .53. Interestingly, the mean shows that the teachers are more interested in student self-response after they have completed their writing than during the writing process.

Summary of Teacher Scales

The items on the teacher questionnaires fit on the seven summary scales on Table 3.1:

> Helpfulness of Response during the Writing Process
>
> Helpfulness of Response after Writing
>
> Helpfulness of Response from Different Responders
>
> Frequency of Response-Related Teaching Techniques
>
> Written Response from Teachers
>
> Response from Peers
>
> Response from Writer

Each scale alpha, mean, standard deviation and variance, and the mean and standard deviation of the average item are reported in Table

Q2C = Q1C
Helpfulness of comments
on completed writing and
helpfulness of comments
on early drafts

$t = -1.07$
$(df = 543)$

Q1C = Q23
Helpfulness of comments
on early drafts and
frequency of grades on
completed writing

$t = .54$
$(df = 545)$

Q2C = Q23
Helpfulness of comments
on completed writing and
frequency of grades on
completed writing

$t = 1.57$
$(df = 544)$

Q2D
Helpfulness of grades on
completed writing

Q2D/Q23
Helpfulness of grades on
completed writing and
frequency of grades on
completed writing

$t = -5.93**$
$(df = 540)$

Q22
Frequency of marking
problems on completed
writing

Q22/Q2D
Frequency of marking
problems on completed
writing and helpfulness of
grades on completed
writing

$t = 17.31**$
$(df = 540$

Q1D
Helpfulness of grades on
early drafts

Q1D/Q22
Helpfulness of grades on
early drafts and frequency
of marking problems on
completed writing

$t = -2.77*$
$(df = 536)$

$* p < .01.$ $** p < .001.$

Figure 3.4. Teachers' assessments of the relative helpfulness and frequency of response
from teachers: matched pair t tests.

Q3A
Helpfulness of response
from peers

Q3A/Q1B
Helpfulness of response
from peers and
helpfulness of response
from peers on early drafts

$$t = -3.83*$$
$$(df = 544)$$

Q1B = Q2B
Helpfulness of response
from peers on early drafts
and helpfulness of
response from peers on
completed writing

$$t = .31$$
$$(df = 544)$$

Q20
Frequency of work in
peer groups on completed
writing

Q20/Q2B
Frequency of work in
peer groups and
helpfulness of response
from peers on completed
writing

$$t = 8.58*$$
$$(df = 547)$$

* $p < .001$.

Figure 3.5. Teachers' assessments of the relative helpfulness and frequency of response from peers: matched pair *t* tests.

3.3. These scales are relatively independent of one another (Freedman 1985 reports the Pearson product-moment correlation matrix for the scales).

Influences on Teachers

Once the questions are fit onto the seven summary scales, they can be treated as essentially seven questions. I next look at potential influences on the teachers' responses to the groups of questions that could come from the following personal characteristics and aspects of their teaching situations: (1) socioeconomic status of students taught, (2) setting of the school (urban, rural, etc.), (3) grade level taught, (4) geographical region of the teacher's school (Northeast, South, etc.), (5) size of the school, (6) age of the teacher, (7) amount of teaching experience, and (8) teacher's gender.

Of importance here is the analysis that looks at how teachers teaching high numbers of students at the poverty level respond to the question-

Table 3.3

Teacher Scales: Summary of Scale Means,
Standard Deviations, and Variance

	Number of Items	Alpha	Scale Mean (*sd*)	Scale Variance	Average "Item Mean and Standard Deviation" (divided by number of items)
Response during process	2	.62	7.41 (.91)	.82	3.71 (0.46)
Response after writing	6	.67	18.85 (2.75)	7.58	3.14 (0.46)
Responders	6	.69	19.60 (2.32)	5.36	3.27 (0.39)
Teaching techniques	10	.69	31.81 (3.88)	15.05	3.18 (0.39)
Response from teachers	6	.70	14.42 (3.47)	12.06	2.40 (0.58)
Response from peers	4	.66	13.19 (2.10)	4.39	3.30 (0.52)
Response from writer	2	.53	6.48 (1.19)	1.42	3.24 (0.60)

$N = 560.$

naires (Tables 3.4 and 3.5). Since this group is not well represented in the sample, it seems important to determine whether the teachers who did teach low-income students answered the questions in ways significantly different from the others. On only one scale are there significant differences in the way teachers of large versus small numbers of poverty-level students respond — the ways teachers give written response (Table 3.4). Teachers with no poverty-level students use grades and written responses more often and find them more helpful than do teachers with low-income students (Table 3.5).

It is reasonable to suppose that higher income students are more likely to be college-bound and to respond to grades, the traditional reward structure in schools. By contrast, teachers with more than 51 percent of their students at the poverty level use written response and grades least often and find these types of response least helpful. The pattern is difficult to interpret for teachers of moderate numbers of poverty-level students, since those with 11 to 25 percent of their students at the poverty level use this mode less frequently either than

Table 3.4

Influence of Students' Socioeconomic Status on Summary
Scales for Teachers

	Degrees of Freedom	Sum of Squares	Mean Squares	F-test
Response during process				
Between groups	4	.46	.12	.54
Within groups	525	112.53	.21	
Response after writing				
Between groups	4	.22	.06	.24
Within groups	456	103.89	.23	
Responders				
Between groups	4	1.47	.37	2.30
Within groups	397	63.53	.16	
Teaching techniques				
Between groups	4	.61	.15	1.02
Within groups	537	81.13	.15	
Response from teachers				
Between groups	4	5.65	1.41	4.22*
Within groups	503	168.23	.34	
Response from peers				
Between groups	4	1.19	.30	1.07
Within groups	523	145.87	.28	
Response from writer				
Between groups	4	3.05	.76	2.11
Within groups	526	189.59	.36	

*$p < .01$.

those with 10 percent or fewer at the poverty level or than those with 26 to 50 percent (with these last two groups having about the same mean).

Since large numbers of low-income students live in large urban areas and in rural areas, the analysis for teachers teaching in different settings also gives clues about how teachers of non-mainstream populations answer the questions (see Tables 3.6 and 3.7). Differences in response across school settings, although interesting in their own right, provide no support for a theory of differences for teachers in poorer as compared to wealthier areas. Teachers in urban areas and in rural areas, which are more likely to have higher concentrations of poverty-level students,

Table 3.5

Scale Average "Item Means" for Student Socioeconomic Status
on Summary Scale for Response from Teachers

Student Socioeconomic Status	Response from Teacher: Scale Average "Item Mean"
No students at poverty level	2.48 $(sd = .61)$ $(n = 210)$
10% or fewer at poverty level	2.39 $(sd = .56)$ $(n = 181)$
11–25% at poverty level	2.19 $(sd = .58)$ $(n = 62)$
26–50% at poverty level	2.38 $(sd = .51)$ $(n = 37)$
Above 51% at poverty level	2.10 $(sd = .55)$ $(n = 18)$

do not answer questions similarly. The main difference is that teachers in rural areas and small towns place more emphasis on self-response whereas those teaching in the suburbs and in large urban areas are similar in their lack of emphasis on self-response. Perhaps there is more stress on self-reliance in less densely populated areas.

Another difference across geographic settings is the value of in-process response. This type of response, promoted so much in the professional literature, is valued less in small towns and in small urban settings. In-process response is valued as much by teachers of inner-city students as by teachers in the suburbs. Perhaps recent thinking about the theoretical importance of in-process response is slower to reach teachers in smaller towns. Furthermore, conservative influences in these areas might create a resistance to such innovations.

The influences of other teacher traits and aspects of the teaching conditions are shown on the supplementary tables E.1–E.11 in Appendix E. Aside from the differences for teachers of students at different income levels, written comments and grades are given more frequently and

Table 3.6

Influence of School Location on Scales for Teachers

	Degrees of Freedom	Sum of Squares	Mean Squares	*F*-test
Response during process				
Between groups	5	2.98	.60	2.86*
Within groups	527	109.81	.21	
Response after writing				
Between groups	5	1.20	.24	1.07
Within groups	457	102.82	.23	
Responders				
Between groups	5	.35	.07	.43
Within groups	399	65.23	.16	
Teaching techniques				
Between groups	5	1.38	.28	1.83
Within groups	540	81.25	.15	
Response from teachers				
Between groups	5	1.38	.28	.80
Within groups	506	174.15	.34	
Response from peers				
Between groups	5	1.51	.30	1.09
Within groups	526	146.81	.28	
Response from writer				
Between groups	5	4.08	.82	2.27*
Within groups	529	189.83	.36	

* $p < .05$.

considered more helpful by teachers of higher grades (Tables E.1 and E.2); teachers in foreign American schools, in the South, North Central, and West as compared to those in the Northeast and in foreign non-American schools (Tables E.3 and E.4); teachers in larger schools, especially those with enrollments between 1000 and 2499 but not those over 2499 (Tables E.5 and E.6). Also interesting are influences on peer response. It is preferred by teachers of grades 4–6 (Tables E.1 and E.2) and by older teachers (Tables E.7 and E.8). Finally, teachers with more experience, as well as older teachers, use more of the teaching techniques (Tables E.9 and E.10) as do females (Table E.11), who also favor self-response.

Table 3.7

Scale Average "Item Means" for School Location on Two
Summary Scales: Response during the Process and Response
from Writer

School Location	Response during Process: Scale Average "Item Mean"	Response from Writer: Scale Average "Item Mean"
Rural	3.73 (sd = .50) (n = 45)	3.41 (sd = .49) (n = 43)
Small town	3.67 (sd = .50) (n = 163)	3.20 (sd = .61) (n = 169)
Suburban	3.78 (sd = .38) (sd = 160)	3.30 (sd = .63) (n = 161)
Urban—large	3.72 (sd = .41) (n = 63)	3.32 (sd = .51) (n = 61)
Urban—not large	3.57 (sd = .55) (n = 79)	3.10 (sd = .63) (n = 78)
Other	3.83 (sd = .32) (n = 23)	3.15 (sd = .61) (n = 23)

Summary of Results for Teachers' Surveys

The teachers' surveys uncovered how successful teachers of writing
(K–12), mostly in the U.S., feel about the helpfulness of different types
of response to student writing and how frequently they use different
response-related teaching techniques in their classrooms. The results
show consistencies and inconsistencies among the teachers about response, and show how the teachers' personal traits and the characteristics
of their teaching situation affect their opinions.

A summary of the opinions held by the teachers who completed the
questionnaires follows:

1. *Response during the writing process promotes student learning
   significantly more than response to completed pieces of writing,
   but other than individual conferences, it is unclear what kinds of
   response during the process are most and least helpful.* The teachers
   are inconsistent in their opinions about the helpfulness of all

other in-process techniques (that is, of peer groups, written comments, grades, and student self-assessments).

2. *The individual conference is more helpful to student learners than any other type of response.* During the process, the conference is the only type of response that is consistently considered helpful. The conference is also rated the most helpful type of response to final pieces of writing.

   However, it is difficult for the teachers to hold individual conferences very often. Conferences occur less often than other types of response that are considered less helpful.

3. *For final versions, peer-response groups follow close behind conferences in being the most helpful way to respond.* Peer-response groups, although not considered as helpful as conferences and although used relatively infrequently, are used more frequently than conferences.

   Peer groups are used especially profitably and frequently by teachers of grades 4–6. They are considered least useful and are used least frequently by teachers of students in grades K–3 and 10–12. Teachers of grades 7–9 find them of average helpfulness and use them an average amount. They are used more frequently and are considered more helpful by the older teachers.

4. *The teacher is the most helpful responder to students' writing* (more helpful than classmates, other teachers, parents, or other adults).

5. *The teacher's response is not helpful when it comes in the form of grades or written comments on final versions of students' writing.* The latter two types of response to final versions are among the least helpful.

   Some teachers give grades and write comments frequently and others do not. The pattern is independent of the frequency of the teacher's other response practices. However, grading and writing comments occur more frequently as students get older and as the school size increases; school size is larger for secondary than elementary schools. Grades and written comments are most common and most highly valued in the northeastern U.S. and in non-American schools abroad.

   Grades and written comments are the only type of response related to the socioeconomic status of the students. In general, grades and written comments occur less commonly when teachers teach substantial numbers of poverty-level students; however, if 26 to 50 percent of their students are at the poverty level, the teachers write comments and give grades in patterns much like those for teachers with classes with fewer than 10 percent of such students.

Overall, grade giving and writing comments is a relatively infrequent and unhelpful activity.

6. *The most frequent teaching practice involves discussions of topics the students are writing about.* The next most frequent practice is a selective focus on different writing problems, and then an emphasis on the importance of the students' considering the audience they are writing for. Next most frequent are both written and oral comments during the writing process. Then come comments about students' writing strengths as well as their weaknesses. In descending order of frequency are teachers' using models of student writing, their students meeting in peer groups, publishing their students' writing, holding conferences, and using professional models.

Students' Opinions about Response

The items on the secondary students' questionnaires were also grouped and summary scales were computed. The student summary scales show the consistency of the student's answers to questions asking about the frequency and helpfulness of the response they received from these teachers about their writing.

Amount of Writing

As background to the students' views of their teachers' response practices, several items on the student questionnaire focused on the general instructional situation. The first student summary scale on Table 3.8 contains two questions that ask whether or not students feel they write a lot in the class of the survey teacher. The means for these questions indicate that students fairly consistently feel that they do more writing in this class than is usual in their school experience.

Types of Writing Taught

The students do not distinguish between the types of writing they are producing, with the exception of report writing (Q14). The other questions about writing type form a single scale (Table 3.8) with an alpha of .63.[7]

Paired *t* tests comparing the means for items on this scale (Figure 3.6) indicate that the students as a group say they write mostly analytic

Table 3.8

Student Summary Scales

	Means	Standard Deviation	Corrected Item-Total Correlation	Rescaled Corrected Item-Total Correlation
Amount of writing				
Q1 Write for this class	2.61	.54	.41	
Q2 Write for class compared with other classes	4.25	.95	.41	
			Alpha .52	
Types of writing taught				
Q9 Time writing journals for self	1.47	1.21	.37	
Q10 Time writing between self and teacher	1.57	1.25	.32	
Q11 Time writing personal experience essays	2.03	1.18	.45	
Q12 Time writing poems, plays, etc.	2.05	1.29	.33	
Q13 Time writing to find new ideas	1.85	1.18	.43	
Q15 Time writing personal essays	2.33	1.20	.28	
			Alpha .63	
Helpfulness of response during the writing process and after writing				
Q28 Comments on writing before paper completed	3.30	.96	.44	
Q28A Talk with teacher before paper completed	3.20	1.16	.48	
Q28B Talk with students before paper completed	2.77	.98	.31	
Q28C Written comments from teacher before paper completed	2.97	1.32	.46	
Q28D Grades given before paper completed	1.78	1.53	.39	
Q28E Teacher asks for comments before paper completed	2.11	1.44	.53	
Q29 Comments on completed writing	3.44	.81	.42	
Q29A Talk with teacher about completed writing	2.98	1.28	.52	
Q29B Talk with students about completed writing	2.35	1.19	.43	
Q29C Written comments from teacher on completed writing	3.34	.92	.41	
Q29D Grades given to completed writing	3.03	1.03	.38	
Q29E Own comments on completed writing	2.07	1.44	.54	
			Alpha .80	

Continued on next page

Table 3.8 — *Continued*

	Means	Standard Deviation	Corrected Item-Total Correlation	Rescaled Corrected Item-Total Correlation
Helpfulness of response from different responders				
Q30 Comments on writing from others	2.80	1.09	.45	
Q30A Comments from friends about writing	2.75	1.09	.49	
Q30B Comments from parents about writing	2.58	1.33	.55	
Q30C Comments from teacher about writing	3.60	.70	.39	
Q30D Comments from other teachers	2.25	1.55	.59	
Q30E Comments from other adults	1.98	1.49	.67	
Q30F Comments from brothers/ sisters	1.62	1.45	<u>.56</u>	
			Alpha .80	
Frequency of response-related teaching techniques				
Q16 Teacher writes comments before paper completed	2.64	1.08	.29	.28
Q17 Teacher writes comments on completed paper	3.30	.95	.32	.33
Q18 Teacher talks about writing before paper completed	2.97	.98	.50	.50
Q19 Teacher talks about completed writing	2.79	.97	.53	.54
Q20 Students talk about writing before paper completed	2.98	.95	.38	.38
Q21 Students talk about completed writing	2.54	1.01	.40	.39
Q22 Receive grades on completed writing	3.59	.82	.20	.19
Q23 Teacher informs about writers' audience	2.25	1.08	.30	.30
Q24 Make up own topic to write about	2.70	.98	−.01	
Q25 Teacher gives topic to write about	2.72	.96	−.02	
Q26 Class discussion about topic	3.17	.89	.32	.30
Q27 Teacher comments on strong-weak writing	3.30	.87	<u>.49</u>	<u>.50</u>
			Alpha .66	.71
Response from teachers				
Q16 Teacher writes comments before paper completed	2.64	1.08	.38	
Q17 Teacher writes comments on completed paper	3.30	.95	.25	
Q18 Teacher talks about writing before paper completed	2.97	.98	.48	
Q19 Teacher talks about completed writing	2.79	.97	.52	
Q27 Teacher comments on strong-weak writing	3.30	.87	.40	

Continued on next page

Table 3.8 — *Continued*

	Means	Standard Deviation	Corrected Item-Total Correlation	Rescaled Corrected Item-Total Correlation
Response from teachers, *continued*				
Q28A Talk with teacher before paper completed	3.20	1.16	.50	
Q28C Written comments from teacher before paper completed	2.97	1.32	.49	
Q28D Grades given before paper completed	1.78	1.53	.31	
Q29A Talk with teacher about completed writing	2.98	1.28	.48	
Q29C Written comments from teacher on completed writing	3.34	.92	.41	
Q29D Grades given to completed writing	3.03	1.03	.36	
Q30C Comments from teacher about writing	3.60	.70	.48	
			Alpha .77	
Response from peers				
Q20 Students talk about writing before paper completed	2.98	.95	.47	
Q21 Students talk about completed writing	2.54	1.01	.51	
Q28B Talk with students before paper completed	2.77	.98	.57	
Q29B Talk with students about completed writing	2.35	1.19	.57	
Q30A Comments from friends about writing	2.75	1.09	.50	
			Alpha .76	
Response from writer				
Q28E Teacher asks for comments before paper completed	2.11	1.45	.62	
Q29E Own comments on completed writing	2.07	1.45	.62	
			Alpha .76	

N = 715.

essays. The students claim next most frequently to write fiction and personal experience essays. They say they write significantly less frequently to explore ideas. Less frequent still is correspondence with the teacher, and least frequent of all is writing journals for themselves.

There is no parallel scale for the teachers for types of writing, since the teachers show no consistent pattern for the types of writing they are teaching. With respect to types of writing, there is a conflict between

Q15
Essays

Q15/Q12
Essays and poems, plays,
stories

$t = -4.45**$
$(df = 707)$

Q12 = Q11
Poems, plays, stories and
personal experience essays

$t = -.28$
$(df = 708)$

Q13
Find new ideas

Q11/Q13
Personal experience essays
and find new ideas

$t = 3.59**$
$(df = 714)$

Q10
Correspond with teacher

Q13/Q10
Find new ideas and
correspond with teacher

$t = -4.54**$
$(df = 705)$

Q9
Write journals for self

Q10/Q9
Correspond with teacher
and write journals for self

$t = -2.05*$
$(df = 708)$

$*p < .05.$ $**p < .001.$

Figure 3.6. Students' assessments of the relative frequency of different types of writing taught: matched pair *t* tests.

the professional literature and pressures of the school curriculum and the community; often the curriculum and the community expect secondary teachers to teach analytic writing while professional articles question the usefulness of genre classifications, the five paragraph essay, and programs that limit the kinds of writing students do. Because of the consistent picture painted by the secondary students, it is possible that the teachers conform to the external demands on them, at least in their students' eyes, but that they are reluctant to admit their actions in a professional arena such as the one implied by this questionnaire. Thus, they respond randomly. Or alternatively, the students may not discriminate among the genres. They perceive school writing as writing analytic essays, fiction, and personal experience pieces, when in fact there is more random variety in school than they recognize.

Helpfulness of Response during and at the End of the Process

The next set of questions concerns one aspect of how students perceive the helpfulness of different types of response to their writing. The secondary students are more consistent than their teachers in their sense of the helpfulness of different types of response both during and after the writing process. The most reliable scale for the students includes their answers to questions about response both during and at the end of the process (Table 3.8).[8]

The students' hierarchy of values is different from their teachers' (compare Figure 3.7 with Figure 3.1). The item means on this student scale show that the students find some types of response more helpful than others. Unlike their teachers, the students prefer written comments on their final versions significantly more than any other type of response. They next prefer individual conferences during the process. Then they prefer grades on their final versions, conferences on their final versions, and comments written by their teacher on their drafts. Significantly less helpful, they say, are responses from their peers on their drafts, followed by responses from their peers on their final versions. Their self-assessments are not seen to be particularly helpful either during the process or at the end. And perceived significantly less helpful still are grades during the process.

From the students' point of view, the teacher's written comments most clearly make the teacher's values accessible. And understanding the teacher's values is crucial at least to succeeding in school, if not learning to write. The following student expresses this point of view:

> Comments from teachers on my papers and talking over my mistakes, helps me the most. This gives me as a student, a chance to read what my teacher thinks and also to discuss it with him/her. The teacher obviously can't write down everything he/she thinks. This method would help me the most.

Grades seem to reflect an individual student's mastery of writing; students use grades to gauge their improvement, and to measure how "right" or "correct" their writing is, how well they follow what they think are the "rules" of good writing. One student says,

> I think my teacher helps me a lot, because if it's not done the right way you'll get a bad grade. And getting a bad grade really

Q29
Final versions

Q29/Q29C
Final versions and written
comments on final
versions

$t = -26.66**$
$(df = 707)$

Q29C = Q28
Written response on final
versions and response
during the process

$t = -.89$
$(df = 712)$

Q28A
Conferences during the
process

Q28A/Q29D
Conferences during the
process and grades on
completed writing

$t = 3.17*$
$(df = 713)$

Q29D = Q29A
Grades on completed
writing and conferences
on completed writing

$t = -.94$
$(df = 713)$

Q29A = Q28C
Conferences on completed
writing and written
comments during the
process

$t = 1.16$
$(df = 711)$

Q28B
Peers during the process

Q28C/Q28B
Written comments during
the process and peers
during the process

$t = -3.33**$
$(df = 711)$

$* p < .01.$ $** p < .001.$

Figure 3.7. Students' assessments of the relative helpfulness of response during the
writing process and after writing: matched pair *t* tests.

Continued on next page

Q29B
Peers on completed
writing

Q28B/Q29B
Peers during the process
and peers on completed
writing

$$t = 10.13**$$
$$(df = 711)$$

Q29B/Q28E
Peers on completed
writing and self-response
during the process

$$t = -3.79*$$
$$(df = 711)$$

Q28E = Q29E
Self-response during the
process and on final
versions

$$t = .99$$
$$(df = 712)$$

Q28D
Grades during the process

Q29E/Q28D
Self-response on final
versions and grades
during the process

$$t = -4.19**$$
$$(df = 708)$$

* $p < .01$.   ** $p < .001$.

Figure 3.7, continued.

> hurts, so the next time you'll do it the correct way, so you can
> see some improvement, and better grades.

Another remarks,

> When I am learning to write better [,] comments from my teacher
> and examples of how it should be done help me the most because
> they show me where my flaws are and how to improve.

To students, written comments on final versions help them infer the
"rules" or how writing "should be done," while grades indicate their
level of success in mastering the "rules."

Helpfulness of Response from Different Responders

The next summary scale on Table 3.8 examines the helpfulness of
different responders. The item means show that the secondary students

agree with their teachers (see Figure 3.2) about who the most helpful responders are, except that they value their parents' comments more than their teachers value what their students' parents say. The students place their parents third, after classmates and before other teachers and other adults (Figure 3.8). In free responses to the question, "When you are trying to write better, what helps you most and why?" many students

Q30C
Teacher

Q30C/Q30
Teacher and general
response from others

$t = -19.43*$
$(df = 711)$

Q30 = Q30A
General response and
response from classmates

$t = 1.29$
$(df = 713)$

Q30B
Parents

Q30A/Q30B
Classmates and parents

$t = 3.34*$
$(df = 713)$

Q30D
Other teachers

Q30B/Q30D
Parents and other
teachers

$t = 5.58*$
$(df = 709)$

Q30E
Other adults

Q30D/Q30E
Other teachers and other
adults

$t = 5.27*$
$(df = 709)$

Q30F
Siblings

Q30E/Q30F
Other adults and siblings

$t = 6.44*$
$(df = 711)$

*$p < .001$.

Figure 3.8. Students' assessments of the relative helpfulness of different responders: matched pair t tests.

mention their current teacher and some mention their friends; however, every now and then a student mentions a parent. One student says it helped "to talk to my mother or teacher to ask what I can do to make it [the piece of writing] better. To read it to my friends, mother and teacher."

In-Process Response versus Final Version Response

Unlike their teachers, secondary students find response after finishing writing significantly more helpful than response during the process (Table 3.9). This finding is consistent with the findings about the importance to students of written comments and grades on final versions.

Frequency of Response-Related Teaching Techniques

The next summary scale is the first of two focusing on the amounts of different types of writing activities that students engage in as part of the class, including the amounts of various types of response. As many of these activities as possible were paralleled to the teacher questions about teaching techniques. This scale subsumes most response-related activities in the classroom (Table 3.8). All items asking about the frequency of different teaching techniques fit on this scale, with the exception of the two items concerning topic assignment.

The question (Q22) asking how often the teacher gives grades on final versions of the student's writing only has an item-total correlation of .19 on the final scale; however, it is included because the scale alpha is not raised by removing it. The item probably does not fit well on the scale because there is so little variance in the responses to it.

Table 3.9

Comparison of Students' Judgments about the Helpfulness of
Response during the Process versus Response to Final Versions

	Mean Helpfulness (4 = most helpful; 1 = least helpful)	t Test
Response during the process	3.30 (sd = .96)	−3.23* (df = 711)
Response to final versions	3.44 (sd = .81)	

*p < .001.

Students perceive that grades are given universally by their teachers on completed versions of their writing.

The item means indicate that the students report that their teachers almost always write comments on their completed writing. A high frequency of their teachers comment on what is strong as well as what is weak in their writing. Their teachers also hold class discussions about topics before the students write. Least frequent is their teacher's informing them about an audience. Other techniques between the extremes, in order of frequency from high to low, are: student talk during the writing process, teacher talk during the writing process, teacher talk about completed writings, teachers' written comments during the process, student talk about completed writing.

Response from Teachers

The next scale combines items having to do with the helpfulness of certain types of response and the frequency with which the students receive the response. The first set of items concerns response from the teacher (Table 3.8).

Unlike the teachers' summary scale on teacher response, the questions on the student summary scale include both oral and written teacher response. The means show that the students as a group feel that comments from their teachers written on their final versions are the most helpful and most frequent type of teacher response. In these comments their teachers almost always rate strengths as well as weaknesses. The frequency and helpfulness scores match. Students also find conferences with their teacher during the process to be helpful, and they report that their teachers hold conferences somewhat frequently.

Response from Peers

The next set of items concerns the helpfulness and frequency of peer response (Table 3.8). Students report that peer response is used often but that it is only somewhat helpful. They prefer this type of response during the process and find that it occurs most frequently then.

Response from Writer

As with the teachers, two items form a summary scale about self-response, a practice the students find relatively unhelpful at any point during writing (Table 3.8).

Summary of Student Scales

The student summary scales simplify this part of the student questionnaire to the equivalent of eight items. The student scales are:

> Amount of Writing
> Types of Writing Taught
> Helpfulness of Response during the Writing Process and after
>   Writing
> Helpfulness of Response from Different Responders
> Frequency of Response-Related Teaching Techniques
> Response from Teachers
> Response from Peers
> Response from Writer

The student scales' alphas, the scale means, standard deviations and
variances, and the mean item scores and item standard deviations are
summarized in Table 3.10. Freedman (1985) shows that these summary

Table 3.10

Student Scales: Summary of Scale Means,
Standard Deviations, and Variance

	Number of Items	Alpha	Scale Mean (*sd*)	Scale Variance	Average "Item Mean and Standard Deviation" (divided by number of items)
Amount of writing	2	.52	6.86 (1.28)	1.63	3.4 (0.64)
Types of writing	6	.63	11.30 (4.33)	18.73	1.88 (0.72)
Response during and after process	12	.80	33.33 (7.94)	63.11	2.78 (0.66)
Responders	7	.80	17.58 (5.98)	35.79	2.51 (0.85)
Teaching techniques	10	.71	29.53 (5.07)	25.72	2.95 (0.51)
Response from teachers	12	.77	35.88 (6.97)	48.52	2.99 (0.58)
Response from peers	5	.76	13.41 (3.72)	13.82	2.68 (0.74)
Response from writer	2	.76	4.18 (2.58)	6.67	2.09 (1.29)

N = 715.

scales are relatively uncorrelated, although they are slightly more highly correlated than the teachers' are.

Influences on Students

The key influences on the students' replies include their personal characteristics of gender, achievement level, and grade level.

Gender

The students' gender significantly affects their responses on five of the eight summary scales, four of these at the .001 level (Table 3.11). The means on Table 3.11 show that for most items the females give significantly higher scores. On the scale about the types of writing

Table 3.11

Influence of Student Gender on Scales for Secondary Students

	Average "Item Mean" for Males	Average "Item Mean" for Females	*t* Test
Amount of writing	3.39 (*sd* = .66) (*n* = 349)	3.47 (*sd* = .61) (*n* = 356)	−1.75 (*df* = 698)
Types of writing	1.76 (*sd* = .71) (*n* = 346)	2.00 (*sd* = .72) (*n* = 349)	−4.30** (*df* = 693)
Response during and after process	2.69 (*sd* = .65) (*n* = 343)	2.86 (*sd* = .66) (*n* = 352)	−3.48** (*df* = 693)
Responders	2.32 (*sd* = .88) (*n* = 344)	2.70 (*sd* = .78) (*n* = 354)	−6.10** (*df* = 679)
Teaching techniques	2.93 (*sd* = .50) (*n* = 338)	2.97 (*sd* = .51) (*n* = 353)	−0.98 (*df* = 688)
Response from teachers	2.94 (*sd* = .59) (*n* = 339)	3.03 (*sd* = .58) (*n* = 353)	−2.09* (*df* = 688)
Response from peers	2.54 (*sd* = .76) (*n* = 346)	2.82 (*sd* = .70) (*n* = 355)	−4.98** (*df* = 690)
Response from writer	2.01 (*sd* = 1.26) (*n* = 348)	2.16 (*sd* = 1.13) (*n* = 356)	−1.61 (*df* = 702)

* $p < .05$. ** $p < .001$.

taught, the females report being taught more of the types of writing. On the scale about the helpfulness of response, females say that response to their writing is more helpful than do males. On the scale about response from different responders, the trends for females to give higher scores remain in effect. Also on the scale for teacher response, the females report more frequent and more helpful teacher response. On the scale about peer response, the females report more frequent and more helpful peer response.

Achievement

Student achievement level influences the students' responses on three of the scales, two at the .001 level (Table 3.12). The means for the levels of achievement for the scales are also included in Table 3.12. On scales where there are significant differences, higher-achieving students report that they write more, write more frequently in the different types of writing, and find peer response more helpful and receive it more, than do their lower-achieving counterparts.

Grade Level

Grade level affects responses on three scales: amount of writing, classroom activities, and peer response (Table 3.13). The means for each grade level for these three scales are reported in Table 3.14. Student writing increases progressively from grade 7 to 8 to 9, decreases in grade 10 (back to the eighth-grade level), and increases steadily from grade 10 to grade 12. Response on classroom activities follows the same trend. Students judge their peers more helpful as the students' grade level increases, except for the tenth graders who, more than students in any other grade, find their peers least helpful.

Summary of Results for Secondary Students' Surveys

Half of the secondary teachers in the study distributed questionnaires to four of their students: two high-achieving students and two low-achieving students, with one male and one female at each level. These students gave their opinions about response in their classrooms.

The key findings from the student surveys are:

1. *Students report that response to completed pieces of writing promotes their learning significantly more than response during the writing process.* The students are consistent in their opinions about the relative helpfulness of different types of response.

2. *As a group, students claim that written comments on finished pieces are more helpful than any other type of response. Following*

Table 3.12

Influence of Student Achievement Level on Scales for
Secondary Students

	Average "Item Mean" for High-Achievers	Average "Item Mean" for Low-Achievers	*t* Test
Amount of writing	3.54 (*sd* = .59) (*n* = 356)	3.33 (*sd* = .67) (*n* = 357)	−4.46** (*df* = 699)
Types of writing	1.97 (*sd* = .68) (*n* = 354)	1.79 (*sd* = .77) (*n* = 346)	−3.27** (*df* = 683)
Response during and after writing	2.79 (*sd* = .65) (*n* = 354)	2.77 (*sd* = .68) (*n* = 349)	−0.48 (*df* = 699)
Responders	2.56 (*sd* = .83) (*n* = 352)	2.47 (*sd* = .88) (*n* = 354)	−1.34 (*df* = 702)
Teaching techniques	2.99 (*sd* = .49) (*n* = 351)	2.92 (*sd* = .52) (*n* = 348)	−1.78 (*df* = 695)
Response from teachers	3.02 (*sd* = .55) (*n* = 352)	2.95 (*sd* = .62) (*n* = 348)	−1.49 (*df* = 685)
Response from peers	2.74 (*sd* = .74) (*n* = 355)	2.63 (*sd* = .74) (*n* = 354)	−1.99* (*df* = 707)
Response from writer	2.04 (*sd* = 1.36) (*n* = 357)	2.13 (*sd* = 1.23) (*n* = 355)	0.95 (*df* = 704)

*$p < .05$. **$p < .001$.

*these written comments, they find individual conferences during
the process most helpful, followed by grades on their finished
pieces.* They find least helpful, in order, peer response at any
point, self-response at any point and grades on drafts. Females
find all responses significantly more helpful than males do.

3. *Students do not find peer-response groups very helpful, but they
   see them as used by their teachers fairly often.* Groups are seen
   as most helpful and are believed to be used most often during
   the writing process.

   Females like peer groups better and find them used more often
   than males do. Higher-achievers like them better and find them
   used more often than lower-achievers. Tenth graders like them

Table 3.13

Influence of Student Grade Level on Scales for Secondary Students

	Degrees of Freedom	Sum of Squares	Mean Squares	*F*-test
Amount of writing				
Between groups	5	12.32	2.46	6.30**
Within groups	700	273.64	.39	
Types of writing				
Between groups	5	3.68	.74	1.39
Within groups	695	364.60	.53	
Response during and after writing				
Between groups	5	4.80	.96	2.20
Within groups	690	300.38	.44	
Responders				
Between groups	5	2.68	.54	.73
Within groups	693	506.07	.73	
Teaching techniques				
Between groups	5	4.38	.88	3.49*
Within groups	687	176.81	.25	
Response from teachers				
Between groups	5	3.45	.69	2.04
Within groups	688	233.11	.34	
Response from peers				
Between groups	5	14.66	2.93	5.52**
Within groups	696	369.79	.53	
Response from writer				
Between groups	5	10.53	2.11	1.27
Within groups	699	1161.03	1.66	

* $p < .01$.   ** $p < .001$.

least and find them used least often. Otherwise, peer groups' use and value rise steadily with grade level until they peak at grade 11.

4. *Students see self-response as even less helpful and perceive it to be used less frequently than peer response.* However, students from the South value self-response most, followed by those from the foreign American schools and then from the Northeast.

5. *As a group, students rate the teacher as the most helpful responder to their writing; however, they value their parents' responses more*

Table 3.14

Scale Average "Item Means" for Student Grade Level on Scales:
Amount of Writing, Teaching Techniques, and Peer Response

Grade Level	Amount of Writing: "Item Mean" Student Response	Teaching Techniques: Average "Item Mean" Student Response	Response Peers: Average "Item Mean" Student Response
7	3.23 (sd = .70) (n = 106)	2.85 (sd = .47) (n = 102)	2.57 (sd = .73) (n = 104)
8	3.39 (sd = .64) (n = 151)	2.87 (sd = .50) (n = 148)	2.60 (sd = .75) (n = 150)
9	3.44 (sd = .63) (n = 105)	2.98 (sd = .51) (n = 102)	2.73 (sd = .71) (n = 104)
10	3.32 (sd = .66) (n = 62)	2.87 (sd = .54) (n = 62)	2.36 (sd = .77) (n = 62)
11	3.43 (sd = .65) (n = 137)	3.04 (sd = .51) (n = 135)	2.84 (sd = .74) (n = 137)
12	3.65 (sd = .49) (n = 145)	3.03 (sd = .49) (n = 144)	2.81 (sd = .70) (n = 145)

than their teachers value parents' responses. Females value all responders more than males do.

6. *The students report that their teachers' most frequent teaching practice includes giving grades and writing comments on the students' finished pieces of writing.* They find that their teachers comment on strengths as well as weaknesses. Their teachers discuss topics with the students before the students write, and the students have opportunities to talk about what they are writing about.

Unlike males, females indicate that they experience the different response-related activities in their classrooms. Students at some grade levels experience more of the different response-related activities than students in other grades. In grade 10, students experience a dip, which is compensated for by a rapid increase in grade 11 and another in grade 12.

7. *The students claim that they write significantly more in the classes of these teachers than in their other classes. They report writing*

mostly analytic essays, followed by fiction, and then personal experience essays.

High achievers write more and write more of the different genres than low achievers. Seventh graders, the youngest students, write less than students at any other grade level; however, they are followed by tenth graders. Ninth and eleventh graders write about the same amount, and twelfth graders write the most. Females write more of the different genres than males.

Discussion of Results from Teachers' and Students' Surveys

The teachers and students disagree about the kinds of response that are most important in the teaching and learning of writing. The teachers value response during the writing process; the students value response to their final versions. The students are most concerned with written comments and say they learn a great deal from grades; the teachers do not value these modes of response.

At the secondary level, students have been conditioned by thousands of hours spent in American schools where evaluation with respect to one's peers, not individual learning and accomplishment, is the mark of success. Thus, it is little surprise that even in classrooms where teachers focus their attention on the teaching-learning process, students still focus their attention on evaluation.

The written comments that accompany final versions of student writing most often serve to justify grades, to explain an evaluation. Successful teachers do not see comments as a pedagogical key. The pedagogical danger in the students' feelings is that they may be concentrating on pleasing the teacher because the teacher is the examiner and the evaluator, but the teacher-pleasing may cause the student to worry about pleasing for the sake of a grade rather than pleasing for the sake of learning. The most serious danger is that students, in trying to please, relinquish ownership of their writing.

A comparison of the teachers' and students' average item means for each parallel summary scale is revealing (Tables 3.3 and 3.10). On every scale except response from teachers, the teachers see instruction as more helpful and/or more frequent than their students. On the scale for response from teachers, the students' average item mean of 2.68 is higher than their teachers' average of 2.40.

We saw much evidence of students' releasing ownership to their teachers during the ethnographies (see Sperling and Freedman in press; Greenleaf 1985). And Perl and Wilson (1986), in their ethnographies of successful teachers, describe a case in which only through interventions from the researcher, who was observing and working with the teacher, could they devise ways to overcome the students' lack of caring about writing and ultimately about what they were learning. The complexity and difficulty of this issue cannot be underestimated. In the end, though, we must remember that the comments and the grade provide the most official and permanent record of the teacher's response; they are the tangible bit that the student "takes away" from a class.

Once the teachers and students get beyond the issue of grades and written comments, they agree that in the teaching and learning of writing, students need, indeed must receive, individualized instruction. Both the teachers and the students indicate that the school, with instruction organized to take place for large groups, works against teachers' being able to devote sufficient time to a primary type of individualized response, conferences. The students, however, seem more satisfied than their teachers.

Peer-response groups are a common substitute for conferences; however, teachers have inconsistent opinions about their helpfulness during the writing process, and students find them relatively unhelpful at any time. Much research remains to be done to understand how peer response can be used productively.

Overall, both the teachers and the students recognize that of the possible responders, the teacher is the most helpful responder to student writing; however, teachers tend to underrate the help parents can and do give their children.

Whereas the teachers indicate that they do not consistently assign writing according to genre classifications, their students feel differently. The secondary students as a group say that they most often write analytic essays. The students' clarity and their teachers' lack of consistency indicate that the teachers might not have wanted to admit what types of writing they were teaching or that they teach all genres equally. It is difficult to believe that the students understood what we mean by the different genre labels while their teachers do not, or that there would be idiosyncratic emphasis on different genres among the teachers — the only other explanations for the teachers' inconsistencies. In the area of genre, current advice from the profession conflicts with mandates of the curriculum and the community. Whereas professionals advise that students should write in a wide range of genres, the secondary curriculum that prepares students for college (and most of the students intend to go to college) focuses on expository writing, on writing in academic modes for academic purposes.

Both the teachers and their students seemed to enjoy completing the surveys and to appreciate having the opportunity to express their opinions about the teaching of writing. Many of the students, in particular, appreciated being able to tell someone about their teacher. As one student remarked:

> I would like to say I'm glad I was able to do this survey, it was an enjoyable experience. Like I mentioned before I enjoy writing very much thanks to my dear sweet teacher whose name I won't mention; but I would like to thank her and you for making it possible for [me] to do this survey. I also would like to thank her for introducing and really helping [me] into the world of writing. I know she won't see this but I still would like to thank her and I will do just that.

First Ethnographic Analyses: Response Practices in Two Ninth-Grade Classrooms

How do the response practices of the two successful ninth-grade teachers in the ethnography compare with those of the teachers in the surveys? The surveys indicate what a large number of successful teachers say about how they respond to student writing and what their students say about the response practices of these teachers. The ethnography provides detailed observations of two teachers' classrooms. With the national surveys, it is possible to identify patterns in the reported response practices of successful teachers. With the ethnography, it is possible to add detail to the patterns and to indicate how different teachers vary, given the patterns. Since the two teachers in the ethnography were selected to be different from one another, they provide some sense of the variation we might expect.

The two teachers in the ethnography provided frequent and numerous types of response to their students' writing, unlike the teachers that had been described in past surveys and observational studies (e.g., Applebee 1981, 1984; Dillon and Searle 1983; Graves 1978). Classifications of the response in these two classrooms into the traditional categories of the peer group, the conference, and written comments do not adequately capture what the ethnographers observed. First, the usual labels for response excluded some of the response that we observed. Additionally, the usual labels seemed too general; responses that would be labeled identically seemed to function differently and to have different characteristics. For example, some conferences are initiated by the teacher and occur in private settings; others are initiated by the students as an aside to work in a peer group and are held in front of and sometimes in interaction with students other than the writer. The conferences Graves (1983) describes for elementary students take place in teacher-led, small groups, while the conferences Freedman and

Sperling (1985) describe occur in a college teacher's office. Although all these events are labeled conferences, the differences might be as great as the similarities.

The first step in describing response in the two classrooms involved developing a coding system for characterizing the response. Coding categories emerged from the data and allowed verification of the research team's observations about the distribution and description of response.[9] The coding also pointed to similarities and differences between these two classes and those in the national survey as well as to similarities and differences across the two classrooms themselves.[10]

Unit of Analysis: The Episode

In the classroom talk, the boundaries of response activities could be drawn in various ways. We coded units of response that we called "episodes." In teacher and student talk, the episodes consist of topically-related chunks of talk, separated by well-marked, change-of-subject intonation or lexical markers such as "O.K., now . . ." In the end, the episodes fall into two categories: those involving the teacher and students and that we observed both in person and on videotape, and those directed to focal students — in their peer groups and in written responses to their writing. For the coding, a set of written comments on a single piece of writing and a peer group involving a focal student each count as one response episode. The change-of-subject subdivisions are made on talk during conferences and class.[11]

We recognized and considered coding even finer subdivisions of these response episodes. For example, the episodes are made of smaller chunks or "rounds" (to use the term that Garvey 1977, gives to subsets of larger interactional episodes of adult-child interaction), and rounds are made of turns, and so on. None of these finer subdivisions, however, yielded more information than the episodes. Furthermore, agreeing on the boundaries of smaller units proved difficult. (For more information on episodes, see the Coding Manual in Freedman [1985], and see Mehan's [1979] discussion of topically related sets, 65–71.)

Categories

By studying the episodes in the field notes, supplemented by tape recordings of the classrooms, we decided on coding the following categories:

1. *Responder* (the person who gives the response)
2. *Recipient* (the person who receives the response)

3. *Initiator* (the person who initiates the events that yield the response)
4. *Context* (the situational context — whole-class, peer group, conferences — in which the response episodes occur)
5. *Time* (when the response occurs — whether during the writing process or following final draft)
6. *Target* (whether the response is targeted so that it has the potential of being incorporated directly into the assigned writing)
7. *Text* (whether an already-formed piece of discourse such as a paragraph, an essay, a film, or a speech, serves to coordinate the response)
8. *Pedagogical Focus* (what the orientation for the response is — cognitive-based, text-based, or procedural)

The Coding Manual in Freedman (1985) gives detailed descriptions and examples of all coding categories.

Coding Procedures

Three members of the research team coded the data. Two, the Scribe and the Technician, had collected the ethnographic data and knew them well. The third coder had assisted with data collection from time to time and was familiar with the data, but did not know them as intimately as the others did.

Rather than code all three assignment sequences from each of the classrooms, we selected one assignment in each class that provided a sample of the kinds of response observed across the assignments. The selected assignment was the one on which there was the greatest range of response and during which the researchers and the student and teacher participants agreed that the most teaching and learning was occurring. In Glass's class, it was the saturation report, her second written assignment; in Peterson's class, it was the character sketch of a familiar person, the first written assignment that we observed.

To identify the episodes, we supplemented the field notes taken by the Scribe with researchers' notes. These notes were based on reviews of each day's videotape, of each audiotape that involved a focal student in a peer group, and of written comments on the focal students' writing. The supplemented notes yielded a complete data base for identifying and then coding precisely the response occurring in the classroom.[12]

For a reliability check, the three coders, independently, coded fifteen response episodes from each of the two classes, for a total of thirty episodes. A weighted measure of reliability, Cohen's Kappa (1960), was performed on this coding. Table 3.15 gives the reliability results for each coding category. For all categories, the three coders were reliable, no one disagreeing significantly with any other.

Next, the three coders divided the coding task in a balanced way. For each week of data coded, one primary coder and one secondary coder were assigned on a rotating basis. The rotation system is detailed in Table 3.16. The primary coder coded all the data for the week while

Table 3.15

Inter-Coder Reliability[a]

	Coders		
	1 and 2	2 and 3	1 and 3
Variables			
Responder	77.27%	95.42%	81.82%
	.25**	.65***	.45***
Recipient	90.91%	90.91%	90.91%
	.81***	.81***	.82***
Initiator	81.82%	90.91%	81.82%
	.53***	.75***	.53***
Context	86.36%	95.45%	90.91%
	.77***	.93***	.85***
Time	100%	100%	100%
Target	95.45%	81.82%	86.36%
	.89***	.52***	.61***
Text	81.82%	77.27%	81.82%
	.66***	.54***	.58***
Pedagogical focus[b]			
Cognitive	77.27%	90.91%	86.36%
	.55***	.73***	.81***
Text	59.09%	81.82%	77.27%
		.60**	
Management	63.64%	86.36%	68.18%
	.36*	.70**	.42*
Uncodable	95.45%	95.45%	90.91%
	.83***	.86***	.70***

[a] The three coders are identified by numbers—1, 2, and 3. Column figures represent agreement statistics for each pair of coders. The top figure represents the percentage of agreement between the pair and the bottom figure represents Cohen's Kappa. Where Cohen's Kappa is not given, it is not applicable.

[b] The reliability for the pedagogical focus category is reported for each level of the variable because each episode could have been coded for two types of focus.

* $p < .05$.   ** $p < .01$.   *** $p < .001$.

Table 3.16

Coding Rotation System

Week	Teacher	Primary Coder	Secondary Coder	Number of Spot Checks
1	Peterson	1	3	all episodes
Pre-1 and 1	Glass	3	2	all episodes
2	Peterson	3	1	3
2	Glass	2	1	3
3	Peterson	2	3	2
3	Glass	1	3	2
4	Peterson	1	2	1
4	Glass	3	2	1
5	Peterson	3	1	1

the secondary coder made randomly selected spot checks to ensure continued reliability. No reliability problems were detected by these checks.

The amount of coded data from each classroom was parallel. The selected assignment lasted for four and one-half weeks of 50-minute periods in Glass's class and for five weeks of 40-minute periods in Peterson's class. Data were coded for three focal students in Peterson's class and four in Glass's. In Peterson's class, Candace was dropped from the study because she was frequently absent due to severe personal problems beyond the control of the teacher; hardly any data were available on her. Even with the uneven number of focal students in the two classes, the proportion of focal students to the rest of the students is equivalent: three out of twenty-seven for Peterson and four out of thirty-three for Glass.

Results: Response in Two Ninth-Grade Classrooms

Before performing the statistical analyses of the ethnographic data, we sketched an impressionistic picture of response in the two classrooms. We wanted to know whether the statistical counts would produce a similar picture.

We sketched Glass as a teacher guiding her students along a path of discovery, giving them cognitive tools for learning, independently, how to tackle specific writing problems. In this regard, she appears to depend largely on instruction at a somewhat abstract level, developing with her students concepts and principles, for example, or creating hypothetical writing situations, which her students then draw on to apply to their own writing. Further, she encourages students to reflect on their own writing processes, again a way to abstract from specific experience, with the aim of transferring these insights to future writing situations. Much of the direct response to student papers-in-progress comes from peers, who are guided to work in large part independently from her.

On the other hand, Peterson creates a master/apprentice atmosphere in his classroom. He works closely with individual students on the papers they are writing, giving frequent and direct feedback to them, often on the specifics of their texts, and holding one-to-one conferences in the classroom in order to do so. Practice writings are commonly geared to such specifics as sentence techniques or word choice. In addition, classroom work centers on helping students to think deeply about their topics, getting them to ask unusual and probing questions and to look for contradictions and contrasts. He shows them how to see the differences between details and generalizations as he helps them make use of the information they gather as they write.

Most of the categories on which we did statistical analysis bore out our original impressions of the two teachers. The analysis shows, on a concrete and verifiable level, the similar and contrasting ways in which their individual teaching approaches are actually accomplished in the classroom. The analysis also allows amplification of the results from the national surveys.

The first analyses of the ethnographic data are based on 467 coded response episodes on the selected assignments, which occurred over an equivalent amount of lesson time in the two classrooms. For each coding category, a Karl Pearson Chi-Square Test for Homogeneity assesses differences across the two classrooms. When this omnibus test shows significance, post hoc pair-wise comparisons (Z tests) between the two teachers are made on each level of the variable. Results are reported in Table 3.17.

Time in Process

The time variable considers when in the writing process response occurs in each class. As the teachers who completed the surveys value in-process response, Glass and Peterson provide most response during the writing process. Although they allow for response to occur at the time final drafts are returned to students, even this response is still really "in-process" in that it does not serve simply to end an assignment but

Table 3.17

Comparisons of Teachers: Types of Response

Type of Response Event	Percent of Response Events within Each Classroom		Tests of Significant Difference	
	Glass ($N = 191$)	Peterson ($N = 276$)	Chi-square	Post Hoc Z
Time			52.04***	
Process	74.3	96.7	($df = 1$)	
Final	25.7	3.3		
	($n = 191$)	($n = 276$)		
Context			46.44***	
Whole class	44.5	21.0	($df = 2$)	5.40***
Peer group	36.6	31.9		1.05
Teacher-student conference	18.8	47.1		−6.86***
	($n = 191$)	($n = 276$)		
Responder			51.04***	
Teacher alone	62.3	86.5	($df = 5$)	−5.95***
Teacher and student(s)	12.6	3.3		3.52***
Teacher and writer(s)	.5	.7		−.28
Student(s)	11.5	4.7		2.58**
Student and writer(s)	5.2	4.7		.24
Writer(s)	7.9	0		4.05***
	($n = 191$)	($n = 275$)		
Recipient			11.19**	
Individual writer	36.1	51.8	($df = 1$)	
Group of writers	63.9	48.2		
	($n = 191$)	($n = 274$)		
Initiator			14.07***	
Responder	63.9	71.0	($df = 3$)	−1.61
Recipient	11.5	16.3		−1.50
Another	21.5	9.4		3.50***
Unknown	3.1	3.3		
	($n = 191$)	($n = 276$)		
Context by initiation				
In-class			2.56	
			($df = 2$)	
Initiator = Responder	88.1	87.9		
Initiator = Recipient	8.3	12.1		
Initiator = Teacher	3.6	0		
	($n = 84$)	($n = 58$)		
Group			8.10*	
			($df = 2$)	
Initiator = Responder	59.7	42.0		2.21*
Initiator = Recipient	9.0	25.9		2.81**
Initiator = Teacher	31.3	32.1		−.10
	($n = 67$)	($n = 81$)		

Continued on next page

Table 3.17 — *Continued*

Type of Response Event	Percent of Response Events within Each Classroom		Tests of Significant Difference	
	Glass (N = 191)	Peterson (N = 276)	Chi-square	Post Hoc Z
Context by initiation, *continued*				
Conferences			81.51*** (df = 2)	
Initiator = Responder	23.5	86.7		8.0***
Initiator = Recipient	26.5	13.3		1.63
Initiator = Teacher	50.0	0		4.90***
	(n = 34)	(n = 128)		
Target			34.03***	
Direct to assignment	80.1	53.6	(df = 1)	
Indirect to assignment	19.9	46.4		
	(n = 191)	(n = 263)		
Text			11.28***	
Not present	24.3	12.2	(df = 1)	
Present	75.7	87.8		
	(n = 189)	(n = 262)		
Pedagogical focus				
Cognitive	42.7	43.8		.28
Text	28.7	31.7		.83
Management	28.7	24.4		1.19
	(n = 279)	(n = 356)		
Pedagogical focus by context				
Cognitive focus			15.32*** (df = 2)	
Class	44.5	26.9		3.10**
Group	36.1	33.3		.48
Conference	19.3	39.7		−3.86***
	(n = 119)	(n = 156)		
Text focus			18.10*** (df = 2)	
Class	33.8	16.8		2.68**
Group	40.0	26.5		1.96*
Conference	26.3	56.6		−4.47***
	(n = 80)	(n = 113)		
Management			26.98*** (df = 2)	
Class	48.8	17.2		4.58***
Group	37.5	36.8		.09
Conference	13.8	46.0		−4.89***
	(n = 80)	(n = 87)		

* $p < .05$. ** $p < .01$. *** $p < .001$.

leads into the next assignment as well. Although both teachers favor in-process response, there are significant differences between them. Glass devotes more response episodes than Peterson (25.7 percent of hers compared to 3.3 percent of his) to final drafts, and Peterson devotes significantly more response episodes than Glass (96.7 percent of his compared to 74.3 percent of hers) to drafts leading to the final draft.

The time variable matches the teacher profiles. Peterson, working closely with students as they produce their papers, needs to devote a great deal of draft time to response. Glass, letting her students work more independently, needs to provide her own response at the end of an assignment, even though she uses this response to help her students transfer their skills to the next assignment.

Context

The context variable considers what size grouping the teacher and students are working in when response occurs: whole-class, peer groups, or one-to-one. There is one major response context, the whole-class lesson, that the surveys do not consider. We found, however, that in the two classrooms in which the ethnography was conducted, a significant portion of the response occurs during such lessons. However, there are significant differences in this kind of response between the two teachers. For Glass, 44.5 percent of the response episodes occur when the class meets as a whole, compared to 21 percent of the response episodes in Peterson's class.

The other contexts for response observed in the classrooms are considered in the surveys: one-to-one conferences and peer groups. For Peterson, 47.1 percent of the response episodes occur as teacher-student conferences, both formal and informal, whereas only 18.8 percent of Glass's do, and these are mostly informal. The differences are significant; however, no significant differences were found between the teachers in the percentage of response episodes that occur in peer groups (36.6 percent of Glass's response episodes and 31.9 percent of Peterson's).

The contexts for response for Peterson are at odds with the actual patterns in the surveys but are in line with the surveyed teachers' preferences. That is, he provides for more conferences than peer groups. In contrast, Glass, like the bulk of surveyed teachers, provides for more peer groups than conferences. These practices, in fact, match their individual teaching approaches — the former to work on a specific level, something that can only be successfully accomplished by working with one student at a time on a particular paper, and the latter to work on a general level, something that can be most efficiently achieved when large groups of recipients are present at the same time.

Responder

The responder variable considers who gives response, and how often. In both classes, as in the surveys, the teachers are the principal responders to their students. However, in the two classrooms, teacher response often occurs in conjunction with student response, something not anticipated by the surveys or by past research on response. Glass responds in conjunction with student response significantly more often than does Peterson (12.6 percent of her response episodes compared to 3.3 percent of his). Peterson acts as sole responder for a significantly larger number of response episodes (86.5 percent of his) as compared to Glass (62.3 percent of hers).

In both classes, student response occurs less frequently than teacher response. However, in Glass's class, students, alone without the teacher, act as responders significantly more often than in Peterson's class (11.5 percent of the response episodes in her class as compared to 4.7 percent in his). A similar situation holds for writers giving self-response. In fact, while this kind of response occurs in Glass's class (7.9 percent of the response episodes), it does not occur in Peterson's. No difference was found in the two classes for situations in which either the teacher or student as responder works in conjunction with one or more writers as self-responder.

The findings that Glass responds significantly more than does Peterson in conjunction with student responders, that more response occurs in her class with student responders acting alone and that there is student self-response, supports her being more a "cognitive guide," providing opportunities for her students to take the reader-responder's point of view and to learn about writing through this complementary route.

Recipient

The recipient variable considers the receiver(s) of the response. The recipient is not considered on the surveys. Rather, it is assumed that one student is the recipient and that all students receive response equally. However, in the two observed classrooms, students receive response in a variety of ways. In each class, response episodes sometimes include one student writer as recipient of the response and sometimes a group of student writers (either a small group or the whole class). Response in Glass's class is geared more toward groups of writers (63.9

percent of her response episodes) than to individual student writers (36.1 percent of her response episodes). Peterson's response episodes are more evenly distributed among individuals (51.8 percent of his response episodes) and larger numbers of students (48.2 percent).

Initiator

The initiator variable considers who, responder or recipient, asks for response to occur. In both classes, more episodes are initiated by the person who is giving the response (the responder — generally, the teacher) than the person who is receiving it (the recipient — always, the student). Overall, the teacher most frequently initiates the response. While there are times when the student writer initiates response, in Glass's class the responder/recipient-as-initiator ratio is only 63.9:11.5 percent, and is similar to that in Peterson's class, 71:16.3 percent. This homogeneity between teachers is undoubtedly attributable to both teachers' being the class "leaders" as well as principal responders, taking lessons (and response) in the directions they have earlier planned for the students to follow. It is unclear whether the amount of student-initiated response is relatively low or high. Although it seems that it might be desirable for students to initiate more response, it is possible that the teachers provide so many opportunities for response that the students seldom have to ask for it themselves. Indeed, little is known about optimal levels of student-initiated response or the conditions that lead to student initiation.

A significant difference exists between the two classes for the situation in which someone outside the response episode, namely the teacher, sets up response to take place between others within the response episode, namely two or more students, where one or more students act as responder and one or more as recipient. Significantly more episodes are set up this way in Glass's class (21.5 percent of her response episodes) than in Peterson's class (9.4 percent of his).

Context by Initiation

The context by initiation category in the ethnographies illuminates the findings from the survey. The oral contexts observed in the ethnographies are whole-class discussions, peer groups, and individual conferences; the initiation patterns include teacher-responder as initiator, teacher setup of student response, and student as initiator.

During class discussions, both teachers, acting as responders, initiate the response well over 80 percent of the time (Glass, 88.1 percent; Peterson, 87.9 percent). This similarity between teachers is closely related to the finding for the single variable initiator, which shows the teacher/responder-as-initiator to be prevalent in both classrooms, where the teachers serve as principal class "leaders."

When she is present during peer groups, Glass initiates significantly more response episodes than Peterson does when he is present (Glass initiates 59.7 percent of the response when she is present during peer groups compared to 42 percent for Peterson). There are no differences between the two teachers in the number of times they set up response episodes to occur in groups between student responders and recipients. But there is a significant difference in the two classrooms when teachers interact with peer groups, and the recipient of response, that is the student, acts as initiator. In these situations, recipients initiate significantly more response episodes in Peterson's class (25.9 percent of the group episodes) than in Glass's (9 percent).

When the context is the one-to-one conference, the differences between teachers are pronounced. Peterson initiates significantly more response episodes than Glass — 86.7 percent of his conference episodes compared to 23.5 percent of hers. In this context there are no significant differences between teachers when recipients initiate response, even though this occurs for 26.5 percent of Glass's conferences compared to 13.3 percent of Peterson's. However, the situation in which the teacher sets up one-to-one conferences between students and then gets out of the way so pairs of students can then act as responders and recipients occurs for 50 percent of conference response episodes for Glass as opposed to none at all for Peterson.

When we look at context and see how the initiating of episodes transpires, the results support, by implication, our sense of the two teachers. Specifically, both teachers, taking the role of responders, initiate response episodes with peer groups more than do student recipients. But Glass, as responder, initiates more episodes with peer groups than does Peterson. His student recipients initiate more episodes than do hers. Used to working as an apprentice to their teacher, students in Peterson's class might have felt at liberty to call on him for group consultation. Such consultation is not in keeping with the independence that Glass expects of her groups, so they are perhaps more reticent about calling her over. Initiating group consultations had to be her responsibility.

The same picture, though with converse percentages, holds for the context of the one-to-one conference. The one-to-one conference is the modus operandi in Peterson's class, a pedagogical approach that allows him to work closely with each student and that he, naturally, would initiate to a great extent. Such conferences are incidental to Glass's approach, being initiated almost equally by herself as responder and by students as recipients. However, essential to her teaching is the notion of student independence, and unique to her class (set against Peterson's) is her arranging one-to-one meetings to occur between students — this type of initiating accounting for a full 50 percent of the one-to-one conferences in her classroom.

Target

The target variable considers the amount of response targeted to work that is directly versus indirectly related to the assignment. The surveys do not examine the target of the response. But the ethnography uncovers that significant differences exist between the two teachers regarding whether the writing being responded to has the potential of being incorporated into the writer's final draft (direct target) or whether it does not (indirect target). Glass devotes 80.1 percent of her response episodes to writing that is directly targeted to the assignment compared to Peterson's 53.6 percent.

These findings for the variable target reach the essence of the two teachers' approaches to teaching writing, with Glass teaching on a more general or abstract level and with Peterson on a more specific level. Peterson, working on lower levels of abstraction, needs multiple and diverse specific texts to respond to in order for students to be able to evolve their own generalities and make connections to future assignments. Thus response is often targeted to texts that are only indirectly related to the assignment but that provide these diverse sources. From Glass, students already have abstractions and principles, and it is necessary to apply these to the task at hand, getting for the assignment they are working on as much diverse feedback as Glass, their peers, and they themselves can provide.

Text

The text variable considers whether concrete text — that is, a student paper, a speech, a film, a piece of professional writing — serves to coordinate response episodes. Although not examined in the survey, text emerges in the ethnography as an important consideration. While both teachers frequently use text to coordinate response, Peterson shows a significantly higher percentage of "text-coordinated" response episodes (87.8 percent) than does Glass (75.7 percent).

Findings for the variable of text further delineate the profile of the two teachers. For Peterson's approach to response, text necessarily needs to be present to coordinate response episodes, as response tends to be directed and specific. For Glass, working with concepts and principles, effective teaching often demands that hypothetical situations guide response, thus the more frequent absence of text to coordinate response episodes.

Pedagogical Focus

The pedagogical focus variable considers whether response focuses on cognitive processes, concrete text, or issues of management. Although the findings about the teachers' values reported in the next chapter touch on this issue, this variable is not explicit in the survey. For both teachers, response episodes are more often cognitive in focus than text- or management-focused. For Glass, 42.7 percent of the focus for response episodes is cognitive, compared to 28.7 percent being text-focused and 28.7 percent management-focused; and for Peterson, 43.8 percent of the occurrences of pedagogical focus in response episodes are cognitive, compared to 31.7 percent being text-focused and 24.4 percent being management-focused. The differences across the teachers are not significant.

We had expected that both teachers, in spite of their different approaches, would place most of their pedagogical focus on cognitive processes. Glass, we had anticipated, would tend to focus the content of her response on an abstract but cognitive level, and Peterson, we had anticipated, would focus his on a concrete but still cognitive level. The academic agenda underlying the successful teaching of writing includes an underlying emphasis on the cognitive processes of the writer. As it addresses their students' writing, the content of these two teachers' responses follows that prescript. It is not, then, the nature of the *content* of their responses that differs, but rather their *approaches,* as the other findings illustrate. More detailed analyses in Chapter 4 will help us understand the workings of their teaching in more depth, especially with respect to this category.

Pedagogical Focus by Context

When the occurrences of pedagogical focus are analyzed according to the context in which they appear, virtually the same differences surface between teachers as in the analysis of context. In Glass's class, each kind of pedagogical focus occurs significantly more in a whole-class context (44.5 percent of response with a cognitive focus occurs in the context of the whole class, 33.8 percent of response with a text focus does, and 48.8 percent of response with a management focus does) than they do for Peterson (26.9 percent of response with a cognitive focus occurs in the context of the whole class, 16.8 percent of response with text focus does, and 17.2 percent of response with a management focus does). In Peterson's class, each kind of pedagogical focus occurs significantly more in the context of the teacher-student conference (39.7 percent of response with a cognitive focus occurs in the context of the teacher-student conference, 56.6 percent of response with a text focus does, and 46 percent of response with a management focus does) than they do for Glass (19.3 percent of response with a cognitive focus occurs in the context of the teacher-student conference, 26.3 percent of response with a text focus does, and 13.8 percent of response with a management focus does). There are no significant differences between teachers in how the two types of pedagogical focus (cognitive and management) are distributed when the context is the small group (Glass, 36.1 percent of cognitive focus compared to Peterson's 33.3 percent; Glass, 37.5 percent of management focus compared to Peterson's 36.8 percent). For the text focus, the two teachers differ in the group context (40 percent of response with a text focus occurs in the group context for Glass, compared to 26.5 percent of response with a text focus for Peterson).

Summary of Results for Ethnography

The observed patterns of response in the two classrooms show that

1. *In both classes, most response occurs during the writing process.* Even response to final versions is often targeted toward the next piece of writing and occurs during the process of writing that next piece. Thus, response during the process and response to final versions often overlap.

2. *Both teachers provide a substantial amount of response during whole-class discussions, with Glass providing this type of response more often than Peterson.* The teachers initiate most of the response in the whole-class context.

3. *The relative frequency of peer-response groups and individual conferences varies across the two classrooms, with Peterson holding more conferences than peer groups and with Glass focusing more on groups than conferences.* However, because Glass relies more on whole-class teaching, the amount of response in peer groups is not significantly different for the two teachers. When the teachers enter the peer groups, they vary according to how much they initiate response, with Glass initiating more response than Peterson.

The nature of the conferences varies in the two classrooms. Peterson initiates the conference as a private meeting between himself and a student. Glass's students initiate conferences, usually in the form of questions for Glass that arise when they are working in groups; Glass often does not respond herself, but sets up a response from the members of the group to the writer.

4. *In both classrooms, the teacher is the most frequent responder; however, how the teacher responds varies.* In particular, Peterson responds mostly alone, whereas Glass more often responds in conjunction with other students. Correspondingly, students receive response mostly in group settings (whole-class or peer group) in Glass's class. Peterson's students receive about half of their response as individuals and half in group settings.

    In both classrooms, the teacher usually initiates the response. Students request response relatively rarely, although they sometimes make the request. This pattern is especially prominent during whole-class discussions.

5. *Teaching practices vary in the two classrooms. More than Peterson, Glass targets her response to the piece of writing that the student is working on, but not to text itself. More than Glass, Peterson coordinates his response to particular texts, but not necessarily those the student is working on.*

6. *In both classrooms, most response is cognitively focused rather than text- or management-focused.* Only in conferences do the teachers tend to talk more about the text itself than about cognitive processes involved in text production.

The ethnographies show the kinds of variation in response practices that might be expected between different successful teachers and add detail to the results of the surveys. The analysis reveals how Glass and Peterson, both successful teachers of writing, actually distribute response in their classrooms. Their similarities confirm the survey results, and their differences illustrate some of the disagreements among the survey participants. The differences suggest both that there are different varieties of success in that some activities mesh better with some types of teachers, and that there are some profound institutional obstacles and deep-rooted disagreements in the field, especially when it comes to teaching writing as a social and cognitive process.

Notes

1. Most researchers have studied single types of response in order to explain how each type is accomplished (e.g., conferences [Carnicelli 1980;

Freedman and Katz 1987; Freedman and Sperling 1985; Jacobs and Karliner 1977; Kamler 1980]; peer groups [Gere and Abbott 1985; Gere and Stevens 1985; Nystrand 1986]; written comments [Beach 1979; Hahn 1981; Hillocks 1982; Marshall 1984; Searle and Dillon 1980; Sommers 1982]).

2. The question numbers are keyed to numbers on the elementary form of the teacher surveys in Appendix A.

3. Freedman (1985) shows other options for combining 1, 2, and 3 (questions having to do with the relative helpfulness of response) and explains the reasons for selecting these three sets.

4. Notice that this set and the previous one on the student surveys are parallel to 1, 2, and 3 for the teacher surveys (p. 51). The rationale for the different groupings of these essentially parallel items is given in note 8 below.

5. Before the scales were computed, means were substituted for missing data. Otherwise, if a respondent did not answer one item on the scale, the case would have been dropped and none of that respondent's answers would have been considered.

6. When this entire set of items is grouped together, Q22 (marking problems on final pieces of writing) and Q23 (assigning grades on final pieces of writing) showed weak item-total correlations (the next to the last column on Table 3.1). Deleting Q22 raises the scale alpha from .61 to .62; also deleting Q23 raises the alpha to .65. A new scale that omits Q22 and Q23 points to the advisability of also omitting Q25 (the frequency of sequencing assignments). Whereas the other items with original item-total correlations in the .20s (Q15, Q16, Q18, Q26, and Q27) either remain in the .20s or are raised with rescaling, Q25's correlation drops. By omitting Q25, the scale alpha rises to .69. Thus, for the final rescaling (last column on this scale on Table 3.1), the three inconsistent items are omitted.

7. Q14 had an item-total correlation of only .14, and if it were included, would have dropped the scale alpha to .61.

8. When items about response during the writing process (Q28-Q28E) were scaled separately, the alpha was .69; when response to completed writings (Q29-Q29E) was scaled separately, the alpha was .71. The scale of the combined items in Table 3.1 had an alpha of .80, a significant enough boost to justify a single scale.

9. The research team for the data analysis phase consisted of Cynthia Greenleaf, Melanie Sperling, Leann Parker, and me.

10. Coding and statistical analyses of classroom life miss much that could lead to an understanding of the workings of response. The analyses provide a useful general characterization of response and indicate fruitful directions for subsequent, more detailed analyses.

11. The oral episodes were captured by the room microphones as well as the teachers' wireless microphones and included all classroom discussion, all peer-group discussions when the teachers were present, and all in-class, one-to-one conferences between the teachers and individual students. In addition, the peer-group episodes were captured on separate tapes of groups that involved the focal students. Finally, all of the teacher's written comments to the focal students were collected.

12. Since many observational studies of the teaching and learning of writing in classrooms depend heavily on notes and writing samples, it is important to stress here the crucial contribution of the tape-recorded data. Although the notes were taken by a trained Scribe, and although the Scribe and the Technician reviewed and supplemented the notes at the end of each day of data collection, the notes were an astoundingly incomplete record of response in comparison to the supplemented notes. If a complete record is needed, tape recordings are essential.

4 Values about Writing: Underpinnings and Structuring of Response

Introduction

A comprehensive study of response should examine what motivates responders to react as they do. In part, how anyone responds to writing is determined by individual values about writing itself and about what makes written language strong or weak, interesting or dull, worthwhile or not worthwhile. The response process can be understood as a process of intersecting values. Responders' values affect how they respond; writers' values affect how they respond to their own writing and what they learn from response. In this project, since teachers and/or students are usually the responders and since students are recipients of response, it becomes possible to understand key variables that influence the teaching and learning of writing through observing the clashing and coming together of teacher and student values during the response process.

In this chapter, I first examine the values expressed by those teachers who completed the surveys. In the second section, I discuss what the teachers and students in the ethnographic study value about writing, how the teachers structure response activities to enact their values, and how the teachers', and students' values are similar and different. This second section provides a detailed qualitative analysis of the two classrooms, focusing on in-process response, the main way the teachers and students spend their time (Chapter 3), and looking at teaching and learning from the researchers', teachers', and students' points of view.

Survey Teachers' Values: Reasons for Teaching Writing

Two lists of items on the teachers' questionnaires work together to assess the teachers' values by determining their most and least important reasons for teaching writing.[1] The two lists were used by Applebee (1981). Their replication here allows a direct comparison of the values expressed by this sample with those expressed by Applebee's sample.

To create the question about values, Applebee refined the work of Barnes and Shemilt (1974) who, in a study of British teachers, found

110

two views of writing: the *transmission* view, in which writing is seen as a vehicle for transmitting ideas; and the *interpretation* view, in which writers learn and explore ideas through the act of writing. Applebee's two lists identify four slightly different views. The first list contrasts teaching writing to help writers *transmit information* with teaching writing to help writers *understand their personal experiences;* the second list contrasts teaching writing to help writers *understand concepts* with teaching to help writers *develop skills.*

The following lists indicate the view each item represents:

List 1

Transmit information:

help students remember information

test students' learning of content

summarize material covered in class

Personal experience:

correlate personal experience with topic studied

share imaginative experiences

allow students to express feelings

List 2

Understand content:

explore material not covered in class

force students to think for themselves

clarify what has been learned by applying concepts to new situations

Develop skills:

practice in writing mechanics

teach proper form for types of writing

test students' ability to express themselves clearly[2]

For the analysis, the teachers' responses to each item on the lists were converted to three-point scales that indicated the possible combinations of checks on each item (three points for most important, two points if neither was checked, and one point for least important). The data were analyzed first to see if the values of this sample and Applebee's would prove similar. Applebee found that teachers fell into one of two groups. Either they valued the transmission of information or they valued helping writers understand their personal experience, but they showed no combination of the two sets of values. Likewise, they either valued helping writers understand concepts or helping them develop skills, but not both. I hypothesized as Applebee suggested, "in effective instructional contexts the polarities might collapse. . . . Most effective learning of writing skills occurs when concepts are being applied. . . . Subject-area information is learned best when applied in the context of individual experience" (72).

Elementary Teachers

The elementary teachers in this sample showed multiple reasons for teaching writing. The six factors in Table 4.1 contrast starkly with Applebee's two factors. Besides having multiple reasons for teaching writing, these elementary teachers did not offer the contrasts embedded in the lists; rather, they created contrasts of their own, most of which were difficult to interpret. They seemed to do just what Applebee suggested effective instructors would. The first factor on Table 4.1 (form not thought) indicates that those who used writing to teach the proper forms did not teach writing to encourage thinking; however, both groups may have had students apply concepts to new situations, and both may have taught writing to test clear expression. The second factor (concepts, not mechanics) indicates that those who taught writing primarily to have students apply concepts to new situations did not also teach to have the students practice mechanics. Still, the group may or may not have taught writing to teach proper essay form. The third factor (material) groups those teachers who taught writing to have students explore and summarize material. The fourth factor (testing) groups the testers, those who taught writing to test both the students' learning of content and their ability to express themselves clearly. The fifth factor (uses of personal experience) contrasts those who wanted students to correlate their experience with a topic with those who wanted students to share imaginative experiences. The last factor (expressing feelings, not remembering information) indicates that those who taught writing to encourage students to express their feelings did not also aim to have them write to remember information.

Information, skill development, concept development, and the relationship to personal experience are intertwined, even though aspects of the original contrasts that Applebee found for his sample of secondary teachers hold at certain points.

Secondary Teachers

The secondary teachers also offered different values from the secondary sample in Applebee's survey, although their values were more similar

Table 4.1

Reasons Elementary Teachers Teach Writing: Factor Principal Component Analysis with Varimax Rotation

Reasons	Factor 1	Factor 2	Factor 3	Factor 4	Factor 5	Factor 6
To remember information	−0.13247	−0.23936	−0.13261	−0.15891	−0.06453	−0.85827
To correlate experience with topic	−0.09155	0.42025	−0.41289	−0.13967	0.61483	0.29435
To test learning of content	0.22343	0.00046	0.16257	0.70516	0.33134	−0.13470
To share imaginative experiences	0.13000	0.13490	−0.14676	−0.09681	−0.84346	0.04075
To summarize class material	0.16879	0.05042	0.83606	0.06535	0.10337	0.05463
To express feelings	−0.19572	−0.40088	−0.09604	−0.18536	−0.05258	0.69531
To explore out-of-class material	−0.36522	0.13401	0.61039	−0.36116	−0.07687	0.01622
To practice writing mechanics	0.36341	−0.65115	−0.13625	−0.19967	0.31862	−0.06738
To force thinking	−0.70577	0.00635	−0.16850	0.06975	0.04253	−0.01445
To apply concepts to new situations	0.04955	0.80727	0.04492	−0.29658	0.07322	−0.03309
To teach proper essay form	0.79249	−0.06074	−0.11766	0.08978	−0.09659	−0.02574
To test clear expression	−0.19938	−0.16329	−0.21153	0.73036	−0.19806	0.14449
Percent of variance	16.2%	13.4%	12.1%	10.5%	10.4%	9.9%

Note: Variable scores loading on each factor are underlined.
N = 189.

to those expressed by Applebee's sample than were those expressed by this elementary sample. This finding was not unexpected, since the question about values was designed for secondary teachers, this being the only group Applebee surveyed. The major difference between the values of these secondary teachers and Applebee's is that the polar values of these teachers, although existent, are much weaker than those Applebee documented (Table 4.2). These teachers created four, rather than two, factors. Applebee's teachers' first factor contrasted teachers who stress information with those who stress personal experience. This contrast is the weaker second factor for this group; furthermore, two of the six items on the list do not show any contrast: testing content and sharing imaginative experiences. For these teachers, the distinction between stressing information and stressing personal experience proved considerably weaker than it did for Applebee's sample.

Applebee's second factor, the first in this analysis, was strong for these teachers, but two of the original items on the list still did not fit. Although some of these teachers saw their mission more as one of

Table 4.2

Reasons Secondary Teachers Teach Writing: Principal
Component Factor Analysis with Varimax Rotation

Reasons	Factor 1	Factor 2	Factor 3	Factor 4
To remember information	0.16719	0.65089	−0.07203	0.38562
To correlate experience with topic	−0.10127	−0.15751	0.72130	−0.21756
To test learning of content	−0.06805	0.20103	0.06542	−0.78674
To share imaginative experiences	0.03936	−0.71723	−0.09056	0.28536
To summarize class material	−0.05197	0.60737	−0.14633	−0.00166
To express feelings	−0.03234	−0.53533	−0.39647	0.31889
To explore out-of-class material	0.62963	0.04987	0.26431	0.08647
To practice writing mechanics	−0.56529	−0.02761	−0.23184	0.42028
To force thinking	0.59286	0.07451	−0.14862	0.03563
To apply concepts to new situations	0.36793	0.00401	0.64676	0.12267
To teach proper essay form	−0.75553	0.12208	−0.01978	−0.05399
To test clear expression	−0.02081	−0.21490	−0.55755	−0.56943
Percent of variance	18.2%	14.9%	12.1%	10.4%

Note: Variable scores loading on each factor are underlined.
$N = 367$.

helping students develop skills and other teachers saw their mission more as one of helping students understand concepts, both teacher groups had students write so that they could test students' use of clear expression, and so that the students would learn to apply concepts to new situations.

Elementary and Secondary Teachers

To better understand these results, I examined the percentage of the sample, checking each item as most and least valued. Both the elementary and secondary teachers agreed on the primary importance of teaching writing to force students to think for themselves (Table 4.3). The elementary teachers also aimed to use writing to teach their students to share their imaginative experiences and express their feelings. Writing as an art form, as a way of sharing imaginative experiences, although valued at the secondary level, was most valued at the elementary level. The secondary teachers, on the other hand, taught writing to help their students correlate their experiences with the topics being studied. The elementary and secondary teachers also differed in their emphasis on testing content, and differed somewhat in their stress on having students write to express their feelings, explore material not covered in class, and practice writing mechanics.

Comparison of Secondary Teachers with Applebee's Secondary Teachers

Dramatic differences are evident in the values expressed by Applebee's secondary English teachers and the secondary teachers sampled here (Table 4.3). Applebee's teachers placed significantly more stress on mechanics and writing as testing and significantly less stress on writing as thinking, as clarifying concepts, and as relating ideas to personal feelings and experiences.

Most of the teachers in this study aimed to teach writing *to force their students to think for themselves.* These teachers also wanted students *to understand personal experiences, and to connect those experiences to their learning.* Writing became primarily a tool for making learning meaningful to the individual, for making the connections between the self and the academic world, and for creating pieces of art. These teachers believe strongly that writing, thinking, and learning must occur in the context of individual experience. This finding is entirely consistent with Applebee's original point about effective instruction: skills and information are learned when they are "applied in the context of individual experience" (1981, 72).

Table 4.3

Reasons for Asking Students to Write

Reasons	Percent of Teachers Rating as One of Two "Most Important"			Chi-square Tests[a] $(df = 2)$
	Elementary $(n = 189)$	Secondary $(n = 367)$	Applebee's Secondary English $(n = 140)$	
List 1				
To help students remember information	13.8	14.2	18.6	(a) .02 (b) 1.51
To correlate personal experience with topic	44.4	64.3	47.1	(a) 20.14** (b) 12.47**
To test students' learning of content	3.2	16.6	45.7	(a) 21.28** (b) 45.80**
To share imaginative experiences	68.8	42.4	30.0	(a) 35.20** (b) 1.74
To summarize material covered in class	4.8	7.6	13.6	(a) 1.65 (b) 4.28
To allow students to express feelings	66.7	55.3	38.6	(a) 6.66* (b) 11.31**
List 2[b]				
To explore material not covered in class	12.3	6.0	5.0	(a) 6.65* (b) .19
To practice writing mechanics	20.9	12.0	46.8	(a) 7.72* (b) 72.04**
To force students to think for themselves	65.8	70.1	44.0	(a) 1.08 (b) 29.73**
To clarify what has been learned by applying concepts	44.9	46.2	22.0	(a) .08 (b) 25.49**
To teach proper form for writing	16.0	20.7	27.7	(a) 1.71 (b) .81
To test students' ability to express themselves clearly	42.2	47.0	61.0	(a) 1.14 (b) 8.00*

[a] The first chi-squares (a) contrast the elementary and secondary teachers in this sample; the second chi-squares (b) contrast the secondary sample here with Applebee's secondary English teachers. There are two degrees of freedom because there are two groups of teachers and a three-point scale.

[b] For the second list, $n = 141$ for Applebee's sample.

$* p < .05.$ $** p < .001.$

Teacher and Student Values Meet in the Classroom

The second part of this chapter examines the values of Peterson and Glass, the teachers in the ethnography, and the values of their students. The detailed information about how these two teachers and their students play out their values in the course of classroom life yields stories that enrich the findings from the surveys. Classroom descriptions show that Peterson and Glass display similar values to those reported by the teachers in the surveys; both aim to teach their students to think critically and creatively about their world and, in Peterson's class, about the literature they read. Both teachers use writing as one way to help their students reach this goal. Also, like the surveyed teachers, they use writing for other purposes as well.[3] The surveys also indicate that students and teachers disagree about issues of response. The students in these two classes indicate something about the source of these disagreements. All in all, the stories of these two classrooms show the complexity of teaching students to think for themselves and to relate what they learn to their experiences.

Chapter 3 indicates that Peterson and Glass attempt to realize their common goals in significantly different ways. Because of their differences, they show more than one picture of successful practice. Whereas Peterson personally coaches his students during the writing process, Glass stresses the importance of students' writing independently and "guides" her students indirectly. These differences in orientation lead to differences in the response activities that each teacher emphasizes. In Glass's classroom, in-process response occurs mostly during whole-class discussion and peer-group work; in Peterson's it comes in his written comments supplemented by teacher-directed individual conferences and group games that feed into whole-class discussion.

One result of these different orientations is the different ways peer groups operate in the two classrooms (see Freedman and Bennett [1987] for more detail). Peterson's groups generally solve circumscribed problems that are related to learning to think creatively about their writing topics. Glass's students respond to one another's writing in groups. These observed differences in the two classrooms suggest that teachers responding to the survey may have different notions about the use of peer groups. Such differences in successful teachers' in-process response may help explain the unpatterned results about in-process response activities on the national surveys reported in Chapter 3.

To document both the nature of these two teachers' values about writing and the ways they structure response to their students' writing, I analyze (1) the nature of the tasks and activities they design for their students; (2) their talk with their students, both in class and during conferences; (3) their written comments on their students' writing; and (4) their interviews with the research team. I also examine their students' values about writing by looking at (1) the students talk during class; (2) their talk in peer group meetings; (3) their talk in conferences; (4) their talk in their interviews with the research team; and (5) their writing.[4] After discussing each teacher's values and the relationship of those values to response, I conclude the description of the classrooms by following one student in each class throughout the writing of one piece. The case study students were selected to highlight the intersection of teacher and student values during response.

Thinking in Art Peterson's Classroom

Throughout the seven weeks that the research team observed Peterson's class, his students worked on the three major assignments described in Appendix B. Every assignment was a character sketch, with the students moving from writing about a friend or acquaintance; to a more removed and abstracted subject, a famous person; to the most removed and abstracted subject, a character from Charles Dickens's *Great Expectations.* Such a sequence was designed to help Peterson's students understand how to connect their personal experiences to their reading and writing and to think in increasingly more abstract and complex ways. In teaching his students to think critically, to connect their thoughts to their personal experiences, and to communicate those thoughts in writing, Peterson aims ultimately to help his students achieve "wisdom." He writes about the nature of wisdom as it connects to writing: "Whatever wisdom we achieve, comes through hard thinking about our experience before we speak and write, and a willingness to sharpen and refashion our ideas once we've tried them out" (Peterson 1986, 8).

In the next sections, I illustrate how Peterson structures response activities to emphasize thinking. In every assignment, he stresses two key concepts: (1) facts, judgments, and "showing" details; and (2) seeming contradictions.

Facts, Judgments, and Showing Details

Throughout the period of observation, Peterson concentrated on helping his students practice manipulating what he labels "judgment" and "observation" or fact. For example, one day students were asked to make a judgment about Henry, given the fact that "Henry pulls the wings off flies." In numerous such practice exercises and then in applications to their writing, students come to understand and make distinctions between fact and judgment. Peterson personally coaches his students until they can apply their understandings of specific details and wider generalizations to their writing about a character's habits or traits.

Structuring Response Activities

How does Peterson structure response activities to emphasize the distinction between fact and judgment and to connect this distinction to his individual students' writing? He begins by posing situations for his students that help them practice ways of thinking that will be productive as they generate ideas for their own pieces of writing. In a number of activities, he and the students in the class respond to the productivity of individual students' thinking processes. The substance of the first week's whole-class meetings, peer-group meetings, and homework assignments are interwoven by Peterson to focus on facts and judgments (Table 4.4).

For Monday's activities, Peterson begins whole-class discussion by modeling the difference between observation and opinion with two sentences on the chalkboard: Students are asked to explain "the difference between" *Thornhill is selfish* and *Thornhill pushed a man out of a car.* Given the student reply, "The one describes the other one," Peterson elaborates on the connection as a distinction between "seeing" and "judging" what you see. He shows the students a short movie clip from *North by Northwest* (for a second time), and instructs them to "compare information" in groups about what they observe of Cary Grant's character. The group activity is framed and informed by the whole-class discussion about seeing and judging. The students share common, whole-class experiences — the discussion about seeing and judging and the movie. Their group activity functions in the context of each group's return to whole-class activity. The groups are told that after "a couple of minutes . . . we'll see what you've got," that is in the return to the whole-class discussion. Then Peterson reminds the students of the group's task: "Remember I don't want any judgments." When Peterson calls a halt to group discussion about the Cary Grant movie after six minutes, students are asked to report their observations to the class. Peterson reinforces the focus of the lesson: "If you hear a judgment [from a student in another group], and I agree with you, your group gets a point."[5] The ensuing classroom talk is extremely lively; several students seem confused by the fact/judgment distinction while others do not. The combination of compiled information about Cary Grant

Table 4.4

Focus of Students' Response Activities
during First Week in Peterson's Class

Day	Whole Class	Peer Group	Assignments
Monday	Discussion of distinction between *Thornhill is selfish* and *Thornhill pushed a man out of a car.* Distinction between *observation* and *judgment* carried over to analysis of Cary Grant's character based on the first few minutes of the movie *North by Northwest,* which the students watch in class.	Pool information about observed detail of film character's appearance and behavior; guideline questions are: What does he wear? How does he look? What does he say? What do others do? What does he do?	Begin reading *Great Expectations (GE).*
Tuesday	Discussion of "what happens" in the *GE* chapters students are reading on their own.	Pool information about *GE* character, guided by same questions about detail as on Monday, this time charted on a ditto sheet for students to fill out.	Prepare list of people whom they know and who know them, to get ideas for focus of first character sketch assignment.
Wednesday	What constitutes a *pattern* for a character, i.e., given the sentence *Henry pulls the wings off flies,* what can be added about Henry that might also be true of the kind of character who would remove wings from flies?	Practice construction of *patterns* of details to characterize someone by adding pertinent sentences to texts begun by others.	Write paragraph about *GE* character assigned to their group, based on details listed on ditto chart.

Continued on next page

Table 4.4 — *Continued*

Day	Whole Class	Peer Group	Assignments
Thursday	Function of *topic sentence* as a judgment that acts as a connector of other observations within a paragraph.	Listen to individual students' written paragraphs on the *GE* character and notice whether the paragraph has a topic sentence that "connects" details to one another; talk about gaps in detail and missing "evidence"; how sentences can be connected.	Choose one person from their list and apply ditto chart questions about detail to that person.
Friday	How known characters on student lists are different from one another.		

and Peterson's arbitration over students' talk structures the observations developed by everyone in the room. The exercise helps Peterson reach his specific goal of developing students' abilities to recognize and control the difference between fact and judgment.

The next day students are asked to move straight from thinking about Cary Grant into thinking about a *Great Expectations* (*GE*) character their group has been assigned. For the movie, Peterson has written five questions about characters on a ditto sheet: "What does he wear? How does he look? What does he say? What do others do? What does he do?" (see Table 4.4, Peer Group–Monday). The same questions are part of Tuesday's dittoed chart, which students complete as they analyze characters from *GE* in their groups. Peterson does not elaborate on the seeming transfer of focus; it is, in fact, only a seeming transfer. The issues of connection, and perception, relevant to the movie exercise, teased out in the course of the feedback, are wrapped back into the *GE* assignment.

These response activities are not direct response to an individual student's writing in progress. They are noteworthy in that students receive response to their ideas and their thinking processes, both from Peterson and their peers. The response activities are anticipatory,

preparatory to writing. On this Monday, Peterson directly refers to the
GE assignment and indirectly to the character analysis of a friend or
an acquaintance. He says that the day's activities will be "important
for your anecdote assignment," an anecdote being assigned to precede
the first character analysis.

Peterson carries forth these notions about fact, judgment, and detail
as he works with individual students on drafts of their writing. For
example, when Peterson confers with Geraldine about her anecdote,
he first summarizes what he has heard as she read her recounting of
how her sister's boyfriend "sleeps at the beach" and "likes his car."
Then he questions Geraldine about both the facts of the situation and
the judgments she might make:

> *T:* He likes his car?
>
> *G:* He likes his car.
>
> *T:* Why do you think he likes his car so much [unclear]?
>
> *G:* I don't know.
>
> *T:* What kind of car does he have?
>
> *G:* A (unclear). [T nods]
>
> *T:* Okay, so how would you characterize this guy? What
> are his . . . qualities? [G. taps fingers, seems to be
> thinking]
>
> *G:* He's funny and —
>
> *T:* Okay [unclear] he's funny. Okay, that's one thing. But
> what else?
>
> *G:* His most prized possession is his car. And —
>
> *T:* Would he rather . . . work on his car or go out with
> your sister?[6]
>
> *G:* He'd rather go out with my sister [laughs]. I think
> [laughs].
>
> *T:* Why don't you ask him why he likes his car so much?
> You see what you have to have, is to make it work,
> you have to have some reason. You gotta try to figure
> out why he likes his car. /Okay./ Why do most people
> like their car? Because I want you to start with that.
> And then we'll move from there, okay? Because he's
> funny and he likes his car. But "he likes his car" isn't
> a character trait, it's. . . . See . . . what . . . I mean. To
> be humorous that's [unclear]. It's a . . . sign of some-
> thing else. See what I mean? I mean, he might like his
> car because he doesn't like to be . . . pinned down to
> one place. See what I mean?

> *G*:   Uh hum.
> *T*:   Ask him.
> *G*:   Okay. . . .
> *T*:   You gonna see him today?
> *G*:   Probably.
> *T*:   You tell me tomorrow what he says, all right?

Peterson attempts to get Geraldine to go beyond her point that her sister's boyfriend likes his car to what that means about him as a person. Peterson suggests Geraldine needs to know why he is so attached to his car. The one generalization Geraldine makes, "he's funny," is not apparently related to her point about his attachment to his car. Peterson suggests that Geraldine gather more information, spend more time talking to her sister's boyfriend, understand more about his attachment to his car, and then report her findings to Peterson the next day.

After reading Vera's anecdote, he works with her on issues of fact, judgment, and detail. He first responds:

> *T*:   That's good. Except I think you could flesh this
>   out. . . . You gotta get more detail in there. /Yeah./
>   Cause it's, really, it's a good start. Yeah. /Okay./

He then asks Vera to tell him about the different ways her character shows her strength. He wants Vera to give more factual support for her judgment about her character's strength. Vera gives a lengthy explanation, after which Peterson says,

> *T*:   What you wanna do is get the different ways . . . sorta
>   organize around different ways she shows her strength.

Mental Search: Unusual Detail to Seeming Contradictions

Another aspect of teaching his students to think creatively about their topics involves them in finding traits that show contrast. Peterson stresses the importance of writing to interest the reader and coaches his students to select "interesting" detail by looking beyond the obvious, for the unusual, the seeming contradictions, the mystery of people, both for real people and for the characters in *GE*.

Structuring Response Activities

Again, Peterson poses multiple situations that afford his students practice in searching for unusual detail and interesting contradictions. An example, from the third week of observations, illustrates activities that Peterson devises to help his students engage in this aspect of thinking creatively. He begins by modeling how he conducts his own mental searches. He prepares a list of thirty-two questions to ask about characters: "Questions for Character Analysis." The students are encouraged to consider such questions as they think about the people they are writing about. Examples of the questions are "Would you buy a used car from this man? Would he go to the movies by himself? Would he send back a steak in a restaurant?" (The complete list can be found in Appendix F.) The questions are multifunctional. They serve, first, as a heuristic for how to think critically and creatively about characters and thereby generate "interesting detail." They also help students expand the material they have at their disposal for writing character analyses on their own. For example, in one activity, groups are asked to add five more questions of like precision for "finding out what your guy is about."

Although the thirty-two questions stimulate creative thinking and help students generate "unusual" details, they do not require that students see contradictions. However, Peterson uses them in this way as he helps his students understand the connections between the detail they have generated. In particular, throughout Week 3, Peterson holds individual conferences with students about the anecdotes they have written about their character in preparation for the first paper. These conferences occur as peer groups work on a variety of activities. In this case, they are working with the list of thirty-two questions — answering them for their characters, or adding to the list. In the conferences, Peterson discusses comments he has already written on drafts of the anecdotes; with each student, he seems to try to find the complexity within the character portrayal. In many cases, he pushes the individual writers to find and communicate "the contradictions" about the character they are portraying. In other cases, he searches what they have already written and finds the germs of "interesting" ideas that might be elaborated. For example, Laura has described her character as basically crazy-acting. He notices that her examples show the person as also considerate. In conference, he says to Laura,

> A lot of people who act crazy aren't very considerate of other people. But it looks like he is. He has, what, a kind of a combination [student nods]. So why don't you think about making him two-sided. Because his consideration for other people /uh huh/ you have some stories about that. /Uh huh/ And also his craziness. . . . And actually it might be, just think about this, I'm not sure, it might be that his craziness is related to trying to [unclear] for other people.

In Donald's case, Peterson takes a similar approach but, this time, by questioning Donald and pushing him to think more about the character.[7] Peterson begins the discussion:

> *T:* I forget. What was the story about in your anecdote?
> *D:* Uh, he was in a race and, uh, he fell down before he got to the finish line.
> *T:* Yeah, yeah, yeah, yeah. Then . . . then he [unclear] all kinds of excuses.
> *D:* Yeah.
>
> . . . .
>
> *T:* Where does it [another point Donald made] fall under your demonstrating [unclear] his . . . excuses and stuff?
> *D:* Well, he criticizes people, and —
> *T:* Why? Why do you think he does it?
> *D:* Uh, he doesn't want to be criticized. So he criticizes them first.
> *T:* Does that work? People don't criticize him then?
> *D:* Mmm. Well, maybe they do behind his back so he can't hear it.
>
> . . . .
>
> [interruption by another student]
> *T:* So . . . he's got, on the one hand, . . . he doesn't accept any feelings in himself. Right? He makes up all these excuses. Right? On the other hand, . . . he's quick to criticize other people. How do you think he got like that?

After discussing these negative points about Donald's character with Donald, Peterson asks another question to probe for contradiction: "Has he got any desirable traits? Is there anything about him that . . .?" Donald cannot think of any desirable traits, and so Peterson closes the conference with, "Well, try to think of stories in both those cases. Excuses and criticism of other people."

Effects on Students

Peterson's whole-class and small-group, problem-solving activities, coupled with his individualized and personal approach to response during the writing process, yield dramatic results that are easily observed in the students' writing.[8] The case study of Gina[9] writing one piece offers a particularly vivid and gratifying example of the payoff of his teaching and how his values and Gina's merge during the writing process.

Values and Response: Gina's Case

Gina's case shows what Gina learns from the response she receives in Peterson's class and how Peterson's values and Gina's intersect. Gina is writing her character sketch of someone she knows well. She has written the following anecdote:

> (1) I have a friend, her name is Dianne, and she is quite an unusual person. (2) She, in turn, has a best friend whose name is Andrea. (3) Not long ago, Andrea met a special person she was more than excited about. (4) She would carry on for hours on end about how sweet, and kind and handsome he was. (5) By the way, his name is Dan, which is the same as Dianne's boyfriend, but that's a different story. (6) Anyhow Andrea's relationship with Dan bloomed and as is natural, she introduced him to her best friend, Dianne. (7) Now, it is essential to understand that Dianne is the all-american girl. (8) She skis; jogs, plays tennis, has an eternal tan and is extemely "sweet", and most of all, she's rich and makes sure that everyone knows it. (9) Andrea, on the other hand, is not quite as outgoing, she is also sweet, but less complicated and a little more sincere. (10) Andrea brought Dianne over to see Dan quite often, well, maybe not so, about four times, this is over about a month. (11) Often Dan would bring some mutual friends of his and Andrea's all of whom were, as is often the case, madly in love with Dianne. (12) One day, Andrea, Dan, and these friends had a little "party" afterschool, a little to drink and a little to smoke. (13) Suddenly, Dan put his arm around Andrea saying, "Can I have Dianne's phone number? I want to call her, I like her so much!" (14) Andrea could not believe her ears, sure Dianne and she had discussed Dianne's feelings for Dan. (15) But she never thought that they were more than ones of friendship. (16) Andrea, being the most unselfish person alive, simply nodded her head, and recited the precious numbers she herself had dialed dozens of times. (17) That night was endless, nightmares of Dan and Dianne haunted her and true sleep never came. (18) Dianne, in turn, the next day, began to carry on at school about Dan, simply ignoring the pain that Andrea might just be going through. (19) Now Dianne has two Dans to worry about, each unaware of the other's existence and Dianne and Andrea are still "best friends".

Peterson reads this anecdote at home and returns it with only a few written comments:

1. Beside sentence 1 he asks, "Is this true?"
2. He writes "no it isn't" beside the last part of sentence 5.
3. He asks for an example beside sentences 8 and 9.
4. He suggests Gina use fewer words beside sentence 10.

5. He places a paragraph symbol in the margin by sentence 13.

6. Beside sentence 14 he writes, "This is the first time you mention this."

7. He writes "good" beside the first part of sentence 8 and by sentence 16.

He makes one change in Gina's text: He crosses out "saying" in sentence 13 and writes "and said." His global comment about the anecdote is written at the top of the page:

> Basic question: Is this about Dianne or about Andrea? It seemed
> to be about Andrea, in which case we need a lot more about her.
> Try rewriting putting her at the center.

In a follow-up conference Peterson and Gina address the global comment first. They establish the fact that Gina intended the anecdote to focus on Dianne:

> *T1*: Okay... what my basic question here was —
> *G1*: Is it about Dianne?
> *T2*: Yeah, it is about Dianne, right?
> *G2*: It is about Dianne. It's just that I have to tell about Andrea in order to tell this story. I couldn't just say Andrea.

Then he indicates the reason for his confusion:

> *T3*: Okay. So I'll tell you my problem. I think this is really more about Andrea than about Dianne. /Uh hum./ Because... Andrea is the one... who's put in the position where she, right.
> *G3*: Yeah, yeah, yeah.
> *T4*: ... You could write this about Andrea. You could write *this* [the anecdote] about Andrea and you could still write [the character] sketch about Dianne.

He gives Gina a choice; although she wrote her anecdote about Andrea, she could write her full character sketch about Dianne.

The rest of the conference focuses on Peterson's pushing Gina to think more critically about Dianne's character, to prepare Gina for writing the character sketch itself.

> *T5*: All right.... What... is Dianne's main quality as you see it?
> *G5*: Uhm, well, she is pretty phony.
> *T6*: Phony.

G6:   . . . That's the main word. Phony. Uhm . . . she has a
        lot of money and she uses it to get people to like her.
        She thinks that . . . her money is the only thing
        that's . . . in her that's worth anything. So in a lot of
        ways she's very, uhm, /insecure./ Insecure. Well she's
        also secure in that . . . she tries to act as if she *is* secure.
        /Uh hum./ You can really see through that after you
        get to know her. /Uh hum./ . . . She uses her friends
        as a sort of shield. If she wants to do something, and
        because of her insecurity she feels bad about it, she
        tells her friend, "Go do this for me." For example, if
        she wants to, uh, ask somebody to do something for
        her. . . . Her friend said she wanted me to go to the
        movies with her. She was insecure about me saying
        "yes" or "no," whether or not I liked her. So she asked
        her friend to ask me.

T7:   Okay. Okay. So you've got this insecure person, but
        she has certain, uh uhm . . .

G7:   But she tells people in a lot of ways. A lot of people
        think she *is* the most secure person that they've ever
        seen.

T8:   Yeah. Because she has these little, uh, tricks or /Yeah/
        devices, one of which is money.

G8:   Uh hum.

T9:   Another, another, another . . .

G9:   She has lots of clothes, her tennis ability, her skiing
        ability. That stuff.

T10:   Okay, and then she has all these other little manipu-
        lative techniques.

G10:   Yeah. She uses her friends.

T11:   Yeah, right.

G11:   Yeah.

T12:   Okay. So that's good. You've got a person who is
        basically insecure, but is able to cover it up. Of course
        you've got to establish her insecurity. You can't just
        say she's insecure.

G12:   Uh hum.

T13:   I mean, you've got to [unclear] give me some examples
        of how this shows through sometimes. /Uh hum./ But
        then, you get into, the way you, these little techniques
        that she uses. That could be good.

In T5 Peterson asks for the *underlying generalization,* a question that allows Gina to articulate in oral language her essential understanding of Dianne (G5 and G6). Gina sorts out the appearance from the reality. Peterson does not impose his ideas; after all, he has never met Dianne. Gina moves from describing Dianne as phony, to insecure, to apparently secure in G7. Peterson (T9), playing the role of both an interested reader and a teacher, asks Gina to elaborate on the reasons others perceive Dianne as secure. He *coaches Gina in synthesizing* her thoughts by taking one of her judgments, *adding* a piece of support from what she has said, and then *asking Gina to add* further elaboration, by modeling his previous thinking. Specifically, Peterson synthesizes when he suggests that Dianne use "devices" and he adds, "one of which is money" (T8). He then asks Gina for "another, another, another" (T9). And Gina supplies others (G9, G10). Finally, Peterson in T12 *summarizes* what he and Gina have constructed, what will become the essence of Gina's paper; "you've got a person who is basically insecure, but is able to cover it up." Peterson has led Gina to verbalize more than the surface phoniness, to understand its source and its effects. Gina has used oral language in the form of a student-teacher conversation to bring her thoughts together.

Next Gina writes a draft of a character sketch about Dianne. After more written comments, peer-group work, and conferences, she writes a final version of the sketch (see Appendix G). In the discussion that follows, I summarize parts of the sketch and include key paragraphs to illustrate how the thinking Peterson emphasizes and his individual work with Gina help her to think about her own character as she writes the anecdote.

Gina begins with a quotation from Dianne. " 'I couldn't help my best friend with her homework, but I gave her fifty dollars to buy a book. Do you think that's enough?' " After introducing Dianne as a complex person, "envied and admired by some; yet resented and disliked by others," Gina characterizes herself as a "closet analyst" who finds Dianne her "greatest challenge" because of her complex personality. After several one-sentence examples, Gina concludes this introductory section with the following generalization: "It's really incredible how she always manages to find the right words to say and to make people do things completely against their own will and their common sense." Gina continues:

> Although she's not blond, the only way to describe Dianne's looks
> is to say she is the perfect California girl. For one thing, she keeps
> an eternal, never-fade tan. Dianne is tan year-round from her

scalp to the soles of her feet. Dianne has a Colgate smile with pearly white, perfectly aligned teeth. Whenever she flashes her smile you feel like someone turned the sun up too high. She has her own surfboard, her own water skis, and her own water bike (don't ask me where she uses these things, I don't know). She owns OP (Ocean Pacific) clothes by the millions and is eternally listening to the BEACH BOYS on her Sony Walkman (which cost her $250.00)

In spite of the fact that Dianne is usually the center of attention, she is insecure, but she is very good at covering it up. Because Dianne has a lot of money, she believes that ultimately, she can buy everyone and everything. One time she invited me to go to a movie with her, but it so happened that I was busy that night and couldn't go. Well she, immediately assumed that I wasn't going because I didn't like her and offered not only to buy my ticket, but to buy me dinner as well. On Andrea's birthday, instead of going to her birthday party, Dianne gave Andrea thirty dollars.

Dianne believes that those close to her are trying to use her just as she uses them. She is always on the defensive end. I remember the time that. . . .

Incredibly, Dianne can be extremely and afraid of rejection. So shy, that once when she wanted to envite me to a party at the beach, Dianne sent Andrea to ask me because she didn't know me very well and was too afraid to face me and my answer. . . .

To understand Dianne, it is essential to understand her need not only to be accepted, but to have the world revolve around her. . . . If I talked about each of her qualities I would be here for days. So I'll tell one of the best "stories" and you can see what I mean.

At this point, Gina writes from her anecdote:

At the beginning of the year, Dianne liked a guy whose name is Dan. As usual, she convinced Andrea to make sure he liked her back. This she did by having Andrea rant and rave about what a great person Dianne was. Inevitably, he liked her back. As soon as Dianne found out she made no further attempt at becoming friends. She almost ignored Dan. She then proceeded to make Dan's best friend like her, and together they had many "adventures". About four months ago, they went to Lake Tahoe together. While they were there, they got drunk. Later, they went skiing only to get caught by the ski patrol who tried to send them back to San Francisco. They managed to run away and hitchhike back to the city. Everyone always found out about these stories, especially Dan; but then that was the whole point. Later she dropped Dan's best friend for Dan. Dianne gave Dan a dose of adventure too, but later dropped him. This on-again-off-again relationship went on for months until she finally stopped it completely, but only for a few months. Now, she's picked him up again, and he, has become her worshipper. For her birthday, she told him she wanted a gold necklace and a dozen roses. So the poor guy went out, got a paper route and worked for months to get what she wanted. When her birthday came around he proudly gave her the wonderful gifts and all she could say was a cold and simple, "Thanks".

The sketch continues with another paragraph emphasizing Dianne's cruelty and the fact that many people who were previously fooled by Dianne's exterior "are beginning to see that they've been wrong." Gina concludes,

I feel sorry for Dianne. She could have the world if she would just stop worrying about being the center of everything and appreciate all the wonderful things that she has. Especially, I wish she would see how much harm she does to those who care about her. She must be terribly lonely. I wish she would wake up, take the blindfold off, and see the world as it really is.

Indeed, Gina not only has thought a great deal about Dianne's character, but has communicated these thoughts and a full picture of Dianne to her reader.

Peterson's web of response activities is designed to help Gina think critically and creatively about characters in particular and ideas in general. Further, the activities serve to help her communicate her emerging ideas in written form, in ways that would please a broad audience of both Peterson and her peers. Throughout, although Peterson clearly coaches Gina, he aims at getting her to think through and then express her own ideas, not his.

Peterson's students vary in how much they "own" what they write. Gina herself is often frustrated by the hard work involved in the serious thinking that Peterson demands. Revealing glimpses of Gina's values come when she talks to her peers about her feelings about her writing and Peterson's response to it. She participates little during whole-class discussions, but acts as the unequivocal leader in her peer-group meetings.[10] Alone with her peers she complains,

I'm tired of writing. Everything I write he doesn't like. Every time I think it's pretty good, he always gives me something bad. And before, if I had written it for some other teacher, they would have said, "Ah! Beautiful!"

Gina then admits,

The thing is, I don't want to change because of him. You know, that's the way I do it. I mean, if I changed, I'd have to *think* about it. This way I just keep going, you know.

Like most of the students we studied, Gina begins (and may even end) by wanting to "get the most reward for the least effort" (Sperling and

Freedman, in press). On the surface, her complaints to her fellow students could be interpreted as a student rebelling against a distasteful new directive from yet another idiosyncratic teacher. However, when talking with their peers, students often seem to use such "anti-teacher/anti-classroom" talk as a way to bring themselves together as a peer group and as a way to work through some of their most pressing academic problems. Gina's talk about changing shows her engaged in the act of thinking seriously about changing. She may be using this talk to prepare to construct a task that is more difficult than usual for herself. Without doubt, Gina's writing shows that she chooses, "to *think* about it," to construct the more difficult task. As Hayes's (1986) data suggest, students like Gina will not expend so much effort all the time. The data here show that when Gina is pressed or motivated "to think about it," she at least has cognitive and social strategies that will help her out.

Thinking in Mary Lee Glass's Classroom

I next describe how Glass emphasizes the teaching of thinking in her classroom. The statistical summaries of the response episodes (Chapter 3) foreshadow the fact that the ways Glass teaches thinking will show important contrasts with the ways Peterson teaches thinking.

Throughout the ten weeks that we observed Glass's classroom, the students wrote three major papers, and gave oral presentations — some of which were based on the paper topics. The writing topics described in Appendix B include: an interview with a fellow student, a "saturation report" on a place, and an "opinion" essay. As in Peterson's class, the writing activities moved students to increasingly more abstract and potentially more personally distanced subjects.

Like Peterson, Glass believes that to teach students to write well involves teaching them to think independently, critically, and innovatively. In an essay on her philosophy of teaching writing, she says:

> Most important, if the discovery of what we have to say leads us to explore our thinking, to uncover new ideas or relationships or insights that we had not seen before, that, I think, is the "big one."... The teaching of writing must involve a wide range of experiences which encourage the beginner, or the expert, to learn to generate, collect and articulate his thoughts and words, to organize and arrange them, revise and refine them, and to evaluate the product before beginning the next excursion.

In her teaching, Glass stresses two kinds of activities underlying the ability to write well on the topics she poses: *independent research* to gather, synthesize, and focus material, and (friendly) *independent criticism/evaluating* to recognize where the end-product meets and falls short of the writer's own standards.

As with Peterson, every activity in Glass's classroom is informed by her philosophy of teaching writing. Thus, assignments, whole-class discussion, and peer-group work address collectively her hopes for her students' cognitive and academic growth. However, because of her stress on the importance of students' developing independence from the teacher, peer-group response takes a more central role in Glass's in-process response activities than it does in Peterson's. As Glass explains in an early interview with the research team, she does not want to "teach *at* the kids for forty-five minutes . . . group work is really the key activity."

Independent Researcher: Gather, Synthesize, Focus

On each assignment, Glass's independent student researchers gather information, synthesize it, and focus it for a reader. For example, Glass begins the interview project by explaining the work to be done: "Assume that you are a reporter who has been assigned to this personality to (1) write an article (2) do a speech." As the students gather information, they are directed to find "showing" details which must be distinguished from "telling" details (see Caplan and Keech 1980), much as Peterson's students work with facts, judgments, and showing details. What is different here is that, throughout, Glass places more emphasis on self-reliance than Peterson does. Also, once Glass's students have collected details, she emphasizes form more explicitly than Peterson, in particular with her emphasis on synthesis and talk about "finding a focus."[11]

Structuring Response Activities

Glass structures the classroom so that students will receive feedback on their research activities as they are conducting them. However, in contrast to Peterson's class, the response rarely comes from Glass to individual writers; rather, it comes mostly from her discussion and illustration of writing concepts with the whole group. The class discussions often feed into peer-group work as she guides the students in helping one another. In the end, only students see and respond to one another's in-process drafts. Since key group and class activities are spread across stretches of time and change over the course of the school year, this mode of structuring response can best be illustrated by examining the different activities over time. Thus, I will describe response to research activities during the three writing assignments we observed.

In the interview assignment, students write about each other and therefore must gather information from each other. They begin responding to one another's ideas during the four occasions Glass has them work together in pairs to gather details about each other. The students are deliberately not paired with their friends. As they switch between the roles of interviewer and interviewee, each student models his or her information-gathering techniques for the other. These interviews form the core of the classroom activity, while in-class discussion functions on the periphery. The pair sessions require usually at least half a class's period; the first half of the class is spent with Glass modeling questioning strategies, discussing how to get a shy person to talk, and other interview techniques. She even offers herself as a "practice" target for interview questions.

As students gather information, they practice synthesizing and focusing it. In class, Glass asks, "What do you do with all the random bits of stories, information you collect? How do you avoid a 'blow-by-blow' history?" As the students are thinking about how to collect their material into an interesting and cohesive focus, she models the process, using her answers to their questions when she was their "practice" target. One question to her was: "What do you enjoy?" She had answered, and listed on the board:

> reading books
>
> a holiday once in Tahiti
>
> listening to music

The students had also asked: "Can you remember something you did when you were a kid?" Her answer had been:

> feeding the chickens when I was on vacation

She adds this fourth, apparently disjointed detail to the first list, and challenges the students to "find a focus" for all the data. As they question her about this fourth detail, they find that the theme of "escape," which characterizes the first three, links into the fourth because Glass reveals, "When I was a kid, I hated feeding the chickens and was always looking for a way out of it, to escape." On another occasion, the students practice focusing information as they collect objects ("nothing creeping or crawling") from outside the classroom and work together in groups to find a way of jointly characterizing — finding a focus for — each group's assortment.

In the next writing assignment, the saturation report, students receive in-class directions about how to gather information about a place. Not accidentally, during class discussion about the students' activities, the similarity is noted between what the students are to do and what the research team in the back of the classroom is doing: observing carefully, tape recording, taking detailed notes.

After the students have, independently, gathered much of their information for this project, they meet in groups, this time to work on "focusing" the information. They are to "try some fresh eyes and ears" as they address problems that have arisen for them. In class, before these groups meet, Glass directs the students to find a way of generalizing detail into "atmosphere," "the general feeling" of their chosen place.

A discussion in one of the groups shows the students helping Shelley, one group[12] member, solve a problem she is having applying Glass's notions of research to her own writing:

> *Shelley:* I'm having some really big problems.
> *Jim:* What you doing it [the saturation report] on?
> *Shelley:* Girls' softball practice. [Jim laughs]
> *Julie:* The game?
> *Shelley:* Well, no, just the practice. But I'm gonna have to watch some games cause I'm not sure . . . I don't know what to say. Uhm, . . . a lot of . . . like, I don't know . . . there's not that much, you know what I mean. Well, today if you walked out, you'd probably slip in the mud. [laughs] I mean —
> *Julie:* There she goes! [group laughs]

Shelley's problem is that she is "not sure what to say" and feels as though "there's not that much [to say]"; she seems to be having difficulty gathering information. Shelley continues to talk about her place:

> *Shelley:* Well, I can tell you some things. Last practice the ball . . . hit me in the finger and I sprained my finger. Okay, it hit me right here. I've got a big bruise there and my finger snapped. Okay. [laughs] I'm the clumsiest on the whole team. So, uhm . . . it's dangerous.

At this point, probably because of Glass's instructions, Yvette prematurely suggests a "focus" for Shelley:

> *Yvette:* How about, like, the girls' softball practice is . . . is energetic?
> *Shelley:* I don't know. Yeah. Um.

Julie attempts to continue to suggest a focus but stops when she realizes that neither she nor Shelley have enough information for this kind of discussion. So Julie asks a question, but not one that helps Shelley figure out "what to say."

> *Julie:* It's also hard, hard work, you know. The mood would be, okay, the topic. Which are you doing? The game or just the people in the game?
>
> *Shelley:* Just the practice.

Jim continues the apparently premature search for a focus for Shelley and the others join in, with their generalizations.

> *Jim:* Talk about, like, the excitement building up to the game?
>
> *Julie:* No, you can't really talk about comradeship. Oh yeah, team spirit maybe? Something about spirit. . . . It's really important that everybody help each other, encourage each other. . . . Do you know? Well, uh, the attitude would be there's a lot of spirit.
>
> *Yvette:* And it's also, like, competitive.
>
> *Julie:* Yeah, a lot of competitiveness.
>
> *Shelley:* That would be good [unclear].
>
> *Julie:* And . . . verbs. Verbs. What kind of verbs? Sports maybe. How about "practice sports. Many students." That sounds so stupid. Never mind. . . . What do you think?
>
> *Jim:* I'm not very good, uhm, since I don't have mine ready.
>
> *Shelley:* I think that's good enough. [unclear] Yeah.

Shelley closes the discussion, apparently satisfied. The group continues discussing Jim's and Julie's place and how they will focus their material. Apparently, as the talk has moved away from her piece to the writing of the other students, Shelley continues to mull over her observations of her own place, and how she will make sense of her topic. She unexpectedly interrupts the conversation, asking,

> *Shelley:* Okay, how does this sound? The girls' softball practice is a mixture of good spirit and competitiveness.
>
> *Julie:* Yeah, that's good [unclear].
>
> *Yvette:* Good.

Shelley's idea for a focus comes from her synthesis of Jim, Julie, and Yvette's talk.

In the last assignment we observed, the opinion paper, Glass depends more on whole-class discussion than on groups for helping students with their research skills. She asks students to generate a list of topics they are interested in, have personal experience with, and have an opinion about. In an interview with the research team, Glass explains that this project is a culmination of everything the students have been learning — a drawing together of their skills of observation, organization, and evaluation developed throughout the semester. It is also meant to *extend* those skills. This point is explicit in her in-class discussion with her students. She reviews the interview assignment, asking, "Where did you get your information for writing the paper for the interview? And where are you going to get information for this assignment?" Given the answer, "from your mind," Glass recaps the semester's discussion of what organizing one's observations entails ("sorting," "selecting," "showing"). In this way she introduces the notion of a thesis as a logical development from the notion of a focus that the students' have worked with in their earlier projects. A focus points towards the synthesis of particular, chosen details about an observed place, or person; a thesis points towards an argument, or opinion, which entails such a synthesis of information. The opinion paper requires students to choose an issue and to discuss their personal point of view about it. Students are free to select one of the issues they had listed, or to choose one from a dittoed sheet, which contained topics such as: the value of participation in sports (is sport really healthy?) or advice to varied audiences about teenagers (to parents, teachers, etc.). The "thesis statement" is the one intended to capture the direction of the writer's argument, a concept Glass elaborates during in-class discussion while students develop their ideas about the project.

Throughout, Glass's emphasis is on student independence and form as a heuristic for thinking, approaches not stressed nearly so much by Peterson.

Critic/Evaluator

The development of the student as critic/evaluator is, for Glass, the quintessential corollary of developing skills useful to gathering and arranging ideas. She writes:

> The student of writing must learn to evaluate — his own, her peers', the masters' writing. . . . The trick, then, is to find ways to allow students to evaluate their own work, for, after all, they will be on their own when they leave a particular classroom and must succeed or fail in the next writing situation on their own. . . . Clearly, evaluation must become an automatic part of the practice, an informal exercise in expression and revision as well as the formal statement translated into a grade at the end of the quarter, an

easy and comfortable and nonthreatening part of the process of growth and thinking, an acknowledgement that we can all see and hear and judge what is "better" rather than depend entirely upon the teacher who grades the paper to tell us how good it is. If as a result teachers must give up reading everything the student writes, and, rather, let the students do much of that reading and evaluating, so much the better. No, I did not say give up reading papers entirely, for the teacher cannot lose track of where the students are, but we cannot, and we should not, expect them to learn to write better if we are the only ones in the class whose responsibility it is to evaluate.

Glass's stress on students becoming self-evaluators is motivated by her desire for students to be independent of her, to learn to find answers to their own questions, to develop skills of working with little *direct* teacher assistance during the writing process. Although Glass lends support to the groups by moving among them, it is the students who accompany one another the most through the process of producing a paper — from the initial problems, to settling on focal sentences, to helping one another with rough drafts, to the final clean-up of spelling, punctuation, and syntax. Just as she trains researchers mostly by setting up situations in which students can learn to help themselves, so she trains evaluators.

Structuring Response Activities

Because the development of the student as independent critic/evaluator is crucial to Glass's philosophy, the peer-response group supports her pedagogic goals.[13] For the most part, in-class evaluation activities are designed to support what Glass intends students to do with the help of peers in groups and then independently (or without teacher-structured help) after they leave the groups.

In the interview assignment, students practice evaluating one another's work twice in peer groups, once to read and think about each other's rough drafts and the second time to edit one another's final drafts. In both cases, groups work with editing sheets dittoed for them by Glass, completing the sheets after a student has read her paper aloud, and giving them to the student (all editing sheets, notes, and rough drafts are handed in with the final draft when it is formally graded). In the first groups, the response guidelines ask students to consider the following as they evaluate one another's rough drafts.

Answer the questions below in as specific a way as you can, with the idea of being a "friendly" critic whose job is to help the writer improve the paper during revision.

How was the introduction? wow OK so-so boo

Was the focus clear? yes no

Restate it in your own words:

What is the best part of the paper? Why?

What is the part that needs the most work?

Help the writer underline one sentence that needs more "showing" in order to make the picture more clear or interesting.

Other comments?

The questions ask the students to think about both the specifics of organization (attractive introduction, clear focus) and about the less specific business of being a "critic": What is the best part of the paper? Why? What needs the most work?

Again, a segment from one of the peer-group sessions illustrates how the students act as evaluators, identifying and then attempting to help one another solve problems. In Shelley's group, which was discussed in the previous section, productive evaluative talk occurred around a problem that the *writer* identified and that led the group to work collaboratively on a solution. The same holds here. When reading their work aloud, the students tend regularly to offer self-evaluations. Sensitive to their visible audience's needs, they offer clarification and evaluation of their work. Anne, for example, prefaces the reading of part of her draft of her saturation report.

> *Anne*: Oh well, see, I started two different papers and I haven't even finished any of them. So it's kind of . . . I'm not sure which one I'm gonna use. Okay.[14]

Anne reads her draft and concludes with, "How's that? I haven't really done much." Julie replies, "Okay. That's good." After an interruption by Karen to ask a question about her paper, Julie, needing to complete her response sheet about Anne's draft, returns the discussion to Anne's paper:

> *Julie*: Okay. So . . . your focus is on Center Quad, right?[15]
> *Anne*: Yeah.
> *Julie*: But what's the focus?
> *Anne*: "It's the kind of place where you go to read, relax, study, eat, or just — "

Then Julie moves beyond the sheet:

> *Julie*: Do you explain why?
> *Anne*: Not . . . really.
> *Julie*: Can you explain why, maybe?
> *Anne*: Okay. Yeah, well, I'll have to change it a lot.
> *Julie*: Don't worry. Mine is . . . just so bad.
> *Karen*: So's mine. [overlap]

The students fill out their sheets and simultaneously discuss deadlines, the difficulty of the assignment, and the lengths of their papers. Just as the group seems ready to move on to Karen's reading of her piece, Karen reopens the discussion of Anne's paper:

> *Karen*: Yeah, but you [Anne] should get the focus out in the first sentence. It's kind of unclear. You should make sure you get out exactly what the focus is.
> *Anne*: Okay.
> *Karen*: Cause, I realize that your place is Center Quad, but —

Karen gives Anne a rule for focus sentences, which she apparently makes up (Glass has never said such a thing); Anne is ready to accept this rule. But Jeannie interrupts to continue the discussion:

> *Jeannie*: I think you are mostly showing how quiet it is.
> *Karen*: But you know what's really good.
> *Jeannie*: Most people consider the center part of school to be really loud and —
> *Julie*: That's good! That's really good. You should compare the two, like quiet as opposed to . . . um —
> *Anne*: Noisy and active?
> *Julie*: Just like lunchtime, as opposed to 7:30 in the morning, or something like that.
> *Anne*: You can do something like that?
> *Julie*: Yeah, you can do anything you want. See, I decided like in the park. I went at two different times. Once when it was Friday night and nobody was there, and once when it was Sunday afternoon when everybody was there.[16]

Jeannie begins to think about the content of Anne's paper, the substance of the focus rather than its placement. Julie continues on an even more productive tack, going back to Anne's original self-evaluation. Although in Anne's case, after she articulates her problem, the students help her with a solution, in most cases when students identify a problem in their writing, peer solutions do not emerge.[17]

Work on the opinion paper unfolds as peer-group evaluation is supported by in-class modeling and troubleshooting. Groups meet three times — twice to read rough drafts, using new evaluation sheets that ask that students pay attention to their peers' (and by implication of course, to their own) thesis statements, introductions, and structure: "Does the writer show enough evidence? Can you see the connections from one paragraph into the next?" Pairs meet a third time to proofread one another's final version of the paper. Student interactions in groups remain similar.

Summary

It is the duality of the critic and researcher that creates for Glass the real writer; classroom and peer-group activity allow students to practice both roles. Glass's major emphasis is student independence, one of her criterial goals for productive classroom response activities and for learning to write. She believes that self-reliance is particularly crucial for creativity and design. Glass avoids intervening directly in the process of a student's writing of a paper; she works around the edge of the student's writing and thinking, giving opportunities for writers to work out their problems, and giving them time to develop ideas and try out those ideas on others.

Effects on Students

To understand the effects of Glass's teaching on individual students is a complicated matter. The progress one would expect to be able to see would be in students' abilities to search for information (to do research) and in their abilities to evaluate their own writing and the writing of their peers. Theoretically such progress would be reflected in the students' writing as well, but the effects might be less immediate than what one would expect from Peterson's students. In the next section, I follow Julie, one of the more able focal students, as she writes her saturation report.

Values and Response: Julie's Case

In an interview with a member of the research team, Julie indicates that she has always seen herself as a writer. Outside of school she writes "about the sea," and "about why this world's so bad." She also reports, "When I'm not mad at my brother, I write about him." She tells the researcher that when she was eight or nine, "I tried to write a book 'cause I heard the youngest author was six years old. So I tried to write a book of my own." She recalls the characters in her book, "Sandy" and Sandy's brother, "Baby Joe." She continues, "I still have it [the book]. I drew pictures and illustrations."

Julie is used to succeeding in school. In class she asks questions that help her understand how to complete the writing tasks and increase her understanding of how to evaluate writing. Reminiscent of Gina in Peterson's class, Julie says to the researchers that in Glass's class writing is hard because "you really have to think. It just amazes me how much you have to think just to write one of her papers." Like Peterson, Glass challenges her highest achieving students, pushing them to think carefully and critically. In the same interview, Julie herself says, "She [Ms. Glass] expects a lot out of you. She really has high expectations for us. . . . Like she expects us to do good, and then we'll do good." By following Julie as she writes her saturation report, one can see how Glass's whole-class and small-group preparation for writing and group-focused response influence Julie as a writer and how Glass's values about the importance of becoming independent researchers, critics, and evaluators intersect with Julie's.

Julie writes her saturation report about Mitchell Park, a local place she visits often and knows well. Julie's first task is to visit Mitchell Park a number of times, take notes, and focus the information she gathers. Glass has asked all the students to keep a log detailing their writing process. In her interview, Julie tells us that keeping the process log helps her in a number of ways:

> Like sometimes, if I don't use as much time [to write the paper], I feel really guilty. And I spend more time the next time. I think it's [writing the process log] something like therapy . . . I discovered a lot of my mistakes by writing in that process log because I start writing. All of a sudden it dawns on me that, it's like a flashback, all of a sudden I see my paper and I can actually see what I'm doing wrong. . . . I can understand what I've done wrong. Even sometimes when the teacher tells me, I just can't understand. I'm just sitting there with a blank look on my face. But when I start writing in that process log, I start really thinking about it, and recalling the events. . . . I learned about myself too. That might sound kind of strange, but I learned how lazy I can get sometimes and when I'm angry. I don't know. It's kind of like a diary.

This type of self-response and introspection is precisely what Glass hopes her students will gain.

In preparation for writing her saturation report, Julie writes in her log on March 8:

> I have asked my mother to bring a tape recorder home to me from work, so that I can tape all the sounds that I don't catch. The tape recorder is for a English assignment dealing with the

five S's. I am going to do it at Mitchell Park. I have not had any
time to go to the park to soak everything up yet. But I have
already gathered the materials I need to write (or whatever)
everything down. I have gotten a notebook, tape recorder, pencils,
etc. I'm gearing to go. All I need is a time to go.

On March 14, about a week later, Julie continues:

On Friday, I went to Mitchell Park at 6:10 p.m. — stayed for 1/2
hour. On Sunday, I went to Mitchell Park for 1 1/2 hrs. I have
made no progress since Sunday because it was raining last night.
It would be hard observing a park with nobody in it while it was
raining, but the other times I went, I collected a lot of information.

In fact, Julie does collect a lot of information; she fills forty pages of
her stenographer's notebook with details about what she sees on her
visits to Mitchell Park.

The same day that Julie writes this log entry, she meets with her
fellow students in class for a peer-group session. Glass directs the group
to help each member with problems and to work on finding a focus
for the details the students are gathering. The group does not discuss
Julie's progress.

On March 20 drafts are due. Julie's first two paragraphs, which
become the focus of peer-group discussion, follow:[18]

(1) "Mala! Mala!" yells a ruddy, dark faced man. The words seem
to roll off his tongue in a series of up and down tones as he cheers
on his volleyball team. (2) He reminds me of Al Pacino, with his
hawk-like brown eyes sunken in their sockets. (3) The breeze stirs
his hair for a moment before he speaks in the pleasant garble of
Spanish.
(4) "Just beat it, just beat it . . ." blares a radio loudspeaker.
Michael Jackson's high pitched voice rivals the "cheep-cheep" of
the birds and "Mommy, he did it," screams of the junivile
delinquents running around. (5) These are just some of the people
from San Jose, San Francisco, Palo Alto, and other parts of the
bay area who come to Mitchell Park for recreation, gatherings,
and picnics, for its large size and friendly atmosphere.

The piece continues, showing different scenes, through Julie's eyes, as
she roams through the park.

In her peer-response group, Julie is supposed to get response to this
draft and to give response to the drafts of the three other students in
her group. The response groups meet on two consecutive days, for
twenty-eight minutes on the first day and twenty-five on the second.
All the members in Julie's group seem nervous about reading their
drafts. The first day begins with delays: numerous apologies for the

poor quality of the drafts and talk about the task. The students even call Glass over to help them get started.

Julie, who is the leader of the group, does not seem happy with her draft. She avoids reading first and is the third and last reader on the first day. When it is her turn, she begins with an apology, "These are really rough ideas that I have. It's not really like a rough draft. . . . Oh well, I won't explain myself to you. You'll know how bad it is when you hear it." In her eyes, what she has written does not even "count" as a rough draft; she is just getting out ideas. She thinks that her peers will easily recognize that what she has written is "bad." She reads her entire piece, with a great deal of expression, and ends by explaining to the others that she doesn't yet have a conclusion. At this point, Karen asks Julie to read her introduction again. Julie complies by rereading the first two paragraphs. Karen listens carefully to Julie's writing. Then Karen questions Julie about what her first paragraph has to do with the rest of the piece. The others ask Julie to reread her focus sentence, which she does (sentence 5). She explains that this sentence comes at the end of the second paragraph. At this point, Karen suggests that she would like the focus to come earlier. Julie says that she could change its placement, but her tone of voice indicates that she doesn't like Karen's suggestion. Jeannie quickly responds that she likes Julie's opening. Julie concludes with self-denigration, which seems to make up for her earlier signal that she did not like her peers' suggestion about moving her focus. The group then agrees that Julie's draft is good. Julie responds, "Are you sure? Are you serious?" Then in a teacherly tone she asks, "Are there any more comments?" The group members reiterate, "No, that's good."

In this group session, Julie follows her usual pattern when she is scheduled to receive feedback in groups. She gets response from her peers but then indicates that she will reject the response. To maintain her peers' friendship after rejecting their advice, Julie manages to get her peers to take back their request for her to change something she has written. Julie admits to the researcher, "I get defensive when people comment on my paper." Also in her interview, Julie reveals more of her feelings about peer response when she answers the questions on the national surveys for students:

> The students, they're really too timid to really tell you what's wrong with it. And personally I don't think that they really know. Like me, when I'm listening to other people, while they're talking, I have to read their paper. I can't listen to them read out loud. So like some people might say it's [peer response] really helpful, but for me it's not too helpful. I usually change it [a piece of writing] according to my own way.[19]

Indeed, Julie acts just as she says she does in groups. Especially interesting is the point she makes about the difficulty of giving thoughtful response, on the spot, to a paper one hears but does not read. A look at Julie's feedback to other students in the group when students read aloud shows her taking a leadership role; like a teacher, she praises students after they read with "okay, that's good" and "yeah, that was good."[20] But generally she is most interested in filling out the evaluation sheet; Glass will see these sheets and Julie wants her written group work to reflect well on her abilities as a critic/evaluator. In this particular group session Julie does not initiate any response other than that asked for on the sheet. Even her response to Anne, which was discussed earlier, begins with Julie's questions to help her fill out her evaluation sheet. Interestingly, Julie begins to apply her suggestion for Anne to her own writing, but she in fact avoids the more difficult thinking about her own place.

> *Julie:* See I . . . I went [to the park] at two different times, once when it was Friday night and nobody was there and once when it was Sunday afternoon when everybody was there. So I'm just doing Sunday.

In her last remark she explicitly avoids dealing with any contrast by "just doing Sunday."

The next day, Jim, who is scheduled to read his paper, is absent. The group talks about mechanical points in their drafts, verb tense and the like. In the middle of the discussion Glass appears, and Julie takes advantage of the opportunity to elicit an on-the-spot conference. Glass relieves some of Julie's tension about writing this piece, telling Julie to get her ideas out before worrying about the details of form. Julie begins the interchange by articulating what she sees as her problem, "Okay, I'm trying to describe how my place is but I keep starting with *is*. I'm trying to say, 'It's a large circle of plotted land.' See? I just said *is*." [Julie laughs.] Glass replies, "Sometimes you have to do that. I didn't mean to suggest that you can't ever use that word." After further discussion of the form of the sentence, the dialogue continues:

> *T:* What you wanna do first of all . . . write it out without worrying about how many *is*'s you use. [Julie laughs.] Write it out and get everything out there that you wanna include in it. Don't bother about *is*'s because looking at what kind of words you use is something that's revision stage as opposed to drafting stage.
>
> *J:* Okay. So first stage you just write?

T: Okay. That's right. . . . Otherwise you're gonna stumble over every word and you'll never get anything on the page.

J: That's why it took me so long.

T: That's exactly right. First time you just wanna get it out fast and see what material in there is something you wanna use. Then when you put it away for a little while and then go back to it, then you think about revising and tightening up and looking at the information and seeing how you can combine with information that came earlier and getting rid of the lazy words that don't do very much. The lazy words are gonna come out in your draft because that's the way we think and talk. That's perfectly natural. You wanna get them out and onto the paper because when you don't have anything to look at on the paper, you don't have anything to revise. [overlap]

J: You can't revise! [laughs]

T: That's exactly right. That's right. I know somebody who writes that way. . . . He does all his revising as he puts things onto the paper. I can't do that. I have to get it out fast and then go back and [unclear] and tighten it up and make it a better shape. So what you wanna do [is] don't worry about that now. You're in a drafting and getting it out stage. What you wanna do is get it onto the paper in some form first. Then put it away for a while. Then make it better.

When asked why Glass has students work in groups to respond to one another's drafts, Julie uses words that, if true, support Glass's rationale about the value of students' working independently:

'Cause usually the students find the same mistakes that the teacher does. Maybe not. Maybe it takes a little longer. But they do. . . . I think she thinks that students can help us also. They do. Because they have a lot of ideas, each student, each one of my friends. They keep saying, "This is kind of wishy-washy. I got lost in there." And you don't realize this when you're reading it to yourself. 'Cause you know what it's all about. So in that way it helps also.

Julie seems to shift her earlier point of view to match Glass's, to think she gets help from other students. But although she gives help, none of her earlier opinions and none of her actions in groups show her getting help from her peers. Julie also demonstrates an interesting confusion as she continues to speculate on why Glass would organize these groups:

> She likes us to, I don't know, she might not really have this in mind, but I think she wants us to read more. Read out loud. And enunciate more.

According to Julie, perhaps reading aloud in groups ties in to the speech curriculum; students learn to enunciate as they read their writing aloud!

On March 21, the day after the last peer-response sessions on the saturation report, Julie writes in her log:

> I have had to observe, soak to collect information for my paper. Then I proceded to sort, and select information that was revelent to my focus. I then started writing with the information I had. I still have to finish the paper and revise it and recopy it. I feel that more descriptions and transitional phrases are needed. Right now, I feel that my paper could be twice as good. It is better than I thought I could do though. It will be much better when I finish. I need help on describing, the introduction, conclusion, and showing. I think that I can straighten out the transitions. Dead wood sentences: before: My eyes sting for a moment before the smell of hamburgers, chicken, and hot-dogs fill my nose.
> after: My eyes sting for a moment before the mouth watering aroma of hamburgers, hot dogs, and chicken fill my nose.
> before: Soon my vision was shattered as an unpleasant, burnt, charcoal smell invaded my senses.
> after: Soon my vision was shattered as the unpleasant odor of burnt chicken, and charcoal invaded my senses causing me to pinch my nose and cough.

Julie uses her own resources, not the in-class help of her peers, as she thinks about her revision. She works hard in her log to develop evaluative criteria and apply them to her own writing. In this log entry she works through her understanding of "deadwood sentences." She attempts to do more than identify the problem as she tests "before" and "after" sentences, essentially adding detail and specificity to the original. "Smell" becomes "mouthwatering aroma"; "an unpleasant odor" becomes "the unpleasant odor" that causes her to pinch her nose. Julie does not seem to understand what Glass means by "deadwood sentences" in that she adds detail but does not remove any "deadwood." Talk during the peer-group meeting related to only one area where she says now that she needs more help — her introduction — but she indicated during the group meeting that she was not satisfied with her peers' responses.

A comparison of the draft that Julie brings to class on March 20 with her final version from March 26 reveals that she makes a number of substantive revisions.[21] Her self-evaluation of her draft during the earlier peer-group meeting seems to have guided much of her revision work. The first draft is merely a compilation of ideas, brief and abbreviated scenes from Mitchell Park, with a somewhat artificial attempt at writing a general focus sentence. Interestingly, Julie also incorporates the advice of her peers which she seemed to reject at the time. The focus sentence appears in the first paragraph, but at the end, not as the first sentence.

In her final piece, Julie succeeds in painting a clear picture of Mitchell Park. What holds the picture together is not the overly general "focus sentence" at the end of the first paragraph but Julie's revealing glimpses of herself as observer. She shows herself to the reader as she walks through the park and watches the people; her actions allow the reader to infer a more specific focus. Julie muses, "When someone says 'Mitchell Park,' what comes to my mind? I immediately see a large grassy area. . . ." She hears a blaring radio and reports, "I plug my ears and wince as another radio is turned on full blast playing foreign folk music featuring bongo drums and banjos. Sitting against the worn out wooden bench, my cheeks warm up from the heat of the sun shining directly above me, and a warm breeze stirs my hair." Julie likes being outside, but the loud people and activity intrude on her pensive mood. She goes on to describe how smoke from a barbecue "smarts my eyes." She gets hungry as she smells the food cooking, but then reports, "My pleasant picture shatters as the stench of something burnt invades my senses. I tried to place myself as far away from this area as I could." After watching a soccer game and children playing in a sandbox, Julie reveals that she is tired of the observational task, "I walk on, tired of watching them play." She passes a bridge and gazes at the water, remarking, "It's very peaceful here despite all the noise. A carefree mood seems to descend upon me as I bathe in the warm sun." She watches a couple kiss while "Behind them, a small blonde haired girl struggles to follow them as she pushes a blue stroller." Julie next admires a woman jogger and again becomes conscious of needing to observe something: "I decide to walk after this lady jogger for a little while since nothing spectacular was happening at the bridge." She happens upon a tennis game where she hopes to "absorb some of their [the players'] skill"; she admits that she is a "bad tennis player." She returns to the place of the volleyball game as the sun sets. Her concluding paragraph reads,

> I shiver as a cool wind ruffles my hair. The sun, not radiating
> any real warmth, means time to go home, I muse. I unlock my
> bike and procede to get on it. As I ride away, I look back and
> think how wonderful it is that so many different kinds of people
> come to Mitchell Park.

Julie enjoys the natural setting and the opportunity to gaze on scenes,
some of which include people; but she has indicated earlier that she is
bothered by noisy music and burning smells. She does not like the
people who invade her natural setting with their too obvious presence.
It is unclear whether Julie really thinks it is wonderful that there are
"so many different kinds of people" in the park. Her concluding
sentence seems to be a formulaic tie back to the first paragraph. And
upon rereading the first paragraph, the noisy scene is not in synchrony
with what Julie likes about the park.

At this point in Glass's classroom organization, lacking trust in her
peers' response and her peers not giving her much substantive feedback,
Julie seems to have little opportunity to get the help with revision that
she indicates she needs in her March 21 log entry. She trusts Glass's
opinions, but Glass rarely gives conferences or written comments during
the writing process.

What Julie benefits from most in Glass's class is the structure that
gives her time to work through her ideas. Ironically, the requirement
of stating an explicit focus, without accompanying adult guidance to
help her articulate her "take" on her topic, seems to have led Julie
into problems. Although she helps her peers, she has difficulty handling
the complexities embedded in her own thoughts. On her own, Julie
seeks informal help from selected friends in talking through ideas for
writing. For example, during her interview Julie tells the researcher
how she and her best friend went together to Mitchell Park when she
was observing there:

> I don't know if you [researcher] remember that I had to go to
> Mitchell Park and observe everything. My friend came with me
> every day, and she'd point out things that I should have noticed,
> and like we have this one-track mind. I'm just looking for this
> thing and she tells me, "You know you can look at this, too."
> And that really helps me.

At another point she tells the researcher, "I always tell my friends my
ideas about what I'm writing about, and then if one of my friends
thinks it's not very good, they'll tell me and help me with it." Such
peer response occurs naturally and helps Julie as she gathers ideas, not

as she revises. It comes from outside the instructional context, without the teacher's knowledge, planning, or direction.

On March 26, Glass collects the final versions of the saturation reports. She puts the students in pairs so that they can help one another with last-minute editing. In her March 26 log entry, Julie discusses how complex she has found writing the saturation report:

> The 5 "S" report was the hardest I've ever done. It took a great deal of time to observe and jot down notes, as well as the rough draft, etc. I had a lot of difficulty in expressing what I thought Mitchell Park was like. By "soaking" everything around me, I realized how much I observed before this report without really realizing it.

Julie is learning through the act of writing. She continues:

> I thought this assignment was interesting, but whether or not I was able to successfully apply what I learned from the last assignments to this one, I don't know. I can't explain why this paper was hard, but it was. Maybe if I had used Mitchell Park as a setting for a fictionous story within my report, it would have been easier.

According to her own account, Julie spent thirteen hours outside of class on her saturation report — five hours gathering information and eight hours writing and revising. In her interview she is asked to choose her best piece of writing for the semester and to tell why she prefers the piece. She selects the report on Mitchell Park and explains, "I like the beginning. I think I worked hardest on this paper." Although left with the vague feeling that she "could have done maybe a little better," she says, "I'm not sure how because I rewrote this paper about six times." Glass's written comments are, for the most part, complimentary and give Julie added guidance for sharpening her prose and checking the appropriateness of her detail. They are detailed because Julie has requested detail.[22]

During the writing process, Julie misses specific in-process feedback from her teacher on the text she produces. However, she has time to use her own self-evaluative resources to produce a piece that makes her think a great deal about her environment. In this particular piece, Julie likely would have been better able to synthesize her experience and understand where her ideas informed her observations with the kind of in-process help from the teacher that Peterson routinely provides. However, given the practice Julie gets in solving her own writing problems, she may in the long run achieve a lasting understanding of principles underlying writing well.

Summary

The teachers in the surveys teach writing for multiple reasons; however, predominant among them is a desire to help their students think more critically about their world. In particular, the teachers are interested in encouraging their students to connect their personal experiences to what they are learning. Although concerned with issues of mechanics, they are not in the forefront of these teachers' minds.

Glass and Peterson have similar goals to those of the other teachers in the surveys. In their classrooms, their underlying values of teaching their students to think critically and creatively drive the response process. However, in spite of their shared beliefs, they structure activities differently because they have different philosophies of how they think students learn. Glass emphasizes general principles that students practice applying by themselves and with the help of their peers to the texts they are writing. Glass plays the role of "guide" to her students who are "explorers." On the other hand, Peterson emphasizes ways of thinking that will help students generate and synthesize their ideas. He helps individual students as they apply these ways of thinking to their specific texts and then helps students solve problems and draw generalizations from the solutions. Peterson plays the role of "master" to his "apprentice" writers. These different approaches to teaching and learning inform and shape the ways Glass and Peterson arrange for response to their students' writing. Whereas Peterson coaches students with individual conferences and written comments on their drafts, Glass relies on guided, peer evaluation and other opportunities for individual self-reflection as resources for her student writers.

Although "response" in these two classrooms makes for different classroom activities and different teacher orientations to students' works-in-progress, significant similarities in the patterns of response-to-writing cross both classrooms.

1. For both Glass and Peterson, response comes in the form of response to ideas in progress as well as to text already written down.
2. The writing process for a single piece takes place over an extended period of time — a month or more on the average.
3. When they respond, both teachers resist telling students what to write or what to think; rather, they set up response situations to

allow their students opportunities to come to know what they think. They want the young writers in their classrooms to begin to see, understand, and come to grips with the complexities in the world. Peterson questions his students and teaches them how to question themselves about their own ideas. Glass works to teach her students to question one another in peer groups and thereby learn to question and guide themselves.

4. Response aims to help students learn to solve the problems they face as writers — both the cognitive problems (getting ideas) and the social problems (learning to write in particular contexts). The writing process is not just a set of procedures — prewriting, writing, revising; rather, it is a problem-solving process, both cognitive and social. Students are explicitly taught to *transfer* the problem-solving strategies they learn on one occasion to the next and from one piece of writing to the next.

5. Response is plentiful and comes in many forms for the same student on the same piece of writing.

Not everything these teachers do works perfectly all the time, and certainly some students gain more than others. Each approach has its costs and its benefits. I have suggested, for example, that peer response in Glass's class can clearly be beneficial, but it is sometimes an insufficient substitute for her feedback during the writing process. On the other hand, when Peterson coaches his students during the process, it is unclear what the students can do independently or whether they understand the concepts behind their writing processes well enough to apply them more independently on future occasions. Individual teachers will always be faced with making decisions about what to emphasize in their classrooms. Certainly, in these two classrooms students stand to learn a great deal. Similarly, from an analysis of response in the classrooms of both Peterson and Glass, we stand to learn a great deal about response to writing in particular and the teaching and learning of writing in general.

Notes

1. See Appendix A, question 10 for the elementary form and question 11 for the secondary form.

2. These lists likely do not fully capture the dichotomies in the field, as consideration of a number of current values are missing. For example, cognitive psychologists consider skill development to include the teaching of thinking skills involved in reaching an audience or in synthesizing ideas and

experience. Skill development here is interpreted only as the teaching of formal text features. For this part of this project, I considered the benefits of being able to compare this sample with Applebee's greater than the benefits that might accrue from revising the lists.

3. The claims in this section about the teachers' and students' values are based on findings from Greenleaf's work on the semantic networks in the oral talk of the teachers and students in both classrooms (in Freedman 1985).

4. The data include the oral data used in Freedman (1985) as well as written comments and student writing that provide information about what the students accomplish.

5. Peterson uses a point system for evaluating group work. Although points are given to groups throughout the semester, and although sometimes elaborate "point-scales" are worked out, groups seem to keep their own scores, and the game never develops into a race.

6. This question comes from a list of thirty-two questions for character analysis that Peterson has distributed and that form the basis for a number of discussions about character analysis. Appendix F contains a copy of the list. His in-class presentation of the thirty-two questions is discussed in the next section on "Mental Search."

7. Donald is one of the four focal students.

8. Sperling (in progress) gives further detail about Peterson's conferences and their connections to student writing.

9. Gina was not one of the focal students; however, we had all data on Gina that we had on the focal students, except interviews. Gina was in Rhonda's group, and so all of her peer-group meetings were recorded. In addition, she left her writing folder, with all of her writing in it, with Peterson. She is selected for focus here because her writing shows most clearly the connections between response activities and revisions and because of the clarity of the recordings of her talk across different response contexts. Further, she articulates more of what she is thinking than other students. Also, her ideas about writing are consistent with those of the focal students as described in Greenleaf's analysis of focal student talk in Freedman (1985).

10. Freedman and Bennett's (1987) final report to the Office of Educational Research and Improvement, "Peer Groups at Work in Two Writing Classrooms," includes a discussion of leadership in peer groups and shows specifically how Gina defines the role of leader.

11. Glass has her students explicitly state a "focus statement" in their writing and practice developing such statements to help her students, at this stage in their learning, develop and hold on to their own sense of focus as they work to control increasingly larger bodies of material.

12. Two focal students, Julie and Jim, are members of this group.

13. A functional analysis of the purpose of the groups in each classroom showed that 54 percent of Glass's groups are intended to serve a response/evaluation function while only 25 percent of Peterson's are designed for this function. Additionally, students spend more time in response groups in Glass's class, her groups lasting an average of twenty-four minutes and his an average of thirteen minutes (Freedman and Bennett 1987).

14. Students typically apologize for their efforts, for a number of possible reasons. In this case Anne's comment seems to go beyond the typical apology (e.g., "This is so bad"), in that she makes a substantive point about her writing.

15. The talk in this group session shows that the distinction between research and evaluation is not clear-cut. It is essentially one of point-of-view — the researcher is in the role of writer-creator; the evaluator is in the role of reader of one's own or another's writing. Of course, writers may simultaneously be writer-creators and reader-evaluators. The point for the transcript is that here the talk about focus is from the point of view of a reader, analyzing a focus that has already been written down.

16. Interestingly, even though Glass does not stress the value of considering conflicts, Julie does so spontaneously.

17. Freedman and Bennett (1987) have found in a subsequent analysis of peer-response groups, using these data, that of the times students *request* help from their peers, they only receive help 12.5 percent of the time.

18. Julie's complete draft, which she reads to her group, as well as her final version, can be found in Appendix G.

19. The interview includes having each student respond to the items on the national survey and to think aloud as they respond, in essence giving a think-aloud protocol as they complete each item.

20. Contrast the feedback Julie gives when students have read aloud with the feedback she gives Sally about her ideas.

21. See Appendix G for the fully revised version of Julie's saturation report.

22. At the beginning of the term, Glass gives students the option of having her mark everything in their papers or having her make selective comments. Julie chooses full marking, as do most of the students in the class.

5 Summary of the Research

This study has asked how response can support the teaching and learning of writing. The project aimed (1) to understand better how response can function in helping students improve their writing, (2) to define more precisely the concept of response, in the hopes of enriching the traditional views and definitions, and (3) to understand how successful teachers accomplish response, and to learn what they do and do not know about response to student writing. The following, more specific questions were asked:

1. Under positive instructional conditions, what is the range of response students receive in school? What characterizes response that students and teachers feel is most helpful? Least helpful?

2. In successful classrooms, what values about writing are being transmitted during response (what is the basis of the substance of the response)?

3. In these classrooms, how are different types of response related to one another during the teaching-learning process?

One part of the study involves a survey of the response practices of 560 teachers, who are judged as among the most successful in their communities, by directors of the sites of the National Writing Projects. The teachers come from all regions of the United States as well as a small percentage from foreign countries, and teach kindergarten through twelfth grade. In addition, 715 students in the classes of half of the secondary teachers (grades seven through twelve) completed surveys about their teachers' teaching practices and their own learning.

The second part of the study involves a close look at the day-to-day response practices of two successful ninth-grade writing teachers: Mary Lee Glass of Gunn High School in Palo Alto, California and Art Peterson of Lowell High School in San Francisco. The successful teachers and their students participating in the research exhibit the following traits:

1. The teachers completing the surveys are highly experienced; they average fourteen years in the classroom. At the time of the

155

observations, Peterson and Glass had taught for twenty-three and twenty-four years, respectively.

2. The students in the classes of the teachers participating in the surveys write more than students in other classes. The pieces are relatively long (an average of one page in class and two to four pages out of class at the secondary level) and are assigned often (most students were writing at the time of the survey). Both secondary and elementary teachers assign an exceptionally large amount of in-class writing. The students have more time than usual (over a week) to complete a piece of written work. In Glass's and Peterson's classes students have between three and six weeks to complete each major piece. During the time of our observation, students are *always* working on at least one piece of writing.

3. The surveyed teachers do not show a consistent pattern with respect to whether or not they sequence the writing their students do according to any kind of plan. However, within the time we observed, when Glass and Peterson both are focusing their students' writing mostly toward a single genre, both Peterson and Glass sequence and plan the kinds of demands they place on their students over a period of months. One kind of task leads to the next, and what is learned during one writing occasion is intended to transfer to the next.

4. The secondary teachers in the surveys, like both teachers in the ethnography, are almost all English teachers (95.6 percent) with degrees in English (61.2 percent with B.A.s and 52.9 percent with M.A.s or working on advanced degrees in English). Peterson's degrees are in history, however.

5. A high percentage of the surveyed teachers (52.8 percent) report teaching fewer classes than the usual teacher at his or her school; only 2.4 percent teach more than a normal load. Although Peterson teaches a normal load, Glass teaches only three classes because she is department chair. And as a group, the surveyed teachers have only about twenty-five students in their classes. Peterson's class has twenty-seven students, and Glass's has thirty-three.

6. The surveyed teachers perceive more of their students as above-average achievers (33.2 percent for elementary teachers and 35.2 percent for secondary teachers) than below average (21.2 percent and 13.5 percent, respectively). Most of the students (75.3 percent) report making A's and B's and say that they plan to complete

four years of college (66.3 percent). The students, on the whole, are not faced with the problems of poverty; only 9.7 percent lack the basic necessities. Relatively few (about 5 percent) are non-native English speakers. The profiles of students in the ethnography are consistent with those in the survey, except that approximately 50 percent of the students in Peterson's class are nonnative speakers.

7. Although a large percentage of the teachers nominated to participate in the surveys teach in schools with low percentages of poverty-level students, the participating teachers who teach high numbers of such students do not respond to the surveys in any markedly different ways from the rest of the sample, other than that they rely less on grades and written comments.

Question 1: The Range and Helpfulness of Response

In both the survey and the ethnography the range of response is great, and its perceived helpfulness varies according to when in the process it occurs and whether students or teachers judge its helpfulness. The following findings are related to question 1:

1. Response occurs mostly during the writing process. According to the surveyed teachers, in-process response is most helpful. It occurs not only to drafts of student writing, but also to ideas and plans.

2. Although successful teachers agree that the most helpful response occurs during the writing process, such response appears to be the most difficult to accomplish. Students prefer response to final versions. Also, the surveyed teachers are inconsistent in their opinions about the effectiveness of different kinds of in-process response, other than individual conferences, which they do not have sufficient time to conduct. Some find peer-response groups helpful; others do not. Some find written comments during the process helpful; others do not. Some find helping students respond to themselves during the process helpful; others do not.

   The teachers in the ethnography structure in-process respond differently, with Glass guiding her students, who are working alone or in small groups, to respond independently and with Peterson coaching his students directly to probe their ideas.

3. Individual conferences are a preferred mode of teaching writing for both teachers and students. However, teachers have difficulty structuring their classrooms so that they can devote a sufficient

amount of time to conferences. Peterson does manage to provide regular conferences at the secondary level. His conferences are brief, generally supplement written comments, and often focus on helping students apply a point made in class to their individual pieces of in-progress writing.

4. Grading and written comments on final versions occur more often as students get older, but from the teachers' points of view, these are not preferred forms of response. However, students persist in valuing written comments and grades much more than their teachers do. The high premium students place on grades creates conflict for the teachers in the ethnography. For many of the ninth-grade students we watched, grades loom larger than what they learn. These students seem to be caught in an institutional bind; grades (the school's and society's measure of learning) and the response that accompanies grades (and often justifies them) are confused with and become more important than the feedback that is more essential to helping them learn. The students are interested in the product of learning more than the learning process.

5. Peer-response groups are more highly regarded by teachers than by their students.

6. Parent response is more highly regarded by students than by their teachers.

7. The ethnography shows that a substantial amount of response occurs during whole-class discussion.

Question 2: Values Transmitted during Response

Above all else, the surveyed teachers expect writing to help their students learn to think for themselves and then connect their personal experiences to their writing; response is largely aimed at achieving these ends. They place little emphasis on the teaching of writing to drill students in mechanics. These values are significantly different from those of the secondary teachers Applebee (1981) surveyed.

Furthermore, unlike Applebee's secondary teachers, the elementary teachers in these surveys have multiple reasons for teaching writing. These secondary teachers divide much more weakly into the skill-oriented and content-oriented groups Applebee found, with more teachers, even at the secondary level, using writing for multiple and not mutually exclusive ends.

Peterson and Glass exemplify two versions of what it means to use writing as a way of teaching students to think deeply about their experiences and communicate those experiences to others. In both classrooms students learn to define their writing process not as a set of procedures involving planning, writing, and revising, but instead as social and cognitive activities underlying writing well. Both teachers stress the development of these activities through the way they set up response. Glass places her students in the roles of independent researchers and critic/evaluators. They are to think critically about the information they gather and the written form it takes. Peterson places his students in the roles of perceptive thinkers who learn to understand people in their world and in the world of books by examining the differences between facts and judgments and by learning to look for and articulate the interesting contradictions in individual personalities.

Question 3: Relationship among Types of Response

Glass uses peer-response groups as the central focus of her instruction. In these group sessions students help one another gather information and evaluate pieces of writing. Response is arranged almost always to work directly toward discussion of what a student is writing, rarely on a practice piece. Although such peer groups are not uniformly successful, Freedman and Bennett (1987) discuss some features that encourage their success. Glass never holds formal, individual conferences, although conferences occasionally occur at a student's initiation while the student is working in a peer group.

In Peterson's classroom peer-group meetings are brief and serve mostly to allow students time to practice solving specific problems related to thinking about characters. Groups are integrated with and oriented back into whole-class discussion. Individualization is accomplished as Peterson writes comments on students' drafts and other preliminary writing and meets with students in individual conferences. Unlike Glass, Peterson frequently arranges response to practice pieces.

6 What Have We Learned and Where Do We Go from Here?

This study of successful teachers of writing and their students tells important stories about response. First, successful response is guided by a strong and consistent philosophy of teaching writing. Successful teachers can articulate that philosophy to other teachers, to parents and school administrators, and to their student writers. The teachers in the surveys and in the ethnography also are conscious of why they teach the way they do and can explain their reasons for the decisions they make while teaching; Glass and Peterson do in class what they say they do. Although there are differences across their classrooms and although the surveys show that there is disagreement and confusion among even the most successful teachers about in-process response, as a group these teachers are attempting to teach their students to think more deeply and critically and to relate their personal experiences to what they are learning. We have much to learn about how to elaborate on such teaching and how best to carry it out; nevertheless, we do know that a strong and clearly articulated sense of values underlies successful teachers' response to writing.

Successful teachers of writing do not all teach the same way. Although they share certain values and goals, their basic philosophies of teaching and learning may differ. We know little about the varieties of success. Do some teaching philosophies match best with the needs of some learners? What are the costs and benefits of various approaches to teaching for various types of learners?

Regardless of teachers' philosophies, several necessary conditions underlie successful response. First, it leaves the ownership of the writing in the hands of the student writer. Successful teachers provide plentiful guidance but resist taking over the writing of their students. Peterson, in his conferences, provides a model for how to question students about their meaning and help them think more critically without writing their papers for them. Second, it communicates high expectations for *all* students. At no point in the process do successful teachers accept less than what the student is capable of, and they believe all students are highly capable. Third, accompanying their high expectations, these teachers give students sufficient help during the writing process to allow them to write better than the students themselves thought was possible. The teacher assumes the responsibility of setting up classroom activities so that students will succeed. Giving help does not mean writing students' papers for them; rather it means allowing students time and providing support while they work to communicate their ideas. These teachers provide support without providing formulas and without using prepackaged curricula.

There are a number of difficulties that even the most successful teachers face when planning responses to students' writing. Although many successful teachers devise ways to provide individual, teacher-led conferences during the writing process, the organization of the typical school does not support individualized teaching of this type; and so even successful teachers do not always individualize instruction in this way. Furthermore, individual conferences may not best support an approach to teaching that stresses helping students gain independence from the teacher. In some cases teachers lean heavily on peer groups for elaborated response to writing. Successful teachers are ambivalent about the success of peer groups. The ambivalence likely has at least two sources. First, students tend not to trust the opinions of their peers as equivalent to the opinions of their teacher and sometimes work to subvert peer response. Accomplishing both conferences and peer response successfully are difficult because, as long as students are trying to write for a grade and are anxious to relinquish responsibility of their writing to their teacher who awards the grade, conferences can easily become sessions in which students manipulate teachers to tell them "answers." Likewise, peer groups can turn into group sessions in which students help each other get their writing "right" or can be devalued as useless by students. Radical reorganization of classrooms will be needed in order to make *writing* and *learning* more important or even as important as *grading* from the students' points of view.

Future research needs to address a number of questions that remain unanswered here because of the nature of the participants in this study. First of all, the students these teachers teach are mostly middle class, native speaking, college bound, and live in suburbs and small towns. Even though teachers of substantial numbers of poverty-level students in urban and rural areas answered survey questions in basically the same way as their counterparts in more affluent settings, we still need to know why so few teachers from urban, rural, and poorer areas were represented in the sample. Is the National Writing Project not reaching many of these teachers or at least the more successful of these teachers? Do most of our successful teachers avoid these settings, and if so, why?

For example, are the settings so difficult to teach in that they discourage success for all but a select few? Perhaps a better knowledge of the teachers' incentives would help us understand what pulls teachers to one setting versus another. Prestige seems to go to teachers of wealthy, college-bound students. How might the incentives be changed to attract more of our successful teachers to poorer urban and rural schools? How might the NWP include more of these teachers? We need to study successful teachers in these settings to learn more about their teaching conditions, their reasons for teaching where they do, and their methods for teaching.

Second, participants in this study were mostly language arts and English teachers. More research needs to be done on successful teachers of writing across the curriculum. What it means to respond to writing in a science class, for example, might be very different from what it means to respond to writing in an English class. We need to know how writing and response to writing best function across disciplines.

Third, the teachers were identified through the sites of the National Writing Project; therefore, they reflect the philosophies of the NWP. It would be interesting, if possible, to gather a sample of successful teachers of writing who are not connected to the Writing Project and compare them to these teachers. The primary obstacle to such an endeavor is the difficulty of finding successful teachers of writing who have not in some way been influenced by the NWP. As of its 1986 annual report, the NWP has provided training to approximately 450,000 teachers of writing; even among teachers who have never participated in the Project, its philosophies are widely known, and for the most part, they reflect current thinking in the profession. It was possible to gather this sample because of the existence of the tight national network of the Writing Project, and since there is no other similar network, it would be difficult to gather a comparable sample of successful teachers nationally. Still, in order to broaden the definitions of success, we need to try to compare other samples of successful teachers to this sample.

This study also raises several general questions about the teaching and learning of writing. The first has to do with the sequencing of writing instruction. We have seen that writing can be taught. However, students need to be allowed to spend substantial amounts of time on even small pieces of writing (of only a few pages in length in the end), with frequent in-class activities that help them become better able to complete the piece well. Further, pieces of writing can be designed to lead from one to another. In the classes we observed, we saw a coherent block of three assignments, each one leading to the next, with the final assignment being a culmination of the first two. The teachers in the survey and in the observational study have a clear sense of what they teach and why. However, there is little evidence that they feel that they can depend on their students' coming into their classes with previously learned skills in writing, beyond the most mechanical; there is little evidence that they can count on their students' building on what they learn in this class in their future classes, in any specific ways. Both Glass and Peterson were involved in curriculum reforms at their schools, but during our observations, we saw little evidence that even they depend on the curriculum outside their classes. The students seem to feel that they have to adjust to each teacher individually. The situations Glass and Peterson find themselves in are radically different from the one Perl and Wilson (1986) describe in which the entire school district of Shoreham-Wading River is working to create communities of writers. In part, the ethnographies document the complications that successful teachers face in school districts unlike Shoreham. We need large-scale studies of the effects of students' greater educational experiences on what they take away from individual classrooms. We need to experiment with ways of providing students with more coherent educational experiences across time.

Although this research has yielded a great deal of information about successful response to student writing, successful teachers cannot continue to work in isolation if there are to be lasting changes and substantial improvement across time in the teaching and learning of writing. The statistics remain dismal about any large-scale change in writing classrooms in this country. The National Assessment of Educational Progress's 1984 report reveals that "fully one-third of the seventeen-year-olds and two-fifths of the thirteen-year-olds report that they receive little or no writing instruction." Further, students report writing no more papers in 1984 than they did in 1974. Most discouraging of all, students are not writing any better in 1984 than in 1974, although a little more time is being devoted to writing instruction.

The teachers who participated in this study are doing their share; but as a profession, we must learn from them to develop ways for writing teachers to improve conditions in their own classrooms and to coordinate their efforts with those of other teachers. But simultaneously, as a profession and as a society, we must protect our best teachers from bureaucratic moves that can obstruct successful teaching, whether they come from communities censoring books or from school administrators in individual schools and districts, or in state agencies introducing "reforms" that enforce behavioral objectives, mandate ill-conceived competency tests, or introduce curriculum "kits" of prepackaged writing instruction. The real reforms that are needed are reduced student loads;

opportunities for stimulating, supportive, and truly professional teacher training and then faculty development; encouragement for teachers across disciplines to use writing to support student learning; and incentives to keep successful teachers in our schools, especially those that encourage more of them to work in schools with high concentrations of poverty-level students.

References

Anderson, R. 1982. Acquisition of cognitive skill. *Psychological Review* 89:369–406.

Applebee, A. N. 1981. *A study of writing in the secondary school.* Urbana, Ill.: National Council of Teachers of English.

Applebee, A. N., and J. A. Langer. 1983. Instructional scaffolding: Reading and writing as natural language activities. *Language Arts* 60:168–75.

Applebee, A. N., et al. 1984. *Contexts for learning to write: Studies of secondary school instruction.* Norwood, N.J.: Ablex.

Applebee, A. N., J. A. Langer, and I. Mullis. 1986. *Writing: Trends across the decade, 1974–1984.* National Assessment of Educational Progress. Report No. 15-W-01. Princeton, N.J.: Educational Testing Service.

Babbie, E. 1973. *Survey research methods.* Belmont, Calif.: Wadsworth Publishing.

Barnes, D., and D. Shemilt. 1974. *From communication to curriculum.* Harmondsworth, Eng.: Penguin.

Beach, R. 1979. The effects of between-draft teacher evaluation versus student self-evaluation on high school students' revising of rough drafts. *Research in the Teaching of English.* 13 (2): 111–19.

Bereiter, C., and M. Scardamalia. 1982. From conversation to composition. In *Advances in instructional psychology* (Vol. 2), edited by R. Glaser. Hillsdale, N.J.: Erlbaum.

Bereiter, C., and M. Scardamalia. In press. Cognitive coping strategies and the problem of "inert knowledge." In *Thinking and learning skills,* edited by S. Chipman et al. Hillsdale, N.J.: Erlbaum.

Braddock, R., R. Lloyd-Jones, and L. Schoer. 1963. *Research on written composition.* Urbana, Ill.: National Council of Teachers of English.

Brannon, L., and C. Knoblauch. 1982. On students' rights to their own texts: A model of teacher response. *College Composition and Communication* 33:157–66.

Bridwell, L. 1980. Revising strategies in twelfth grade students' transactional writing. *Research in the Teaching of English* 14 (3): 197–222.

Britton, J., et al. 1975. *The development of writing abilities: 11–18.* London: Macmillan Education.

Brown, A.L. 1982. Learning how to learn from reading. In *Reader meets author/bridging the gap,* edited by J. A. Langer and M. T. Smith-Burke. Newark, Del.: International Reading Association.

Brown, A.L., A. S. Palinscar, and L. Purcell. In press. Poor readers: Teach, don't label. In _The academic performance of minority children: A new perspective,_ edited by U. Neisser. Hillsdale, N.J.: Erlbaum.

Bruner, J. 1983. _Child's talk: Learning to use language._ London: Oxford University Press.

Bureau of the Census. 1980. _Census geography: Data access descriptions._ Washington, D.C.: U. S. Department of Commerce.

Bureau of the Census. 1984. _Statistical abstract of the United States._ 104th ed. Washington, D.C.: Government Printing Office.

Calkins, L. 1983. _Lessons from a child on the teaching of writing._ Exeter, N.H.: Heinemann.

Caplan, R., and C. Keech. 1980. _Showing-writing: A training program to help students be specific._ Berkeley, Calif.: University of California, Bay Area Writing Project.

Carpenter, G., F. Baker, and F. Scott. 1903. _The teaching of English in the elementary and secondary school._ New York: Longmans, Green, and Co.

Carnicelli, T. A. 1980. The writing conference: A one-to-one conversation. In _Eight approaches to teaching composition,_ edited by P. Donovan and B. McClelland. Urbana, Ill.: National Council of Teachers of English.

Cazden, C. 1979. Peekaboo as an instructional model: Discourse development at home and at school. _Papers and Reports on Child Language Development_ 17:1–19.

Clark, H., and E. Clark. 1977. _Language and psychology._ New York: Harcourt Brace Jovanovich.

Cohen, J. 1960. A coefficient of agreement for nominal scales. _Educational Psychological Measurement_ 20:37–46.

Dillon, D., and D. Searle. 1983. _Teacher response to student writing: Its nature, origin, context, and effect._ Final report to the Social Studies and Humanities Research Council of Canada (Grant Number 410-81-0337).

Elbow, P. 1973. _Writing without teachers._ London: Oxford University Press.

Emig, J. 1971. _The composing processes of twelfth graders._ Research Report No. 13. Urbana, Ill.: National Council of Teachers of English.

Flavell, J. 1981. Monitoring social cognitive enterprises: Something else that may develop in the area of social cognition. In _Social cognitive development: Frontiers and possible futures,_ edited by J. Flavell and L. Ross. Cambridge: Cambridge University Press.

Flower, L. 1980. _Problem-solving strategies for writing._ New York: Harcourt Brace Jovanovich.

Freedman, S. 1981. Evaluation in the writing conference: An interactive process. In _Selected papers from the 1981 Texas Writing Research Conference,_ edited by M. Hairston and C. Selfe. Austin: University of Texas at Austin, 65–96.

Freedman, S. 1985. _The role of response in the acquisition of written language._ Final report to the National Institute of Education, NIE-G-083-0065.

Freedman, S., and J. Bennett. 1987. _Peer groups at work in two writing classrooms._ Final Report to the Office of Educational Research and

Improvement/Department of Education, Center for the Study of Writing, OERI-G008690004.

Freedman, S., and A. Katz. 1987. Pedagogical interaction during the writing process. In *Writing in real time: Modelling production processes,* edited by A. Matsuhashi. Norwood, N.J.: Ablex.

Freedman, S., and M. Sperling. 1985. Teacher student interaction in the writing conference: Response and teaching. In *The acquisition of written language: Response and revision,* edited by S. W. Freedman. Norwood, N.J.: Ablex.

Gagne, R. 1974. *Essentials of learning for instruction.* Hinsdale, Ill.: Dryden Press.

Gere, A. R., and R. D. Abbott. 1985. Talking about writing: The language of writing groups. *Research in the Teaching of English* 19 (4): 362–79.

Gere, A., and R. Stevens. 1985. The language of writing groups: How oral response shapes revision. In *The acquisition of written language: Response and revision,* edited by S. W. Freedman. Norwood, N.J.: Ablex.

Goody, J., and I. Watt. 1963. The consequences of literacy. *Comparative Studies in Society and History* 5:304–26, 332–45.

Graves, D. 1978. *Balance the basics: Let them write.* New York: Ford Foundation.

Graves, D. 1983. *Writing: Teachers and children at work.* Exeter, N.H.: Heinemann.

Greenfield, P. 1984. A theory of the teacher in the learning activities of everyday life. In *Everyday cognition: Its development in social context,* edited by B. Rogoff and J. Lave. Cambridge, Mass.: Harvard University Press.

Hahn, J. 1981. Students' reactions to teachers' written comments. *National Writing Project Network Newsletter* 4:7–10.

Hayes, J. R. 1986. Paper presented at the annual meeting of the American Educational Research Association, San Francisco.

Healy, M. K. 1980. *Using student writing response groups in the classroom.* Berkeley, Calif.: Bay Area Writing Project.

Heath, S. B. 1983. *Ways with words: Language, life, and work in communities and classrooms.* Cambridge: Cambridge University Press.

Heath, S. B., and A. Branscombe. 1985. "Intelligent writing" in an audience community: Teachers, students, and researcher. In *The acquisition of written language: Response and revision,* edited by S. W. Freedman. Norwood, N.J.: Ablex.

Hillocks, G. 1982. The interaction of instruction, teacher comment, and revision in teaching the composing process. *Research in the Teaching of English* 16:261–78.

Jacobs, S., and A. Karliner. 1977. Helping writers to think: The effect of speech rate in individual conferences on the quality of thought in student writing. *College English* 38:489–505.

Kamler, B. 1980. One child, one teacher, one classroom: The story of one piece of writing. *Language Arts* 57:680–93.

Kinneavy, J. 1971. *A theory of discourse.* Englewood Cliffs, N.J.: Prentice-Hall.

Langer, J. 1986. *Children reading and writing: Structures and strategies.* Norwood, N.J.: Ablex.

Leontiev, A. N. 1981. *Problems of the development of the mind.* Moscow: Progress Publishers.

Marshall, J. D. 1984. Process and product: Case studies of writing in two content areas. In *Contexts for learning to write,* edited by A. Applebee. Norwood, N.J.: Ablex.

McNamee, G. 1980. The social origins of narrative skills. Unpublished doctoral dissertation, Northwestern University.

Mehan, H. 1976. Assessing children's school performance. In *Worlds apart,* edited by J. Beck, et al. London: Collier Macmillan.

Mehan, H. 1979. *Learning lessons: Social organization in the classroom.* Cambridge, Mass.: Harvard University Press.

Moffett, J., and B. J. Wagner. 1976. *Student-centered language arts and reading, K-12.* Boston: Houghton Mifflin.

Mohr, M. 1984. *Revision: The rhythm of meaning.* Montclair, N.J.: Boynton/Cook.

Murray, D. 1984. *A writer teaches writing.* 2d ed. Boston: Houghton Mifflin.

Ninio, A., and J. Bruner. 1978. The achievement and antecedents of labeling. *Journal of Child Language* 5: 1–15.

Nystrand, M. 1986. *The structure of written communication: Studies in reciprocity between writers and readers.* Orlando, Fla.: Academic Press.

Ochs, E. 1979. Planned and unplanned discourse. *Syntax and semantics.* New York: Academic Press.

Olson, D. 1977. From utterance to text. *Harvard Educational Review* 47:257–79.

Palinscar, A. S., and A. L. Brown. 1984. Reciprocal teaching of comprehension-fostering and monitoring activities. *Cognition and Instruction* 1 (2): 117–75.

Perl, S., and N. Wilson. 1986. *Through teachers' eyes: Portraits of writing teachers at work.* Portsmouth, N.H.: Heinemann.

Peterson, A. 1986. Thinking made easy: Ten tentative steps toward wisdom. *The Quarterly: Newsletter of the National Writing Project and the Center for the Study of Writing* 8 (3): 8–9, 17.

Purves, A. 1984. The teacher as reader: An anatomy. *College English* 46:259–65.

Rogoff, B., and W. Gardner. 1984. Adult guidance of cognitive development. In *Everyday cognition: Its development in social context,* edited by B. Rogoff and J. Lave. Cambridge, Mass.: Harvard University Press.

Scribner, S., and M. Cole. 1981. *The psychology of literacy.* Cambridge, Mass.: Harvard University Press.

Searle, D., and D. Dillon. 1980. The message of marking: Teacher written responses to student writing at intermediate grade levels. *Research in the Teaching of English* 14 (3): 233–42.

Snow, C., and C. Ferguson. 1977. *Talking to children.* Cambridge: Cambridge University Press.

Sommers, N. 1982. Responding to student writing. *College Composition and Communication* 33:148–56.

Sperling, M. In progress. A study of student-teacher conferences in a ninth-grade writing class. Unpublished doctoral dissertation, University of California, Berkeley.

Sperling, M., and S. Freedman. In press. A good girl writes like a good girl: Written response gives clues to teaching and learning. *Written Communication* 4 (4).

Street, B. 1984. *Literacy in theory and practice.* Cambridge: Cambridge University Press.

Traugott, E. 1985. Literacy and language change: The special case of speech act verbs. Paper presented at the Conference on Language, Literacy, and Culture. Stanford University, Stanford, Calif.

The twelve top public high schools in the U.S. *Money Magazine* 10 (9): 103.

Vygotsky, L. S. 1978. *Mind in society.* Cambridge, Mass.: Harvard University Press.

Wertsch, J. V. 1979. From social interaction to higher psychological processes: A clarification and application of Vygotsky's theory. *Human Development* 22:1–22.

Wertsch, J., N. Minick, and F. Arns. 1984. The creation of context in joint problem-solving. In *Everyday cognition: Its development in social context,* edited by B. Rogoff and J. Lave. Cambridge, Mass.: Harvard University Press.

Wood, D., J. Bruner, and G. Ross. 1976. The role of tutoring in problem solving. *Journal of Child Psychology and Psychiatry* 17: 89–100.

Appendixes

Appendix A
The National Writing Project Surveys

Survey of Excellence in Teaching: Elementary Form

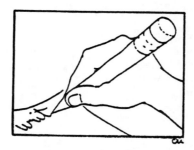

You have been selected to participate in this survey by the National Writing Project because you have been identified as an outstanding teacher of writing in your region.

With this survey, we want to learn more about how excellent teachers across the country teach writing.

> You can answer most of the questions by *circling a number.* In some cases, you will be asked to fill in blanks.
>
> If you notice a problem in any question, please write us a note beside that question.
>
> Read all directions carefully—*especially those in italic type.*
>
> Because this is the first national survey of its kind ever done, you are making an important contribution to professional knowledge. We appreciate your participation in this study.
>
> All your answers will be strictly confidential.

Project sponsored by National Institute of Education
NIE-G-83-0065

We would like your opinions about the helpfulness of various kinds of responses students get on their writing. How helpful do you think each of the following is for elementary level students? *Please circle the appropriate number for each question.*

	Not at all helpful	Not too helpful	Some- what helpful	Very helpful
1. Helpfulness of response on **early** drafts	1	2	3	4
a. Individual conferences with teacher about **early** drafts of writing	1	2	3	4
b. Peer response groups' reactions to **early** drafts	1	2	3	4
c. Teacher's written comments and marks on **early** drafts of writing	1	2	3	4
d. Teacher's grades on **early** drafts of writing	1	2	3	4
e. Getting students' self-assessments about their own **early** drafts of writing	1	2	3	4

If you use other types of response on **early** drafts, please specify:

2. Helpfulness of response on **completed** writing	1	2	3	4
a. Individual conferences with teacher about **completed** pieces of writing	1	2	3	4
b. Peer response groups' reactions to **completed** pieces of writing	1	2	3	4
c. Teacher's written comments and marks on **completed** pieces of writing	1	2	3	4
d. Teacher's grades on **completed** pieces of writing	1	2	3	4
e. Getting students' self-assessments about **completed** pieces of writing	1	2	3	4

If you use other types of response on **completed** writing, please describe:

3. Helpfulness of response from different people	1	2	3	4
a. Classmates or other friends	1	2	3	4

	Not at all helpful	Not too helpful	Some-what helpful	Very helpful
b. Parents	1	2	3	4
c. **You** as teacher	1	2	3	4
d. **Other** teachers	1	2	3	4
e. Other adults	1	2	3	4

If your students receive response from anyone else, please specify:

> We want to get a sense of your class and the kinds of students that you teach. Please answer the following questions about your class.

4. What grade(s) do you teach?

_____ grade(s)

5. How many students are enrolled in your class?

_____ students

6. Approximately what percentage of the students in your class usually speak a language other than English outside of school?

_____ %

7. Approximately what percentage of the students in your class come from the following kinds of families?

Note: *Your answers should add up to 100%.*

Well-to-do families with few if any financial problems... _____ %

Families who can afford the basic necessities of food, clothing, and shelter .... _____ %

Families who cannot afford the basic necessities of food, clothing, and shelter .... _____ %

8. Do your students use a computer or word processor as part of your class?

1 Yes

2 No

9. Basing your answer on all your experience as a teacher, please compare the students in your current class with those from other classes you have taught. Approximately what percentage of the students in this current class are of the following ability levels?

Note: *Your answers should add up to 100%.*

Below average ability............................... _____ %

Average ability...................................... _____ %

Above average ability............................... _____ %

10. Below are two lists of reasons why teachers ask students to write. **Within each list,** please indicate the **two** most important and the **two** least important reasons for asking *this particular class* to write.

List 1 Reasons for asking students to write	Most important **(Check 2)**	Least important **(Check 2)**
To help students remember important information	_____	_____
To correlate personal experience with the topic being studied	_____	_____
To test whether students have learned relevant content	_____	_____
To share imaginative experiences (e.g., through stories, poems)	_____	_____
To summarize material covered in class	_____	_____
To allow students to express their feelings	_____	_____

List 2 Reasons for asking students to write	Most important **(Check 2)**	Least important **(Check 2)**
To explore material not covered in class	_____	_____
To provide practice in various aspects of writing mechanics	_____	_____
To force students to think for themselves	_____	_____
To clarify what has been learned by applying concepts to new situations	_____	_____
To teach students the proper form for a report, essay, or other specific type of writing	_____	_____
To test students' ability to express themselves clearly	_____	_____

Please be sure you have 8 checks for question 10, 2 for each column of each list.

11. In your *total writing curriculum* for *this same class,* approximately how much of your focus is on each of the following types of writing? *Circle the appropriate number for each question.*

	None	A very minor percent	Less than half	About half	More than half
Writing for oneself (lists, journals, diaries)	0	1	2	3	4
Writing to correspond with others (letters, dialogue journals)	0	1	2	3	4

	None	A very minor percent	Less than half	About half	More than half
Writing to convey personal experiences (nonfiction personal narratives)	0	1	2	3	4
Writing to provide an aesthetic experience (poems, plays, short stories)	0	1	2	3	4
Writing to discover or generate ideas (free writing, learning logs)	0	1	2	3	4
Writing to present facts or events (book reports, news reports, **short** research reports)	0	1	2	3	4
Writing to analyze and synthesize ideas (critical or persuasive prose, literary criticism, longer research papers)	0	1	2	3	4
Other kinds of writing (please specify):					

12. How much time does a student have to work on a typical writing assignment for this class?

＿＿＿＿＿ days?

13. In your *last meeting* with this class, did your students do any *in-class* writing?

1   Yes   2   No

⬇

If *yes,* which of the following did they do? *Circle all numbers that apply.*

1   Copying, note-taking, or sentence-level exercises
2   Up to 250 words (one page)
3   251 to 500 words (one to two pages)
4   501 to 1000 words (two to four pages)
5   Over 1000 words (more than four pages)

14. Are students in this class *now* working on any piece of writing *at home*?

   1   Yes   2   No
   ⬇

If *yes*, which of the following are they doing? *Circle all numbers that apply.*

   1   Copying, note-taking, or sentence-level exercises
   2   Up to 250 words (one page)
   3   251 to 500 words (one to two pages)
   4   501 to 1000 words (two to four pages)
   5   Over 1000 words (more than four pages)

The following questions concern your teaching techniques in *this same class*. We are interested in learning the extent to which you use different techniques. Please *circle the appropriate number for each question.*

	Almost never	Some-times	Often	Almost always
15. When a topic is introduced, how often is there in-class discussion (whole class, small group, or individual) about it before students begin writing?	1	2	3	4
16. How often do you use examples of professional writing to help these students improve their writing?	1	2	3	4
17. For each writing assignment, how often do you try to make these students aware of the audience(s) for whom they are writing?	1	2	3	4
18. When responding to problems in the writing of these students, how often do you focus on a selected few of their problems?	1	2	3	4
19. In this class, how often do you use examples of student writing to help these students improve their writing?	1	2	3	4
20. When students in this class are working on a piece of writing, how often do you have them work in peer response groups?	1	2	3	4

	Almost never	Some-times	Often	Almost always
21. When these students produce rough drafts, how often do they receive written or oral comments on them?	1	2	3	4
22. How often do you mark every problem or error that you see in a finished piece of the writing of these students?	1	2	3	4
23. How often do you assign grades to their finished pieces of writing?	1	2	3	4
24. When responding to the writing of these students, how often do you let them know about both strengths and weaknesses?	1	2	3	4
25. In this class, how often do you give assignments sequenced according to a plan you or other experts have devised?	1	2	3	4
26. When these students write, how often do you publish their work for class members or for other readers outside of this class?	1	2	3	4
27. How often do you have individual conferences (either formal or informal) with these students to discuss their writing?	1	2	3	4

We need to gather background information about your school in order to compare teaching situations in different settings.

28. Which of the following best describes the area in which you teach? *Circle the appropriate number.*

    1   Rural (open country, not in a town)
    2   Small town which is not part of a large metropolitan area
    3   Suburb in a large metropolitan area
    4   Central city of a large metropolitan area
    5   City which is not part of a large metropolitan area
    6   Some other kind of place
        (please describe): _____

29. In what kind of school do you teach? *Circle the appropriate number.*

    1   Public
    2   Private, nonparochial
    3   Parochial

30. What are the grade levels at your school?

    Grade _____ through grade _____

31. Approximately how many students are enrolled in your school?

    _____ students

32. What is the normal **class** load each term for a teacher at your school?

    _____ classes

Please provide the following background information about yourself. Again, all your answers will remain confidential. *Circle the appropriate number or fill in the blanks.*

---

33. Sex: 1   Male
          2   Female

34. Year of Birth: 19_____

35. How many years of full-time classroom teaching experience have you had (including this current year)?

    _____ year(s)

36. What was your undergraduate major? *Please circle the appropriate number.*

1	Education	5	Foreign language
2	English		(please specify): _____
3	Math or science	6	Other
4	History or social science		(please specify): _____

37. Have you completed a master's degree (MA, MAT, MS, MEd)?

    1   Yes   2   No
                     ⬇

    ⬇   If *no,* are you working toward this degree?
                   1   Yes   2   No
                         ⬇

If *yes,* what is your specialty? *Please circle the appropriate number.*

1	Education	5	Foreign language
2	English		(please specify): _____
3	Math or science	6	Other
4	History or social science		(please specify): _____

38. Have you completed a PhD or EdD?

    1   Yes   2   No
               ⬇

    ⬇   If *no,* are you working toward this degree?

            1   Yes   2   No
              ⬇

If *yes,* what is your specialty? *Please circle the appropriate number.*

1	Education	5	Foreign language
2	English		(please specify): _____
3	Math or science	6	Other
4	History or social science		(please specify): _____

39. Please use the space below to tell us about any other experience or training that you feel has been helpful to your preparation for teaching.

> Thank you for getting this far. Please answer these last few questions so that you can help us complete our picture of expert teaching.

40. You were selected to complete this questionnaire because you are considered an outstanding teacher of writing. What do you think makes you so successful?

41. What advice would you give other teachers of writing to help them become more effective?

42. One of our main interests in this survey is to find out more about how expert teachers respond to student writing. Can you give us any additional insights on the topic of response to student writing that you think might be helpful to other teachers of writing?

43. Do you have a copy or description of a favorite assignment? If so, we would appreciate your including a copy or description of it in the packet in which you return this questionnaire.

44. Do you have an outline or any other information concerning the goals of the class on which you focused in questions 5 through 28? If so, we would appreciate your including a copy (or copies) in the packet in which you return this questionnaire.

45. Is there anything else you would like to tell us about how you teach writing or how you think it should be taught?

Thank you for your help.

Survey of Excellence in Teaching: Secondary Form

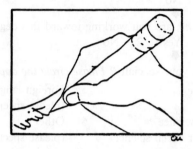

You have been selected to participate in this survey by the National Writing Project because you have been identified as an outstanding teacher of writing in your region.

With this survey, we want to learn more about how excellent teachers across the country teach writing.

> You can answer most of the questions by *circling a number.* In some cases, you will be asked to fill in blanks.
>
> If you notice a problem in any question, please write us a note beside that question.
>
> Read all directions carefully—*especially those in italic type.*
>
> Because this is the first national survey of its kind ever done, you are making an important contribution to professional knowledge. We appreciate your participation in this study.
>
> All your answers will be strictly confidential.

Project sponsored by National Institute of Education
NIE-G-83-0065

We would like your opinions about the helpfulness of various kinds of responses students get on their writing. How helpful do you think each of the following is for secondary level students? *Please circle the appropriate number for each question.*

	Not at all helpful	Not too helpful	Some-what helpful	Very helpful
1. Helpfulness of response on **early** drafts	1	2	3	4
a. Individual conferences with teacher about **early** drafts of writing	1	2	3	4
b. Peer response groups' reactions to **early** drafts	1	2	3	4

	Not at all helpful	Not too helpful	Some-what helpful	Very helpful
c. Teacher's written comments and marks on **early** drafts of writing	1	2	3	4
d. Teacher's grades on **early** drafts of writing	1	2	3	4
e. Getting students' self-assessments about their own **early** drafts of writing	1	2	3	4

If you use other types of response on **early** drafts, please specify:

2. Helpfulness of response on **completed** writing	1	2	3	4
a. Individual conferences with teacher about **completed** pieces of writing	1	2	3	4
b. Peer response groups' reactions to **completed** pieces of writing	1	2	3	4
c. Teacher's written comments and marks on **completed** pieces of writing	1	2	3	4
d. Teacher's grades on **completed** pieces of writing	1	2	3	4
e. Getting students' self-assessments about **completed** pieces of writing	1	2	3	4

If you use other types of response on **completed** writing, please describe:

3. Helpfulness of response from different people	1	2	3	4
a. Classmates or other friends	1	2	3	4
b. Parents	1	2	3	4
c. **You** as teacher	1	2	3	4
d. **Other** teachers	1	2	3	4
e. Other adults	1	2	3	4

If your students receive response from anyone else, please specify:

4. Please answer the questions in this chart about your **Monday** classes. Enter the class titles and then *circle the appropriate numbers* in answer to the questions.

	Period			
	1st	2nd	3rd	4th
Class title	_____	_____	_____	_____
What grade level(s) do you teach in this class? Circle *all* that apply.	7th 10th 8th 11th 9th 12th	7th 10th 8th 11th 9th 12th	7th 10th 8th 11th 9th 12th	7th 10th 8th 11th 9th 12th

How do students enroll in this class?	1 required
	2 option in a
	  required
	  area
	3 elective
		1 required
		2 option in a
		  required
		  area
		3 elective
			1 required
			2 option in a
			  required
			  area
			3 elective
				1 required
				2 option in a
				  required
				  area
				3 elective

How would you describe the ability level of the students who take this class?	1 above avg. 2 average 3 below avg. 4 mixed	1 above avg. 2 average 3 below avg. 4 mixed	1 above avg. 2 average 3 below avg. 4 mixed	1 above avg. 2 average 3 below avg. 4 mixed
How long does this class last?	1 year long 2 semester 3 other	1 year long 2 semester 3 other	1 year long 2 semester 3 other	1 year long 2 semester 3 other
Do you teach writing in this class?	1 yes 2 no	1 yes 2 no	1 yes 2 no	1 yes 2 no
Do any students use a computer or word processor as part of this class?	1 yes 2 no	1 yes 2 no	1 yes 2 no	1 yes 2 no

Period			Additional classes on Monday and on other days (if applicable)	
5th	6th	7th		
7th 10th 8th 11th 9th 12th	7th 10th 8th 11th 9th 12th	7th 10th 8th 11th 9th 12th	7th 10th 8th 11th 9th 12th	7th 10th 8th 11th 9th 12th

1 required
2 option in a
  required
  area
3 elective
	1 required
	2 option in a
	  required
	  area
	3 elective
		1 required
		2 option in a
		  required
		  area
		3 elective
			1 required
			2 option in a
			  required
			  area
			3 elective
				1 required
				2 option in a
				  required
				  area
				3 elective

1 above avg. 2 average 3 below avg. 4 mixed	1 above avg. 2 average 3 below avg. 4 mixed	1 above avg. 2 average 3 below avg. 4 mixed	1 above avg. 2 average 3 below avg. 4 mixed	1 above avg. 2 average 3 below avg. 4 mixed
1 year long 2 semester 3 other	1 year long 2 semester 3 other	1 year long 2 semester 3 other	1 year long 2 semester 3 other	1 year long 2 semester 3 other
1 yes 2 no	1 yes 2 no	1 yes 2 no	1 yes 2 no	1 yes 2 no
1 yes 2 no	1 yes 2 no	1 yes 2 no	1 yes 2 no	1 yes 2 no

We want to learn about your practices when you teach writing and about the kinds of students that you teach. We will ask you to answer questions No. 5 through No. 28 about *one* of your classes. This class, identified in question 5 below, is selected arbitrarily to enable us to compare your answers with those of other teachers across the country.

5. Please think about your *second period class on Mondays* (as you listed it in the chart in question 4). Do you teach writing in this class?

      1 Yes   2 No ➡ If *no,* look at the chart in question 4 for the next class in which you do teach writing. Answer the questions below with reference to that class.

    Indicate the period and title of the class you are focusing on.

    period: _____

    title: _____

6. What is the enrollment in this class?

    _____ students

7. In your school, what is the usual enrollment in a class of this type?

    _____ students

8. After students in this class leave high school, what percentage of them do you think are likely to get additional education or training? We recognize the exact percentage may be difficult to predict; just give your best estimate of the percentage of your students who are likely to go on to the following levels.

    Note: *Your answers should total 100%.*

    No further education past high school .... _____ %
    Vocational training only .... _____ %
    One or two years of college .... _____ %
    At least 4 years of college .... _____ %

9. Approximately what percentage of the students in this class usually speak a language other than English outside of school?

    _____ %

10. Approximately what percentage of the students in this class come from the following kinds of families?

    Note: *Your answers should total 100%.*

    Well-to-do families with few if any financial
    problems. .... _____ %
    Families who can afford the basic necessities of
    food, clothing, and shelter .... _____ %
    Families who cannot afford the basic necessities of
    food, clothing, and shelter .... _____ %

11. Below are two lists of reasons why teachers ask students to write. **Within each list,** please indicate the **two** most important and the **two** least important reasons for asking *this particular class* to write.

List 1 Reasons for asking students to write	Most important **(Check 2)**	Least important **(Check 2)**
To help students remember important information	_____	_____
To correlate personal experience with the topic being studied	_____	_____
To test whether students have learned relevant content	_____	_____
To share imaginative experiences (e.g., through stories, poems)	_____	_____
To summarize material covered in class	_____	_____
To allow students to express their feelings	_____	_____

List 2 Reasons for asking students to write	Most important **(Check 2)**	Least important **(Check 2)**
To explore material not covered in class	_____	_____
To provide practice in various aspects of writing mechanics	_____	_____
To force students to think for themselves	_____	_____
To clarify what has been learned by applying concepts to new situations	_____	_____
To teach students the proper form for a report, essay, or other specific type of writing	_____	_____
To test students' ability to express themselves clearly	_____	_____

Please be sure you have 8 checks for question 11, 2 for each column of each list.

12. In your *total writing curriculum* for *this same class,* approximately how much of your focus is on each of the following types of writing? *Circle the appropriate number for each question.*

	None	A very minor percent	Less than half	About half	More than half
Writing for oneself (lists, journals, diaries)	0	1	2	3	4
Writing to correspond with others (letters, dialogue journals)	0	1	2	3	4

	None	A very minor percent	Less than half	About half	More than half
Writing to convey personal experiences (nonfiction personal narratives)	0	1	2	3	4
Writing to provide an aesthetic experience (poems, plays, short stories)	0	1	2	3	4
Writing to discover or generate ideas (free writing, learning logs)	0	1	2	3	4
Writing to present facts or events (book reports, news reports, **short** research reports)	0	1	2	3	4
Writing to analyze and synthesize ideas (critical or persuasive prose, literary criticism, longer research papers)	0	1	2	3	4
Other kinds of writing (please specify):					

13. How much time does a student have to work on a typical writing assignment for this class?

_____ days

14. In your *last meeting* with this class, did your students do any *in-class* writing?

1   Yes   2   No
⬇

If *yes,* which of the following did they do? *Circle all numbers that apply.*

1   Copying, note-taking, or sentence-level exercises
2   Up to 250 words (one page)

3	251 to 500 words (one to two pages)
4	501 to 1000 words (two to four pages)
5	Over 1000 words (more than four pages)

15. Are students in this class *now* working on any piece of writing *at home*?

1 Yes   2 No
⬇

If *yes,* which of the following are they doing? *Circle all numbers that apply.*

1 Copying, note-taking, or sentence-level exercises
2 Up to 250 words (one page)
3 251 to 500 words (one to two pages)
4 501 to 1000 words (two to four pages)
5 Over 1000 words (more than four pages)

The following questions concern your teaching techniques in *this same class.* We are interested in learning the extent to which you use different techniques. Please *circle the appropriate number for each question.*

	Almost never	Some- times	Often	Almost always
16. When a topic is introduced, how often is there in-class discussion (whole class, small group, or individual) about it before students begin writing?	1	2	3	4
17. How often do you use examples of professional writing to help these students improve their writing?	1	2	3	4
18. For each writing assignment, how often do you try to make these students aware of the audience(s) for whom they are writing?	1	2	3	4
19. When responding to problems in the writing of these students, how often do you focus on a selected few of their problems?	1	2	3	4
20. In this class, how often do you use examples of student writing to help these students improve their writing?	1	2	3	4

	Almost never	Some-times	Often	Almost always
21. When students in this class are working on a piece of writing, how often do you have them work in peer response groups?	1	2	3	4
22. When these students produce rough drafts, how often do they receive written or oral comments on them?	1	2	3	4
23. How often do you mark every problem or error that you see in a finished piece of the writing of these students?	1	2	3	4
24. How often do you assign grades to their finished pieces of writing?	1	2	3	4
25. When responding to the writing of these students, how often do you let them know about both strengths and weaknesses?	1	2	3	4
26. In this class, how often do you give assignments sequenced according to a plan you or other experts have devised?	1	2	3	4
27. When these students write, how often do you publish their work for class members or for other readers outside of this class?	1	2	3	4
28. How often do you have individual conferences (either formal or informal) with these students to discuss their writing?	1	2	3	4

We need to gather background information about your school in order to compare teaching situations in different settings.

---

29. Which of the following best describes the area in which you teach? *Circle the appropriate number.*

    1   Rural (open country, not in a town)

    2   Small town which is not part of a large metropolitan area

    3   Suburb in a large metropolitan area

4   Central city of a large metropolitan area

5   City which is not part of a large metropolitan area

6   Some other kind of place
(please describe): _____

30. In what kind of school do you teach? *Circle the appropriate number.*

1   Public

2   Private, nonparochial

3   Parochial

31. What are the grade levels at your school?

Grade _____ through grade _____

32. Approximately how many students are enrolled in your school?

_____ students

33. What is the normal **class** load each term for a teacher at your school?

_____ classes

Please provide the following background information about yourself. Again, all your answers will remain confidential. *Circle the appropriate number or fill in the blanks.*

---

34. Sex: 1   Male

           2   Female

35. Year of Birth: 19_____

36. How many years of full-time classroom teaching experience have you had (including this current year)?

_____ year(s)

37. What was your undergraduate major? *Please circle the appropriate number.*

1	Education	5	Foreign language
2	English		(please specify): _____
3	Math or science	6	Other
4	History or social science		(please specify): _____

38. Have you completed a master's degree (MA, MAT, MS, MEd)?

1   Yes   2   No
              ⬇

⬇   If *no,* are you working toward this degree?

       1   Yes   2   No
           ⬇

If *yes,* what is your specialty? *Please circle the appropriate number.*

1	Education	5	Foreign language
2	English		(please specify): _____
3	Math or science	6	Other
4	History or social science		(please specify): _____

39. Have you completed a PhD or EdD?

    1   Yes   2   No
                    ⬇

    ⬇   If *no,* are you working toward this degree?

              1   Yes   2   No
               ⬇

If *yes,* what is your specialty? *Please circle the appropriate number.*

1	Education	5	Foreign language
2	English		(please specify): _____
3	Math or science	6	Other
4	History or social science		(please specify): _____

40. Please use the space below to tell us about any other experience or training that you feel has been helpful to your preparation for teaching.

Thank you for getting this far. Please answer these last few questions so that you can help us complete our picture of expert teaching.

---

41. You were selected to complete this questionnaire because you are considered an outstanding teacher of writing. What do you think makes you so successful?

42. What advice would you give other teachers of writing to help them become more effective?

43. One of our main interests in this survey is to find out more about how expert teachers respond to student writing. Can you give us any additional insights on the topic of response to student writing that you think might be helpful to other teachers of writing?

44. Do you have a copy or description of a favorite assignment? If so, we would appreciate your including a copy or description of it in the packet in which you return this questionnaire.

45. Do you have an outline or any other information concerning the goals of the class on which you focused in questions 5 through 28? If so, we would appreciate your including a copy (or copies) in the packet in which you return this questionnaire.

46. Is there anything else you would like to tell us about how you teach writing or how you think it should be taught?

Thank you for your help.

Student Survey

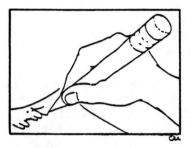

This questionnaire is part of a nation-wide survey by the National Writing Project, a group of teachers dedicated to improving the teaching of writing. We have asked your teacher to give this questionnaire to four students. Your teacher will *not* see your answers.

With this questionnaire, we want to learn what you and other students like you think about the helpfulness of various teaching methods.

> You can answer most of the questions by *circling a number.* For some questions, you will be asked to give a short written answer.
>
> If you notice a problem with any question, please write us a note beside the question.
>
> Read all directions carefully—*especially those in italic type.*
>
> When you finish answering all questions, put your questionnaire back in its envelope and *seal the envelope.* When you seal your envelope, no one who knows you will see your answers.
>
> All your answers will be strictly confidential.

Project sponsored by National Institute of Education
NIE-G-83-0065

Please circle the number beside the answer that best applies to you. *Circle only one number.*

---

1. How often do you write for this class (either at home or in school)?
   - 0 Never
   - 1 Hardly ever
   - 2 Some of the time
   - 3 A lot of the time

2. How often do you write for this class, compared to your other classes?
   - 1 A lot less for this class
   - 2 A little less for this class
   - 3 About the same
   - 4 A little more for this class
   - 5 A lot more for this class

3. How often do you write just because you want to and not for school?

    0   Never
    1   Hardly ever
    2   Some of the time
    3   A lot of the time

4. On the writing you do for this class, what grade do you usually get? Circle the *one* that is most usual for you.

1	A		4	D
2	B		5	F
3	C		6	Other
				(please specify): _____

Please answer these questions about yourself. *Fill in the blanks or circle a number.*

---

5. Birthdate: _____ _____ , 19_____
                  Month   Day   Year

6. Grade: _____

7. Sex: 1   Male
          2   Female

8. When you graduate from high school, what do you plan to do first?
    1   Go to a four-year college or university
    2   Go to a job training program
    3   Go to a two-year college
    4   Go to work full-time
    5   Go to work and then go to college
    6   Go into military service
    7   Other (please describe): _____

For each of the questions below, circle the number that fits best with the writing you do for this class. *Circle only one number.*

	None	Very little of the time	Less than ½ the time	About ½ the time	More than ½ the time
9. Of the time you spend on your writing for this class, how much do you spend on journals or diaries just for yourself?	0	1	2	3	4

	None	Very little of the time	Less than ½ the time	About ½ the time	More than ½ the time
10. Of the time you spend on your writing for this class, how much do you spend writing journals between you and your teacher or letters that you expect to get answers to?	0	1	2	3	4
11. Of the time you spend on your writing for this class, how much do you spend writing essays about your personal experiences?	0	1	2	3	4
12. Of the time you spend on your writing for this class, how much do you spend writing poems or plays or stories that you make up from your imagination?	0	1	2	3	4
13. Of the time you spend on your writing for this class, how much do you spend writing just to find new ideas?	0	1	2	3	4
14. Of the time you spend on your writing for this class, how much do you spend presenting facts or events in the form of book reports, news reports, or **short** research reports?	0	1	2	3	4

	None	Very little of the time	Less than ½ the time	About ½ the time	More than ½ the time
15. Of the time you spend on your writing for this class, how much do you spend writing essays based on your ideas or on your opinions?	0	1	2	3	4

For each of the questions below, circle the number that fits best with what happens in your class. *Circle only one number.*

	Almost never	Some- times	Often	Almost always
16. How often does your teacher write comments on your writing **before** you have put it in its completed form?	1	2	3	4
17. How often does your teacher write comments on the **completed** version of your writing?	1	2	3	4
18. How often does your teacher talk with you about your writing **before** you have put it in its completed form?	1	2	3	4
19. How often does your teacher talk with you about the **completed** version of your writing?	1	2	3	4
20. When you are writing for this class, how often do you and your fellow students talk with each other about your writing **before** it is in its completed form?	1	2	3	4
21. When you are writing for this class, how often do you and your fellow students talk with each other about the **completed** version of your writing?	1	2	3	4

	Almost never	Some-times	Often	Almost always
22. How often do you receive grades on the **completed** versions of your writing?	1	2	3	4
23. How often does your teacher let you know what kinds of people might read each piece of your writing?	1	2	3	4
24. When you are writing for this class, how often do you make up your own topic to write about?	1	2	3	4
25. When you are writing for this class, how often does your teacher give you a topic to write about?	1	2	3	4
26. How often are there discussions in class about a topic before you begin to write about it?	1	2	3	4
27. How often does your teacher make comments about what is strong as well as what is weak in your writing?	1	2	3	4

As a student, you may be getting different kinds of feedback or response to your writing. *In this class,* how helpful to your learning are the following kinds of feedback or response? *Circle only one number.*

	Don't know; never occurs	Not at all helpful	Not too helpful	Some-what helpful	Very helpful for learning to write
28. Comments on your writing **before** the completed version	0	1	2	3	4
a. Talking personally with your teacher **before** your paper is in its completed form	0	1	2	3	4

	Don't know; never occurs	Not at all helpful	Not too helpful	Some-what helpful	Very helpful for learning to write
b. Talking with other students in your class **before** your paper is in its completed form	0	1	2	3	4
c. Written comments from your teacher about your paper **before** it is in its completed form	0	1	2	3	4
d. Grades given by your teacher to your paper **before** it is in its completed form	0	1	2	3	4
e. Your teacher's asking you for **your** comments on your paper **before** it is in its completed form	0	1	2	3	4
29. Comments on **completed** pieces of writing	0	1	2	3	4
a. Talking personally with your teacher about **completed** pieces of writing	0	1	2	3	4
b. Talking with other students in your class about your **completed** pieces of writing	0	1	2	3	4
c. Written comments from your teacher about your **completed** pieces of writing	0	1	2	3	4

	Don't know; never occurs	Not at all helpful	Not too helpful	Some- what helpful	Very helpful for learning to write
d. Grades given by your teacher to your **completed** pieces of writing	0	1	2	3	4
e. Your teach- er's asking **you** for your com- ments on your **completed** paper	0	1	2	3	4
30. Comments on your writing from others	0	1	2	3	4
a. Comments from friends (in- side or outside of class)	0	1	2	3	4
b. Comments from parents	0	1	2	3	4
c. Comments from **your** teacher	0	1	2	3	4
d. Comments from **other** teach- ers	0	1	2	3	4
e. Comments from other adults	0	1	2	3	4
f. Comments from brothers or sisters	0	1	2	3	4

31. When you are trying to learn to write better, what helps you most and why?

32. Please use the space below for any other comments you would like to make.

Thank you for your help.

Appendix B
Assignment Sequences

Mary Lee Glass's Assignment Sequence

1. Interview: 3 weeks

Students spent several days interviewing a classmate, first devising interview questions, then refining and focusing them. What was stressed during this stretch of activity was finding a focus for the interview and gathering specific information in the form of anecdotes about the interviewee.

Students then made oral presentations on their interviewees, with the teacher's stressing their being aware of audience and purpose. They evaluated each other's presentations.

While the students prepared their oral presentations, they were also deciding what to include in their written piece on their interviewees. The rough drafts of these writings were eventually read by each student to his or her peer group, with peers giving written and oral comments as feedback.

At this point, students were to make sure that their papers and the papers of their peers had a focus and that their assertions were developed with specific illustrations. In preparing their final drafts, students were to make use of the feedback they received from their peers as well as a "Writer's Checklist" given to them by the teacher.

On the day final drafts were turned in, students met in pairs to proofread and make final corrections on their papers, and to fill in evaluation sheets on their own and on their partner's papers.

When the teacher returned these writings with her evaluations and feedback, the students reread them, chose one paragraph for revision, and noted their errors on "Needs Improvement" charts.

2. Commercials: 2 weeks

For this oral assignment, groups of students collaborated on written scripts. After reading about the persuasive techniques used in commercials, the groups wrote and performed commercials of their own. Groups spent several days developing ideas, writing scripts, and practicing. The students and the teacher evaluated these commercials on content and performance, evaluating both the individuals and the group as a whole. The written scripts were never collected or discussed as such; they were only important during preparation for the oral presentation and were, for the most part, in the form of notes.

3. Saturation Report on a Place: 3 1/2 weeks

All students chose a place to observe which could be visited several times. They each had a week's time to make three to four visits, taking "copious notes" on what they saw there. The teacher emphasized, and had them write practice paragraphs on, capturing the "character" of their chosen places as well as of other places or people. Students read and evaluated in class two student-written essays on Disneyland and one professional essay on Las Vegas, all examples of writing that had the same purposes as those of this assignment.

Other activities for this assignment included students meeting in groups to discuss the problems they encountered doing the assignment; practicing making and critiquing focal statements; writing and responding to rough drafts as they had for the first assignment; writing, presenting, and evaluating "public service announcements" about their places; and refining and evaluating final drafts as they had for the first assignment.

4. Opinion Essay: 2 1/2 weeks

Students began by generating a list of issues they had opinions about. They refined their lists by pulling out those issues that they knew a lot about. Of these, students were to pick a topic that they not only had an opinion on and information about but also one with which they had personal experience.

Prewriting activities for this assignment included class discussion on techniques for gathering information. Students also learned procedures for generating a thesis and for developing the paragraphs in the body of the essay.

Students were to produce an opinion paper that included a thesis statement and topic sentences. For the first time, Glass stressed essay form. Students accordingly worked in groups on thesis statements. They produced rough drafts that were evaluated in groups as before.

In class, all students read their introductory sentences, which were then evaluated by class vote as to whether or not they sparked reader interest. The teacher emphasized the importance of the introductory paragraph's leading to the thesis in an interesting way. The class discussed how to make their writing interesting to a reader.

Before handing in final drafts, the students identified their thesis sentence, the main idea in the introduction and body paragraphs, topic sentences, and transitional devices. Students then met in proofreading pairs and did final editing and evaluation as they had done previously.

Throughout the eleven weeks, while working on the major assignments, students did several ungraded "practice writings," both in class and at home, and did some work on sentence-combining and using appropriate pronouns.

Art Peterson's Assignment Sequence

1. Character Study of a Friend or Acquaintance: 5 weeks

Students spent several days practicing observations of people. They began by watching a segment of the movie *North by Northwest* and observing Cary Grant — his looks, his speech, his mannerisms, and the like. During this time they began reading Dickens's *Great Expectations* and were assigned characters in the first chapters to observe in much the same way, noting what was said about their looks, speech, mannerisms, and so on. Using their observations of both Cary Grant and the Dickens characters, they discussed character traits in general and the difference between what one observes in a person and what one then infers about that person as a result of the observations. A distinction was made between observation and judgment.

Students also practiced writing paragraphs on people by making judgments about a character in *Great Expectations* and developing them with supporting evidence from the book.

After these practice observations and writings, students began to find a subject for this first paper — someone they knew personally. When they had chosen the person they would write about, they composed an anecdote about their subject. (During this time they continued to discuss the notion of character traits, and they practiced observations, often in groups, competing for points as in group activities that were organized as "games.") Peterson made copies of certain student anecdotes, and the class critiqued them, paying attention to observations and judgments. After having in-class conferences with Peterson, students revised their anecdotes and then critiqued them again in class.

Students then wrote rough drafts of an essay-length character study, in which they incorporated, if they could, the anecdotes they had been working on. There was class discussion of rough drafts, and Peterson held individual conferences on them with students. The rough drafts were eventually read by each student to the peers in his or her group, who filled in response sheets as feedback to each writer. The students focused on finding effective opening sentences, well-written topic sentences, unified paragraphs, good descriptive passages, strong verbs, and smooth transitions from one paragraph to another. When final drafts were turned in, Peterson responded to them in writing and held individual conferences about those he felt needed to be discussed. Only after the conferences did most students get grades on their papers. Students whose papers had already been graded made changes as indicated by Peterson's written responses, without need of a conference.

2. *Character Study of a Well-Known Contemporary Figure: 3 weeks*

As an in-class prewriting activity for this second paper, students generated facts about contemporary rock star Michael Jackson and determined what common threads unified these facts. They each wrote a paragraph about Michael Jackson and critiqued these paragraphs in class.

Peterson discussed finding and using library information, especially in periodicals, to gather data for this second character study. Students read and discussed sample library material; wrote paragraphs in groups, based on that information; composed group paragraphs on contemporary figures whom they chose to work on, sharing their paragraphs with the class; and read newspaper articles that exemplified the kind of papers they were working on, viewing them as models for the writing of introductions and for the presentation of contrasting characteristics within one person.

Meanwhile, students chose a well-known contemporary figure for their second paper. They compiled bibliographies and isolated those qualities of their chosen characters they wanted to write about. All of this information was handed in to Peterson.

On the day students handed in rough drafts, they divided into groups, reading their drafts to their peers and getting feedback via response sheets. Later, Peterson gave students feedback in class about their drafts, as well as in individual conferences, and students worked on revising their drafts. Eventually, students shared their revised rough drafts with their peer groups, who responded to them. Students then wrote final drafts which they gave to

Peterson. The same procedures for revision and grade-giving were followed as for the first paper.

3. Character Sketch of Figure from "Great Expectations": 7 weeks

Preliminary work on this character sketch began when students started reading *Great Expectations* and writing their observations of selected characters from the novel. It was in the final two weeks of our observations in Peterson's class, however, that the intensive work began on this last major assignment. Students practiced for this assignment in groups, each group writing a paragraph about Pip based on a topic sentence provided by Peterson and on supporting evidence that they found in the book. Later, Peterson made copies of some of these paragraphs and students critiqued them in class. They also discussed the kinds of information to include in the introductions, body paragraphs, and conclusions of these third character sketches. When rough drafts were written, the class divided into groups; students read their drafts to their peers, who responded to them, using a response sheet that focused on the characteristics they had written about and whether or not their papers were convincing. Students handed in revisions of these drafts to Peterson, who responded to them as he did for the other two papers in this sequence.

Appendix C
Note-Taking Conventions and Procedures for In-Class Data Collection

A set of note-taking conventions was developed to streamline note taking and to have an efficient and effective manuscript to refer to later when analyzing the data. Note sheets were divided vertically into two columns, one for objective observations and the other for reactions, opinions, interpretations, and hypotheses. Major activity shifts were noted as was clock time at important junctures or key episodes involving response. When the Scribe judged that an episode might need to be analyzed further, the episode was marked by an asterisk.

An identification code headed each set of notes: teacher's last initial, week number, day number. For example, for Glass's class, week two, day four, the code would be "G-02-4." This code was also used on the videotape and on the audiotapes. In this way, data were cross-referenced and indexed.

After class, another set of procedures was followed for checking and adding to the Scribe's classroom notes. First, the Technician, using a contrasting pen or pencil, added objective details that the Scribe may have missed, elaborated on points in the subjective column from her own point of view and, in the left-hand margin, filled in the video counter numbers from her notes that coincided with the activities that the Scribe had described, so that the activities could easily be retrieved on the videotapes during data analysis.

Every night the Scribe read the notes for the day to locate interactions between the teacher and students or among the students themselves (in the whole class or in peer groups) that could be described as "responses" to student writing. Finding such response episodes, the Scribe then coded them in a preliminary way, to indicate the responder and the recipient of the response, the channel of the response (oral, written, nonverbal), and the point in the writer's process when the response occurred (during the process or to final writing).

Finally, the Scribe summarized the day's notes with (1) a list of the day's activities; (2) a list of assignments, both in class and homework; (3) a list of response episodes (listed by code and referenced to a page number); and (4) brief comments that covered anything from classroom events worth noting to difficulties encountered during data collection.

Appendix D
Criteria for Determining What Was to Be Recorded on Camera

On-line decisions about what to get on camera at a given time were guided by the following criteria:

1. In whole-class activities the main channel of communication was between the teacher and the class. The teacher controlled this communication process, calling on particular students to participate, or directing class activities. In this situation, the camera followed the teacher, framing the camera shot so as to get as much of the class as possible on camera with the teacher. Decisions about what portion of the class to include with the teacher were guided by the position of the focal students in the classroom.

2. When students were working individually on an in-class assignment, camera time was divided among the focal students as much as possible. Often two or more focal students could be caught on camera at the same time.

3. If, as often happened in Glass's class, students took turns giving speeches from the front of the room, the camera was focused on the speaker, catching as much of the rest of the class as possible.

4. When students formed peer groups to work on class assignments, the Technician focused on those groups containing focal students. Often more than one such group fit on camera at a time. Since these groups often met over a period of days, the group on camera was rotated from day to day in order to catch each of the focal students interacting with his or her groups, to the extent that this rotation was possible. Sometimes in Glass's class, particular groups went outside of the classroom to work, and it was not possible to film them in this event. When the teacher traveled from group to group, engaging the group members in significant teaching interactions, the Technician followed the teacher.

5. Above all, if focal students were engaged in any activity that seemed significant and important to document, the Technician tried to catch it on video. The Technician's attention had to be divided between the current camera shot and activities taking place beyond reach of the camera involving the focal students. Decisions to focus on focal students were often subjective, amounting to guesses about what might turn out to be significant. For example, a decision might be to focus the camera on a focal student instead of the teacher when the two were engaged in an extended dialogue, but when the teacher and the student were too far away from each other to fit on camera at the same time.

Appendix E
Supplementary Tables

Table E.1

Influence of Grade Level on Scales for Teachers

	Degrees of Freedom	Sum of Squares	Mean Squares	F-test
Response during process				
Between groups	3	.90	1.42	.24
Within groups	486	103.23	.21	
Response after writing				
Between groups	3	.42	.14	.63
Within groups	421	93.61	.22	
Responders				
Between groups	3	.52	.17	1.08
Within groups	366	58.41	.16	
Teaching techniques				
Between groups	3	2.26	.76	5.03*
Within groups	498	74.80	.15	
Response from teachers				
Between groups	3	30.52	10.17	35.68**
Within groups	467	133.15	.29	
Response from peers				
Between groups	3	5.46	1.82	6.66**
Within groups	486	132.97	.27	
Response from writer				
Between groups	3	2.04	.68	1.87
Within groups	485	176.88	.37	

$*p < .01.$ $**p < .001.$

Table E.2

Scale Average "Item Means" for Teacher Grade Level on
Summary Scales for Teaching Techniques, Response from
Teachers, and Response from Peers

Grade Level	Teaching Techniques: Average "Item Mean"	Response from Teachers: Average "Item Mean"	Response from Peers: Average "Item Mean"
K through 3	3.12 $(sd = .40)$ $(n = 47)$	1.90 $(sd = .74)$ $(n = 43)$	3.20 $(sd = .61)$ $(n = 46)$
4 through 6	3.30 $(sd = .36)$ $(n = 112)$	2.12 $(sd = .53)$ $(n = 110)$	3.47 $(sd = .47)$ $(n = 111)$
7 through 9	3.15 $(sd = .39)$ $(n = 179)$	2.50 $(sd = .47)$ $(n = 164)$	3.29 $(sd = .53)$ $(n = 172)$
10 through 12	3.14 $(sd = .40)$ $(n = 164)$	2.66 $(sd = .54)$ $(n = 154)$	3.20 $(sd = .52)$ $(n = 161)$

Table E.3

Influence of Geographical Region on Scales for Teachers

	Degrees of Freedom	Sum of Squares	Mean Squares	*F*-test
Response during process				
Between groups	5	.34	.07	.32
Within groups	519	111.39	.22	
Response after writing				
Between groups	5	1.25	.25	1.10
Within groups	452	102.46	.23	
Responders				
Between groups	5	.75	.15	.91
Within groups	394	65.02	.17	
Teaching techniques				
Between groups	5	1.38	.28	1.85
Within groups	532	79.38	.15	
Response from teachers				
Between groups	5	4.67	.93	2.80*
Within groups	500	166.99	.33	
Response from peers				
Between groups	5	2.37	.47	1.73
Within groups	518	141.51	.27	
Response from writer				
Between groups	5	3.71	.74	2.05
Within groups	522	189.26	.36	

* $p < .05$.

Table E.4

Scale Average "Item Means" for Geographical Region on
Summary Scale: Response from Teachers

School Region	Response from Teachers: Average "Item Mean"
Northeast	2.15 (sd = .61) (n = 56)
North Central	2.43 (sd = .58) (n = 104)
South	2.44 (sd = .59) (n = 153)
West	2.42 (sd = .55) (n = 165)
Foreign American	2.50 (sd = .62) (n = 12)
Foreign non-American	2.19 (sd = .60) (n = 16)

Table E.5

Influence of School Size on Scales for Teachers

	Degrees of Freedom	Sum of Squares	Mean Squares	F-test
Response during process				
Between groups	3	1.13	.38	1.75
Within groups	519	111.39	.22	
Response after writing				
Between groups	3	.66	.22	.97
Within groups	449	101.08	.23	
Responders				
Between groups	3	.07	.02	.14
Within groups	391	65.60	.17	
Teaching techniques				
Between groups	3	.65	.22	1.42
Within groups	528	79.89	.15	
Response from teachers				
Between groups	3	7.25	2.42	7.32*
Within groups	498	164.38	.33	
Response from peers				
Between groups	3	1.45	.49	1.75
Within groups	515	142.98	.28	
Response from writer				
Between groups	3	.36	.12	.32
Within groups	519	192.29	.37	

* $p < .001$.

Table E.6

Scale Average "Item Means" for School Size on Summary
Scale: Response from Teachers

School Size	Response from Teachers: Average "Item Mean"
Under 500	2.24 (sd = .62) (n = 152)
500 to 999	2.38 (sd = .55) (n = 190)
1000 to 2499	2.55 (sd = .55) (n = 151)
Over 2499	2.39 (sd = .54) (n = 9)

Table E.7

Influence of Teacher Age on Scales for Teachers

	Degrees of Freedom	Sum of Squares	Mean Squares	F-test
Response during process				
Between groups	4	.35	.09	.41
Within groups	532	113.21	.21	
Response after writing				
Between groups	4	.57	.14	.63
Within groups	462	104.58	.23	
Responders				
Between groups	4	.72	.18	1.11
Within groups	403	65.68	.16	
Teaching techniques				
Between groups	4	1.66	.42	2.79*
Within groups	544	81.03	.15	
Response from teachers				
Between groups	4	.44	.11	.32
Within groups	510	176.56	.35	
Response from peers				
Between groups	4	2.69	.67	2.44*
Within groups	530	145.77	.28	
Response from writer				
Between groups	4	2.22	.56	1.53
Within groups	533	193.36	.36	

$* p < .05.$

Table E.8

Scale Average "Item Means" for Teacher Age on Summary
Scales for Teaching Techniques and Response from Peers

Teacher's Age	Teaching Techniques: Average "Item Mean"	Response from Peers: Average "Item Mean"
Under 29	3.07 $(sd = .47)$ $(n = 34)$	3.10 $(sd = .63)$ $(n = 34)$
30 to 39	3.13 $(sd = .39)$ $(n = 221)$	3.27 $(sd = .54)$ $(n = 217)$
40 to 49	3.22 $(sd = .38)$ $(n = 218)$	3.34 $(sd = .49)$ $(n = 213)$
50 to 59	3.25 $(sd = .37)$ $(n = 63)$	3.40 $(sd = .48)$ $(n = 58)$
over 60	3.32 $(sd = .27)$ $(n = 13)$	3.40 $(sd = .61)$ $(n = 13)$

Table E.9

Influence of Teacher Experience on Scales for Teachers

	Degrees of Freedom	Sum of Squares	Mean Squares	F-test
Response during process				
Between groups	4	1.02	.26	1.21
Within groups	532	112.54	.21	
Response after writing				
Between groups	4	.83	.21	.92
Within groups	462	104.32	.23	
Responders				
Between groups	4	.76	.19	1.17
Within groups	403	65.64	.16	
Teaching techniques				
Between groups	4	1.72	.43	2.88*
Within groups	545	81.36	.15	
Response from teachers				
Between groups	4	1.42	.35	1.03
Within groups	511	175.63	.34	
Response from peers				
Between groups	4	1.50	.37	1.35
Within groups	531	147.45	.28	
Response from writer				
Between groups	4	.70	.18	.48
Within groups	534	195.46	.37	

* $p < .05$.

Table E.10

Scale Average "Item Means" for Teacher Experience on Scale 4:
Frequency of Teaching Techniques

Experience Level	Average "Item Mean"
5 years or less	3.02 (*sd* = .40) (*n* = 47)
6 to 10 years	3.18 (*sd* = .38) (*n* = 132)
11 to 15 years	3.20 (*sd* = .40) (*n* = 169)
16 to 20 years	3.24 (*sd* = .36) (*n* = 115)
21 years or more	3.17 (*sd* = .40) (*n* = 87)

Table E.11

Influence of Teacher Gender on Scales for Teachers

	Average "Item Mean" for Males	Average "Item Mean" for Females	t Test
Response during process	3.66 $(sd = .46)$ $(n = 106)$	3.72 $(sd = .46)$ $(n = 431)$	−1.17 $(df = 162)$
Response after writing	3.07 $(sd = .48)$ $(n = 97)$	3.16 $(sd = .47)$ $(n = 370)$	−1.79
Responders	3.24 $(sd = .40)$ $(n = 79)$	3.31 $(sd = .41)$ $(n = 329)$	−1.35
Teaching techniques	3.10 $(sd = .40)$ $(n = 106)$	3.20 $(sd = .39)$ $(n = 444)$	−2.26*
Response from teachers	2.36 $(sd = .55)$ $(n = 104)$	2.40 $(sd = .60)$ $(n = 412)$	−0.62
Response from peers	3.26 $(sd = .50)$ $(n = 107)$	3.31 $(sd = .54)$ $(n = 429)$	−0.94
Response from writer	3.07 $(sd = .60)$ $(n = 104)$	3.28 $(sd = .60)$ $(n = 435)$	−3.13**

* $p < .05$.   ** $p < .01$.

Appendix F
Would You Buy a Used Car from This Man? Questions for Character Analysis

1. Would he go to the movies by himself?
2. What would he say if he saw a dog with a can tied to its tail?
3. Does he remember his mother's birthday?
4. Would he send back a steak in a restaurant?
5. What would he do if someone crowded in ahead of him in a movie line?
6. If he were to take up another occupation, what would he want it to be? What job would he be best at?
7. If he accidentally burned a hole in his host's tablecloth, what would he do?
8. Does he favor capital punishment?
9. Does he exercise? How?
10. What would he order as his last meal?
11. What racial, religious, and social groups does he dislike?
12. What kind of pet does he own?
13. How many hours of sleep does he need each night?
14. He comes on a lone hitchhiker on a lonely road. What does he do?
15. If you asked him, would he be able to tell you when his automobile oil is due for a change?
16. If you asked him what "praise" and "punishment" have in common would he be more likely to say they both start with "P" or that they are both "motivators"?
17. Does he always vote?
18. What possessions does he most prize?
19. If he were to cast himself in a classic movie role, what would it be? If you were to cast him in a role, what would it be?
20. If he lost his hair, would he wear a wig?
21. What does the name he chooses to use tell about him?
22. What are the most common remarks those who know him well make about him when he isn't around?
23. What does he wear to bed?
24. What is (or would be) the first thing he notices about you?

25. In what way do you expect he will die?
26. Would he be able to tell you the current price of a loaf of bread?
27. If he were to describe himself in a personal ad, what would he say? If you were to describe him, what would you say?
28. Has he ever made a jigsaw puzzle?
29. If he could watch only one T.V. show a week, what would it be?
30. Can he spell "occurrence" and "recommend"?
31. Does he know what "laconic" means?
32. What does he see as his greatest fear? achievement? failure?

Appendix G
Student Writing Samples

Final Version: Gina's Character Sketch

"I couldn't help my best friend with her homework, but I gave her fifty dollars to buy a book. Do you think that's enough?"

We have here a typical statement made without reservation by a person as complex as Einstein's theory of relativity. She is envied and admired by some; yet resented and disliked by others. She's witty, charming, radiant, and very intelligent. For purposes of anonimity, we shall name her Dianne.

I consider myself a closet analyst. You can probably say I've analized every person I know at one time or another, but my greatest challenge has always been Dianne. She is by far the best manipulator I've known. One time, she convinced her best friend Pamela to have a wild party at her house while Pamela's parents were away. There was also the time Dianne demanded her boyfriend teach her to ride a skateboard, this was during his junior high finals. It's really incredible how she always manages to find the right words to say and to make people do things completely against their own will and their common sense.

Although she's not blond, the only way to describe Dianne's looks is to say she is the perfect California girl. For one thing, she keeps an eternal, never-fade tan. Dianne is tan year-round from her scalp to the soles of her feet. Dianne has a *Colgate* smile with pearly white, perfectly aligned teeth. Whenever she flashes her smile you feel like someone turned the sun up too high. She has her own surfboard, her own water skis, and her own water bike (don't ask me where she uses these things, I don't know). She owns OP (Ocean Pacific) clothes by the millions and is eternally listening to the BEACH BOYS on her Sony Walkman (which cost her $250.00).

In spite of the fact that Dianne is usually the center of attention, she is insecure, but she is very good at covering it up. Because Dianne has a lot of money, she believes that ultimately, she can buy everyone and everything. One time she invited me to go to a movie with her, but it so happened that I was busy that night and couldn't go. Well she, immediately assumed that I wasn't going becuase I didn't like her and offered not only to buy my ticket, but to buy me dinner as well. On Andrea's birthday, instead of going to her birthday party, Dianne gave Andrea thirty dollars.

Dianne believes that those close to her are trying to use her just as she uses them. She is always on the defensive end. I remember the time that one of our mutural friends whose name is Barbara wanted Dianne to come over to meet this cute guy that she liked at the time. Dianne immediately thought that Barbara wanted her to come over so that she could talk to the guy about Barbara and she refused to go to Barbara's house. I told her that she was wrong, that I had gone over to meet him too and that there was no such pretense. Dianne would not believe it. Instead, she went to Barbara's house and turned on the charm. Well, the poor guy fell for it and Barbara was pushed aside. Incredibly, Dianne can be extremely and afraid of rejection. So shy, that once when she wanted to envite me to a party at the beach, Dianne sent Andrea to ask me because she didn't know me very well and was too afraid to face me and my answer. There is this one guy in school that she *really* likes, she's liked him since 7th grade. But she's never had the nerve to *go for it*!

To understand Dianne, it is essential to understand her need not only to be accepted, but to have the world revolve around her. When people are in a group, talking, she immedialety stands in the middle and instantly becomes the center of attention. If I talked about each of her qualities I would be here for days. So I'll tell one of the best "stories" and you can see what I mean.

At the beginning of the year, Dianne liked a guy whose name is Dan. As usual, she convinced Andrea to make sure he liked her back. This she did by having Andrea rant and rave about what a great person Dianne was. Inevitably, he liked her back. As soon as Dianne found out she made no further attempt at becoming friends. She almost ignored Dan. She then proceeeded to make Dan's best friend like her, and together they had many "adventures". About four months ago, they went to Lake Tahoe together. While they were there, they got drunk. Later, they went skiing only to get caught by the ski patrol who tried to send them back to San Francisco. They managed to run away and hitchhike back to the city. Everyone always found out about these stories, especially Dan; but then that was the whole point. Later she dropped Dan's best friend for Dan. Dianne gave Dan a dose of adventure too, but later dropped him as well. This on-again-off-again relationship went on for months until she finally stopped it completely, but only for a few months. Now, she's picked him up again, and he, has become her worshipper. For her birthday, she told him she wanted a gold necklace and a dozen roses. So the poor guy went out, got a paper route and worked for months to get what she wanted. When her birthday came around he proudly gave her the wonderful gifts and all she could say was a cold and simple, "Thanks".

As you can see, Dianne can be quite cruel at times. Because she is insecure, Dianne conveniently makes sure that these stories get around. She knows she leads a soap-operish life, envied by many. Dianne is the symbol of adventure for all of us. Dianne has a way of making everything sound as if it's a secret. Everytime you ask her to tell you her latest story, she pulls you away from the rest of the crowd, to the backlawn or the frontlawn or somewhere "private". Then, she looks at you straight in the eye and begins to speak in a quiet, hushed tone. Somewhere during the conversation, she always manages to say, "Don't tell anyone, please keep it a secret," and then moves on the next person.

Although a lot of people have believed for a long time that Dianne is a sweet, caring, simple-natured person, now, many are beginning to see that they've been wrong. These are the people who dislike her. A lot of the people who admired and became close to her, began to pick up on some of her "qualities" and walked away from her.

I feel sorry for Dianne. She could have the world if she would just stop worrying about being the center of everything and appreciate all the wonderful things that she has. Especially, I wish she would see how much harm she does to those who care about her. She must be terribly lonely. I wish she would wake up, take the blindfold off, and see the world as it really is.

Draft: Julie's Saturation Report

(1) "Mala! Mala!" yells a ruddy, dark faced man. The words seem to roll off his tongue in a series of up and down tones as he cheers on his volleyball team. (2) He reminds me of Al Pacino, with his hawk-like brown eyes sunken in their sockets. (3) The breeze stirs his hair for a moment before he speaks in the pleasant garble of Spanish.

(4) "Just beat it, just beat it . . ." blares a radio loudspeaker. Michael Jackson's highpitched voice rivals the "cheep-cheep" of the birds and "Mommy, he did it," screams of the junivile delinquents running around. (5) These are just some of the people from San Jose, San Francisco, Palo Alto, and other parts of the bay area who come to Mitchell Park for recreation, gatherings, and picnics, for its large size and friendly atmosphere.

(6) Some trees, the ones which still have their leaves, wave and rustle as the breeze goes through it. (7) The sun shines directly overhead, filtering through the leaves which had provided some shade.

(8) "Smack! Smack! Smack! Smack! Smack! Smack! Bung!" of the tennis balls are constantly coming through the laughter, screams, patter, patter of footsteps, clink-clink of bikes, and the "cheep, chirp, kah, kah!" of birds. (9) Smoke smarts my eyes as a wind blows the smell and smoke from a Barbecue grill in my direction. (10) My eyes sting for just a moment before the smell of hamburgers, chicken, and hotdogs fill my nostrils. (11) In my mind, I could visualize a plump, juicy hot dog in a bun, hot and ready to eat. (12) Soon my vision was shattered as an unpleasant burnt, charcoal smell invaded my senses.

(13) Two men, running full speed down the soccer field chased after the black and white ball, with their hair plastered against their faces, dripping perspiration. (14) Their muscles strained against their socks as their cleats flew over the field kicking up dirt. (15) One team wore dark jersies and the other, light green jersies, or shirts. (16) "Let's go! Come on Mike, on the line, on the line. Bill! Bill! Nice shot! Wooo!" shouted one of the players on the dark green team. (17) There was static excitement in the air. (18) Everyone on the green wooden bleachers, leaned forward with their foreheads creased and brows furrowed as they watched the game.

(19) A woman, dressed in a white T-shirt, red shorts and white and blue jogging shoes jogged around and around the field, constantly trying to dodge the bicyclists, little children, and adults using the red pebble/dirt path surrounding the different fields. (20) Her short brown hair bobbed up and down revealing the presence of her white terrycloth sweatband. (21) Sweat stained her shirt and droplets of water dotted her upper lip while she breathed in short gasps.

(22) In the sunken concrete skating rink surrounded by a brick wall, a group of adults practiced something like kung foo. (23) They all performed each movement the same time, moving each part of the body, slowly and deliberately in silence. (24) It seemed like what they were doing was isolated from what everyone else was doing.

Final Version: Julie's 5-S Report on Mitchell Park

"Mala! Mala!" yells a ruddy, dark faced man. The words seem to roll off his tongue in a series of up and down tones. He is casually clad in a white T-shirt, shorts, tennis shoes, and a forest green baseball cap to complete his attire. He reminds me of Al Pacino with his hawk-like brown eyes sunken in their sockets. He stands with his knees bent and arms out-stretched, bringing to mind a tightly coiled up spring as he waits for the volleyball to be served to his team. "Puck!" the dull sound of a hand coming in contact with a ball echos through the air. All the volley players spring up in action as the white volleyball sails over the orange, nylon net. A pleasant, excited garble of Spanish flows the air, while the game continues. These volleyball players are just some of the many people who come to Mitchell Park for recreation, gatherings, and picnics, for its large size and friendly atmosphere.

When someone says "Mitchell Park", what comes to my mind? I immediately see a large grasy area, divided into many fields by bumpy red dirt paths, and dotted with artistic sculptures, tall trees, short trees, pine trees, and so on. All the dirt paths are lined with wooden benches and large dumpsters. Surrounding the park are nicely kept schools, a street, and a library. Several playgrounds are enclosed in the park as well as picnic tables and barbecue grills.

"Just beat it! Just beat it!" blares a radio loudspeaker. Michael Jackson's highpitched voice threatens to drown out the chirping birds, the pitter, patter of small footsteps running past, the clink, clink of the bicycles, and the joyous laughter and shouting all around me. I plug my ears and wince as another radio is turned on full blast playing foreign folk music featuring bongo drums and banjos. Sitting against the worn out wooden bench, my cheeks warm up from the heat of the sun shining directly above me, and a warm breeze stirs my hair.

Smoke smarts my eyes as a stronger breeze blows the fumes from a red, round barbecue grill in my direction. My eyes water and blink rapidly to clear the hazy pictures I was seeing. The wind keeps blowing and soon my nose flares up as the tantalizing aroma of hamburgers, hotdogs, and chicken reach me. Visions of thick, juicy hamburger meat in a toasted bun float around in my mind. My pleasant picture shatters as the stench of something burnt invades my senses. I tried to place myself as far away from this area as I could.

I walked to the opposite side of the park, arriving in the middle of a soccer game. Two men running full speed down the soccer field, toward a white wooden goal post, chase intensely after a black and white soccer ball, with their hair plastered against their faces, dripping perspiration. Their muscles are clearly defined through their socks as their cleats fly over the field, kicking up dirt. One team is wearing dark green shirts and the other light green shirts. Static excietment quivers in the air as the two men near the goal post. All the spectators on the green wooden bleachers by the sidelines lean forward with their foreheads creased while watching the two men.

"Let's go!" shouts a man on the dark green team.

"Come on Mike! On the line, on the line!"

"Bill! Bill! Nice shot!" yells the man on the light green team, obviously pleased with the goal just made.

Continuing on around the park I pass another soccer game and a sand box. In the sand box, two one-stripped swings, and two rings are attached to a four-legged metal frame. A little boy of about five years old plays on the rings, the wind rustling his light brown hair. A blonde haired girl of about the same age plays in the sand with brightly colored shovels and buckets. Two women similarly dressed in blue jeans and a jacket watch the kids from the edge of the sand box.

I walk on, tired of watching them play. I stop by a wooden bridge which is over a creek. On either side of the bridge are tennis courts. Looking down over the slightly curved rail of the bridge, the slow stream of clear colored water moves through the creek, glistening as the sun shines on it. It's very peaceful here despite all the noise. A carefree mood seems to descend upon me as I bathe in the warm sun. A loud, roaring helicopter flies overhead causing the bridge to tremble slightly. A middle-aged couple, the woman, short and plump, her husband(?), tall and skinny, walk silently together holding hands, kissing each other every few minutes. Behind them, a small blonde haired girl struggles to follow them as she pushes a blue stroller.

Soon, a woman dressed in a white T-shirt, red shorts, white and blue jogging shoes, jogs past the bridge. She has been jogging for some time now. I feel admiration for this woman who has the will power and endurance to jog. Meanwhile she cooly dodges little children, boys on their sleek BMX dirt, racing bikes, and other people constantly using the red dirt path. Her short brown hair and shirt are stained with sweat while droplets of water dot her upper lip. Her breathing comes in short gasps.

I decide to walk after this lady jogger for a little while since nothing spectacular was happening at the bridge. I stop following her as I approach the tennis courts. Inside, almost everyone wears white with an occassional glob of color here and there. Being a very bad tennis player myself, I sit on a grey bleacher inside the courts avidly observing two men playing tennis, hoping to absorb some of their skills. Both men had tan, bronze colored skin, but one man had curly brown hair and the other with straight brown hair. Each stroke they made was graceful and smooth.

I close the tennis court gate behind me, leaving the world of bouncing tennis balls. I am back to where I started my journey, near the volleyball game, but the sun has gone down a bit in the sky and the wind blows with more gusto.

Next to the volleyball game which I first observed is a sunken concrete skating rink. Something is taking place their that wasn't before. I decide to go in for a closer look. A group of adults are in the rink practicing something that looks suspiciously like kung fu in slow motion. The group of adults are all silent, with their brows furrowed in deep concentration. Each movement was performed at the same time. Each person of the group moved each part of their body slowly and deliberately. It seems as if these people are in a world of their own, because even children running around playing tag doesn't disturb them.

I shiver as a cool wind ruffles my hair. The sun, not radiating any real warmth, means time to go home, I muse. I unlock my bike and procede to get on it. As I ride away, I look back and think how wonderful it is that so many different kinds of people come to Mitchell Park.

Author

Sarah Warshauer Freedman is Associate Professor of education at the University of California at Berkeley and director of the national Center for the Study of Writing, funded by the U.S. Department of Education. She is also a co-director of the Bay Area Writing Project. In 1985 Freedman edited *The Acquisition of Written Language: Response and Revision.* Her articles have appeared in journals such as *College Composition and Communication, Written Communication, Research in the Teaching of English, Journal of Educational Psychology,* and *English Journal.* She has contributed chapters to books on the writing process and on new directions in writing research. She has been a member of NCTE's Standing Committee on Research since 1981 and has chaired the NCTE Promising Researcher Award. She also served as chair of the American Educational Research Association's Special Interest Group on Research in Writing. She recently completed a study of peer groups in writing classrooms and is currently working with Alex McLeod of the London Institute of Education on a cross-cultural study of the teaching and learning of writing in the United States and the United Kingdom.